Revitalizing Theological Epistemology

Princeton Theological Monograph Series

K. C. Hanson and Charles M. Collier, Series Editors

Recent volumes in the series:

Mary Clark Moschella,
*Living Devotions: Reflections on Immigration, Identity,
and Religious Imagination*

Abraham Varghese Kunnuthara
*Schleiermacher on Christian Consciousness
of God's Work in History*

David Hein
Geoffrey Fisher: Archbishop of Canterbury, 1945–1961

Ronald F. Satta
The Sacred Text: Biblical Authority in Nineteenth-Century America

Catherine L. Kelsey
*Schleiermacher's Preaching, Dogmatics, and Biblical Criticism:
The Interpretation of Jesus Christ in the Gospel of John*

Christian T. Collins Winn, editor
*From the Margins: A Celebration of the Theological Work
of Donald W. Dayton*

Gabriel Andrew Msoka
*Basic Human Rights and the Humanitarian Crises
in Sub-Saharan Africa: Ethical Reflections*

T. David Beck
*The Holy Spirit and the Renewal of All Things:
Pneumatology in Paul and Jurgen Moltmann*

Trevor Dobbs
*Faith, Theology, and Psychoanalysis:
The Life and Thought of Harry S. Guntrip*

Paul S. Chung, Kim Kyoung-Jae, and Veli-Matti Kärkkäinen, editors
*Asian Contextual Theology for the Third Millennium:
A Theology of Minjung in Fourth-Eye Formation*

Bonnie L. Pattison
Poverty in the Theology of John Calvin

Revitalizing Theological Epistemology

*Holistic Evangelical Approaches
to the Knowledge of God*

STEVEN B. SHERMAN

PICKWICK *Publications* · Eugene, Oregon

REVITALIZING THEOLOGICAL EPISTEMOLOGY
Holistic Evangelical Approaches to the Knowledge of God

Princeton Theological Monograph Series 83

Pickwick Publications
A division of Wipf and Stock Publishers
199 W. 8th Ave, Suite 3
Eugene, Oregon 97401

ISBN: 978-1-55635-374-1

Cataloging-in-Publication data:

Sherman, Steven B.

    Revitalizing theological epistemology : holistic evangelical approaches to the knowledge of God / Steven B. Sherman.

    xvi + 278 p.; 23 cm. — Princeton Theological Monograph Series 83

    ISBN 13: 978-1-55635-374-1 (alk. paper)
    Includes bibliographical references (p. 271–278).

    1. Knowledge, Theory of (Religion). 2. Evangelicalism. 3. Pinnock, Clark H., 1937– .
4. Newbigin, Lesslie. I. Title. II. Series.

BT50.S53 2008

To my mentor, Richard J. Mouw,
and
To my wife, Lynn

Contents

Acknowledgements ix

Preface xiii

1 Introduction: The Rise of Postconservative Evangelical Theology 1

2 The Emergence of Postconservative Theological Epistemology 16

3 The Essence and Development

of Postconservative Theological Epistemology 128

4 Lesslie Newbigin's Theological Epistemology:

A Commendable Paradigm for Evangelical Theology 203

5 Constructive Proposal for Revitalizing Evangelical

Theological Epistemology: A Holistic Approach 250

6 Conclusion: Selected Practical Steps for Revitalizing

Evangelical Theological Epistemology 265

Bibliography 271

Acknowledgements

PERHAPS IT GOES WITHOUT SAYING THAT A BOOK REFLECTS NOT MERELY the efforts of one individual but the influence, direction, support, and constructive evaluation of countless others. Acknowledging the many contributors to this work is not so much a matter of deciding who to thank and why, but more a matter of having to eventually find a place to stop, realizing that hundreds of people—whether mentors, professors, authors, pastors, colleagues, fellow students, friends, or family—have helped in making this work move from being a dream to being fully realized.

Even the most generous words of appreciation could not begin to express my sense of gratitude and indebtedness to my advisor-mentor, Richard J. Mouw. As President and Professor of Philosophy at Fuller Theological Seminary, Dr. Mouw's full schedule never precluded his commitment to meeting with me regularly, offering honest and constructive criticism as well as praise and encouragement. His influence upon my life and work stretches beyond the borders of this study. Our conversations over the past eight years have deeply blessed and encouraged me, and have also revealed the great love for God and God's people resident in the heart of my mentor and friend. The world of evangelicalism is much richer for having such an outstanding representative to lead the way forward—richness I anticipate continuing to enjoy for many years to come.

Dr. Wilbert Shenk provided important direction and effective insights, and his quality communication and comments contributed substantially to the success of this study. Thanks also to Dr. Craig Van Gelder, whose patient reading and attention to my work in its final stage were invaluable.

Drawing from the well of wisdom and scholarship characteristic of Fuller faculty has been a distinct honor. I have been a fortunate recipient of Professor Nancey Murphy's unsurpassed commitment to the successful nurturing of students—be it academic excellence or Christian practice—benefiting immensely from her insightful and constructive evaluations during my time at seminary. Often Dr. Murphy provided timely direction, ideas, and critique necessary in the formative stages of my writing, and without which this work would surely have been impoverished.

A word of thanks as well to Dr. Richard Peace, whose early vision and encouragement led to my own vision becoming more than just a dream. And to the rest of the Fuller faculty, administration, and staff, thank you all for seven years of very full and fruitful years of formation and preparation that I will ne'er forget!

Recognition is also due several scholars outside the Fuller community whose efforts helped in shaping and refining my own work. Clark Pinnock, Stan Grenz, Millard Erickson, Roger Olson, and Lesslie Newbigin have produced some of the finest books available in contemporary Christian thought, and I am privileged to have had the opportunity to learn and benefit from their excellent work.

I must also mention my indebtedness to two professors whose passionate teaching and committed Christian living were formative in my decision to pursue academic life as my vocational calling in service to the Kingdom, church, and world. Dr. Richard Goswiller first taught me the importance of striving for balance—for instance, between doing the hard work of study and exegesis while maintaining a vibrant devotional life. Dr. J.P. Moreland demonstrated to me that a Christian academician could simultaneously critique and champion the faith, while also ministering to students pastorally.

It would be remiss not to mention several pastors whose lives and ministries have exceptionally strengthened my own life at various stages throughout this process. Remembered forever will be Pastor Gary Stubblefield's encouragement along with his Christlike mentoring and friendship that helped in serving to shape my own character and focus. Also not soon to be forgotten is the exemplary energy and Christian devotion exuded by Reverend Dr. Mike Sciarra, matched only by his personal encouragement and wonderful fellowship. And I'm also deeply grateful to Dr. David Ho Sang, able pastor, scholar, and friend, whose empathic listening and gracious spirit came to mean so much during the final few years of this project.

I am likewise grateful for the many other friends who have been supportive throughout the process: Arthur Andrews (who read and critiqued an early chapter), Jeff Monk, Ron Hannaford, Bob Thrasher, Tim Morey, Tim Schulz, and Tom Gerber. Still, there could be no greater confidant than fellow PhD graduate, and now New Testament Professor Phil Mayo, whose loyal support and friendship—including spurring me on through the challenges of writing and editing—cannot be accurately measured in words. I trust that our friendship will continue to grow throughout the coming years.

Thanks also to the fine publishing and editorial staff at Wipf & Stock. Editor Charlie Collier's unique combination of professional expertise and interpersonal sensibilities has served to make the publication process a painless and even positive experience. Editorial Assistant Diane Farley also made important contributions toward successful completion of this work.

Finally, a tribute to my amazing family. My faithfully praying parents, whose contribution to the whole process—especially as loving grandparents—can only be estimated in the eschaton. My tireless and welcoming mother-in-law, whose open heart and home were a constant blessing and added source of security for my wife and children. Close friend of the family, Kristi, whose flexibility and trustworthy care for our kids will always be remembered with great affection. To my incredibly patient and merciful children, Chelsea and Nicholas. The two of you really are the best kids on the face of the earth—now please go brush your teeth and take your vitamins!

And to the one human being who more than any other made this work possible, to my faithful and longsuffering life partner, my beautiful and precious wife, whose unending support God has blessed me with in ways beyond description—to you I offer my dedicated praise and gratitude. May our Lord repay your many sacrifices in showering you with his ever-present joy and peace, now and forevermore. To you I dedicate this book.

Preface

Despite the century-old critique of foundationalism and the theological proposals of contemporary thinkers like Pannenberg and Lindbeck, foundationalist theology is not dead. On the contrary, a large cadre of theological modernists appear content to engage in theology in a manner that presupposes the older foundationalist epistemology. At the same time, however, a growing number of theologians are becoming cognizant of the demise of foundationalism in philosophy and are increasingly concerned to explore the implications of this demise for theology. They believe that theology must take seriously the postmodern critique of Enlightenment foundationalism and must capitalize on the attempts of philosophers to formulate alternatives.[1]

YEARS AGO AN OUTSTANDING INSTRUCTOR AT A LITTLE-KNOWN BIBLE college taught a rag-tag group of first-time theology students a lesson that at least one of them ne'er forgot: the importance of striving for balance. Not only did he model it, his commitment to a theological balancing of ontological realism with epistemological humility was something worth emulating. The approach to faith and reason represented by that formative scholar challenged and defeated for this thinker less helpful models stressing either epistemic relativism (void of any restraints against skepticism), or more often, absolutism (suffering the death of hubris and fantasy). The balance Dr. Goswiller spoke of and lived out has not typically been characteristic of evangelical theology in the modern period—especially since the inception of the modernist-fundamentalist debates beginning in the nineteenth century. While not all who would wear the label "evangelical" can rightly be accused of riding the rails of modernity's premiere epistemology—foundationalism—perhaps most have joined themselves to this paradigm, failing to heed Bernard Ramm's sagacious caution regarding theology's relationship to any philosophical system:

1. Grenz and Franke, *Beyond Foundationalism*, 46.

If a theologian rests the case for Christianity completely on some philosophy, and that philosophy be discredited, then the whole case for Christianity is undermined. If Hegel's philosophy is completely routed by twentieth-century philosophers, then all those Hegelian theologians of the nineteenth century believed in the truthfulness of Christianity for all the wrong reasons. They smashed their heads against Hume's advice: Don't believe a religion for all the wrong reasons. . . . I think when a theologian is totally committed to Heidegger, or Whitehead, or Wittgenstein, or any great name of the past, he has not heeded Hume! We may believe the right thing for the wrong reason. Therefore, especially in philosophy, proceed with caution. As the old maxim goes: whoever marries the philosophy of his generation, finds himself an orphan in the next.[2]

A rather acrimonious divorce is underway between evangelical theology and foundationalism[3]—especially among younger evangelical protégés less directly connected with the modernist-fundamentalist controversy than are their professors. These primarily younger evangelical thinkers are almost certainly reading and engaging more of Derrida than Descartes; more interested in doing theology and philosophy for the church than for the academy; more in tune with Wesley's than Warfield's theology; more interested in applying the Bible than defending it; more concerned with the hermeneutics of Gadamer and Ricoeur than (Arno) Gabelein and (A. T.) Robertson; more occupied with the philosophical method of Heidegger than Hegel; more moved by the epistemology of Kierkegaard and Barth than by Kant and Bultmann; and finally, more comfortable with postmodern than modern culture.[4] Such major moves are undoubtedly altering the face of evangelical theology—or more accurately, theol-

2. Ramm, The Devil, *Seven Wormwoods, and God,* 143.

3. Unless otherwise noted, the use of "foundationalism" throughout this paper will indicate "classical" foundationalism (in the rationalist or empiricist sense) and not its "modest" or "soft" versions, which, when intended as the subject matter, will be indicated as either modest or soft foundationalism.

4. Obviously, these statements are overgeneralizations, yet they do provide at least a general sense of the ambiance of younger evangelical moves.

ogy done by evangelicals:[5] even more particularly for this study, theological epistemology written by evangelicals.[6]

Questions are being addressed with respect to what evangelical theology ought to be doing in light of the changing cultural situation. Should the Christian faith continue to be presented and defended mainly according to Enlightenment principles when growing criticism of modern thought is affecting virtually every discipline? Is this critique merely a matter of the latest societal trend, or is this a much larger phenomenon virtually encompassing the West? Ought evangelicalism and its intellectual leaders to "wait it out" or should they "re-vision" their theology? And if something does require reconsideration, exactly what is it, and what might this re-examination entail?

This study is about contemporary evangelical approaches to the knowledge of God, considering—and suggesting—ways Christian philosophers and theologians envision and make use of theological knowledge in the postmodern context.

---

5. Some question the reality of an *evangelical* theology. For instance, Richard Mouw does not think that evangelicalism generates "a very rich theological system," and that the term "evangelical" should be used as "a theological modifier rather than as a noun. The label should not be allowed to stand alone when sorting out theological systems." He continues: "The key features of evangelical thought are best seen as theological *emphases* that have come to have importance in the context of certain kinds of theological struggles" (Mouw, *The Smell of Sawdust*, 72).

6. Although there is some debate as to whether the idea of a theological epistemology is coherent, I have chosen to utilize the phrase throughout this work. As used herein, the phrase might best be understood as broadly referring to the theory or study of the knowledge of God (including, for instance, alleged sources of theological knowledge), especially with regard to its methods and raison d'être, as considered from within a Christian (or more particularly, evangelical) theology framework. (Jürgen Moltmann, for instance, uses "theological epistemology" as the title for a chapter in *Experiences in Theology*.) One possible alternative phrase for theological epistemology is "epistemology of theology," which, while connoting a similar meaning, appears (due to word order) to imply "the study of the study of theology," and thus I do not used the phrase. "Religious epistemology" is yet another potential substitute, but was not selected due to its conceivably much broader intended or implied meaning and application. As can be expected, there are several different renderings of—and debate over—each of these terms and phrases used among scholars, as well as such within subcategories (e.g., the meaning and/or breadth of saving [or salvific] knowledge). No doubt, this necessarily leads to ambiguities, misunderstandings, and a need for more nuanced uses of such terms and phrases. This will be attempted throughout the paper, but inevitably confusion will occasionally overshadow clarity, to which this author can only reply, patience and benefit of the doubt is deeply appreciated.

Introduction

The Rise of Postconservative Evangelical Theology

IN THE SPRING OF 1995, ROGER OLSON'S MANIFESTO-TYPE ARTICLE IN *The Christian Century*[1] served notice to the larger theological world that "postconservative evangelicals" were a force to be reckoned with.[2] These four pages of text have generated thousands more. Even book-length treatments have since appeared on the subject.[3] While not signaling the actual *beginning* of the postconservative evangelical theology enterprise, it succeeded in making the public aware of a new theological movement—with hopes of generating significant interest in the ideas being offered.[4]

While Olson could rightfully be credited with popularizing this new evangelical movement—although in 1995 he seemed more comfortable speaking of it as a *mood*—the theological impetus for postconservative evangelical theology can be traced much earlier: to the transitioning theological work of both Bernard Ramm and, more definitively, Clark H. Pinnock.[5] Both were moving in virtually the same direction: away from a defensive posture of rationalistic evidential apologetics, and toward a more

1. Olson, "Postconservative Evangelicals," 480–83.

2. The terms "postconservative" and "reformist" will be used synonymously within this book. (As a related point, when discussions focus on "openness" theologians it will be helpful to keep in mind that virtually all are postconservative.)

3. Perhaps the most directly relevant is Erickson, *The Evangelical Left*.

4. Olson does claim to have coined the term "postconservative" to describe this new movement (Olson, "Reforming Evangelical Theology," 201). Nevertheless, Clark Pinnock was using the term in 1990 to describe a theological movement within both evangelicalism and post-Vatican II Catholicism. See Pinnock, *Tracking the Maze*, 63–71.

5. See, for instance, Pinnock, *Reason Enough; Tracking the Maze; Wideness in God's Mercy; Flame of Love; The Scripture Principle;* Pinnock and Brow, *Unbounded Love;* Pinnock and Brown, *Theological Crossfire;* Pinnock and others, *Openness of God;* and Ramm, *The Devil, Seven Wormwoods, and God;* and *After Fundamentalism.*

holistic approach to theology and epistemology, with a greater emphasis on the *testimonium* of the Spirit. These two eminent evangelical thinkers also wanted to move evangelical theology into a more direct and constructive engagement with biblical and historical criticism, modern science, and postmodern philosophical challenges. Leaving behind what they saw as an extreme focus on objectivity and scientific method, each sought to develop an evangelical theological method: Ramm settling on a more or less Barthian approach,[6] and Pinnock focusing on a free will theism[7] with a pneumatological emphasis.[8]

Acknowledging the significant, formative contributions of Ramm and Pinnock is but part of the larger—and rapidly developing—story of postconservative evangelicalism; it was Olson's article, serving as a type of manifesto for the movement, that brought significant attention to postconservatism. And thus for this study, we will be consulting his article in setting forth the primary themes of postconservative evangelical theology. Before proceeding along these lines, however, we must make mention of an earlier sort of postconservative manifesto.

Believing that the modern period[9] (as with the medieval before it) had given way to a different historical context, some late-twentieth-century evangelical scholars became concerned that theology must not lag behind in *recontextualizing* the gospel for the post-Enlightenment setting. Relevant nagging questions began to arise within evangelical academia: Would seeking to express the Christian faith (e.g., its historic doctrines) vis-à-vis postmodern categories lead to undermining the gospel? Would it necessarily entail compromising evangelical truth claims, and subjecting Christ to culture? Would scripture be bound to destruction via postmodern philosophy's deconstruction of texts? And would the surrender of absolute epistemological certainty result in a merely disguised form of liberalism?

6. Ramm, *After Fundamentalism*.

7. Also known as "creative love theism." See Pinnock and Brow, *Unbounded Love;* Pinnock and others, *Openness of God*.

8. See Pinnock, *Flame of Love*.

9. Although dating the "modern period" is doubtlessly a subjective enterprise—admitting much overlap with what is now commonly referred to as "pre-modern" and "postmodern" epochs—we can roughly correlate the beginning of the modern era with the year 1650 and the death of the so-called father of modernity, René Descartes. The "end" of the modern era is not infrequently connected with the year 1950 (for several reasons we will discuss later), reflecting a 300-year span of dominance in Western thought.

The response to such questions is where a great gulf can be seen today between "traditionalist" and "reformist"[10] evangelical scholars, each representing different sides of the theological chasm. Whereas traditionalists generally see the move to embrace the postmodern cultural condition for evangelical theology as undesirable accommodation, postconservatives desire to update theology within postmodernity; it is this latter approach that will receive the principal concentration within this detailed discourse.[11] But before moving too far ahead, we must return to the postconservative manifesto topic.

The crucial questions noted a few paragraphs earlier began to be raised to new levels when directly addressed in 1990 by Clark Pinnock in *Tracking the Maze*, where he set out to provide evangelicals a means of *Finding Our Way through Modern Theology from an Evangelical Perspective* (the book's subtitle). While a more in-depth treatment of this book (along will several others works by Pinnock) will be carried out in a later section, his main arguments will be summarized here, for they reflect an agenda for a postconservative theology[12] that would hope to make thorough use of the new cultural condition.

---

10. The terms "traditionalist" and "reformist" are borrowed from Olson, "The Future of Evangelical Christianity," 40–41. Olson characterizes traditionalists as those who uphold "traditional interpretations and formulations as binding and normative," and who tend to "look with suspicion upon any doctrinal revisions and new proposals arising out of theological reflection." In contrast, reformists welcome the "continuing process of constructive theology seeking new light breaking forth from God's word." As expected, not all evangelicals agree with Olson's characterizations—his own reformist-leaning tendencies are evident. Nevertheless, his is the primary model employed in this paper in considering the major and minor differentiations between scholars most interested in protecting traditional visions of the Christian faith and those focused on pioneering new methods and views. Obviously, the theological "webs" of individual scholars and their fraternity intersect at various points, parallel at others, and diverge in varying degree, so that any generalizations are likely to have exceptions, and must be taken as "in the main."

11. It should be understood that there is tremendous diversity among evangelicals of every persuasion as to the appropriateness of enlisting elements of postmodern thought and culture for evangelical theology. Later, we will seek a more detailed differentiation between the different views by adding certain qualifiers to the two main positions spoken of here (e.g., *strict* traditionalists, *radical* postconservatives). Although this may be helpful, the taxonomy remains a subjective one, and doubtless will incur many detractors who envision their own positions as more moderate than I have expressed it. Surely the same can be said for how I view my own theological commitments.

12. Pinnock's own terms used at the time of writing *Tracking the Maze* were "postmodern orthodoxy" (see *Tracking the Maze*, dedication page).

Pinnock draws several conclusions that provide a window on his perspective: theologians do not have to feel pressured to capitulate to the canons of human authority resident within modernity now that criticism has disclosed its faulty reasoning and cultural conditioning; Christian theology should not be primarily rational-propositional in form, but rather see its principal task as exploring and proclaiming the Christian story; Christian doctrine is a second-order reflection or language commenting on the Christian story and performing a servant role in relation to the gospel; the Christian story is original, and the dogma is always a historically and culturally conditioned interpretation, however useful; the gospel message as revealed in the scriptures is foundational to theological knowledge; any Christian theology that fails to correlate the two poles of the word and the context is a failure.

Even more specifically, Pinnock seeks to identify the fundamental two horizons issues in contemporary theology,[13] and what he sees as three types of theological responses, characterized by theologians who primarily fit into one of the following categories: progressives, conservatives, or moderates. Pinnock himself sides with the moderates, presenting what may be viewed as a sort of "postconservative manifesto" that includes nine apparent moves:

1. Greater openness to the humanity of the Bible and biblical criticism, as well as more flexibility regarding the meaning of inerrancy and more hesitancy about the term's usefulness.

2. Legitimacy of evangelical theological pluralism in recognition of diversity in the biblical teaching.

3. New respect for tradition's intrinsic value and the stability it provides.

4. Open discussion about the nature of God and potential need for focusing on the openness of God to the temporal process.

5. Willingness to recover an evangelical model accepting evolution as complementary to creation and origins.

---

13. In short, "the two horizons" refers to the horizon of the biblical text and the horizon of the interpreter. See Thiselton, *The Two Horizons*.

6. Viewing salvation more broadly, including opportunities for the unevangelized, as well as re-envisioning hell in terms of annihilation rather than eternal torment.

7. Movement away from a pessimistic premillennialism to a positive vision of church and society, including the transformation of culture and social/liberation concerns.

8. More sensitivity to the supernatural, e.g., miracles, especially among charismatic and Pentecostal movements.

9. Radical ecumenical openness to cooperate with evangelicals of other denominations.[14]

Since Pinnock's manifesto was penned, virtually each of the "changes in the boundaries" of evangelical theology has been taken up by younger evangelical scholars as the last decade of the twentieth century witnessed an escalating interest and debate among evangelical theologians over the question of reconsidering (or revisioning) evangelical theology.[15] Moreover, as this effort will attempt to demonstrate, further developments across the spectrum of scholarship have been reshaping the face of evangelicalism in the new millennium as well. And while this does not appear to be a total revisioning of categories—Calvinist and Arminian doctrinal distinctions, for instance, show few signs of disappearing—a definite broadening, perhaps even morphing, of taxonomy is occurring with increased intensity:

---

14. See Pinnock, *Tracking the Maze*, 67–68.

15. For instance, see Burnham, *Postmodern Theology*; Clapp, "How Firm a Foundation"; Dorrien, *The Remaking of Evangelical Theology*; Erickson, *The Evangelical Left*; *Postmodernizing the Faith*; Fackre, *Ecumenical Faith in Evangelical Perspective*; Grenz, *Revisioning Evangelical Theology*, Gunter and others, *Wesley and the Quadrilateral*; Hart, *Faith Thinking*; Hauerwas, Murphy, and Nation, *Theology Without Foundations*; Knight, *A Future for Truth*; Murphy, *Beyond Liberalism and Fundamentalism*; Newbigin, *The Gospel in a Pluralist Society*; *Proper Confidence*; *Truth and Authority in Modernity*; Noll, *The Scandal of the Evangelical Mind*; Oden, *After Modernity*; Olson, "Postconservative Evangelicals"; *The Story of Christian Theology*; Phillips, *Faith After Foundationalism*; Phillips and Okholm, *Christian Apologetics in the Postmodern World*; Pinnock, *Tracking the Maze*; *Wideness in God's Mercy*; *Flame of Love*; Pinnock and Brow, *Unbounded Love*; Pinnock and Brown, *Theological Crossfire*; Pinnock and others, *Openness of God*; Placher, *Unapologetic Theology*; Sanders, *No Other Name*; Thiel, *Nonfoundationalism*; Thiselton, *Interpreting God and the Postmodern Self*; Vanhoozer, *Is There a Meaning in This Text?*; Van Huyssteen and Wentzel, *Essays in Postfoundational Theology*; Van Inwagen, *God, Knowledge, and Mystery*; Webber, *Ancient-Future Faith*; Wells, *No Place for Truth*; and *God in the Wasteland*.

to an extent viewed by some observers as "outside the bounds" or "beyond recognition" as evangelical.[16]

The change within evangelical thought that Olson noted in 1995 is occurring within a variety of disciplines. For instance, within *history*, there is a movement underway from the ahistorical to tradition; within *theology*, a change from propositionalism to narrative; and within *apologetics*, a transition from rationalism to embodiment. Importantly, each of these three main arenas has, as a primary concern, theological knowledge[17]—cor-

16. See for instance, Piper, Taylor, and Helseth, *Beyond the Bounds*, and Ware, *God's Lesser Glory*.

17. Recognizing the great diversity in which key terms and phrases (e.g., "knowledge of God") used in this book are defined within (and outside of) evangelical scholarship, I will modestly attempt to delineate several of these crucial terms and phrases: 1) Knowledge of God or Theological Knowledge—the most general expression used to speak of potential or actual human knowledge of God, which may or may not imply personal, corporate, salvific, or direct knowledge of God, depending upon contextual usage. (Even in context, there likely remains some ambiguity for the reader since all human knowledge remains partial and imprecise.) These terms may also connote knowledge pertaining to relationship or fellowship between the Deity and human beings. When speaking specifically within a Christian or evangelical framework, "God" should be taken to refer to the Trinitarian God of the Christian faith, unless otherwise noted. 2) Knowing God—in general, more specifically referring to the divine-human *relationship* or *fellowship*, whether or not connoting *salvific* knowledge. (It will be imperative to keep in mind that *ultimately* only God authoritatively determines the salvific "value" of knowledge.) At least in some cases, "knowing God" assumes or anticipates a faith-based obedient response to God. In addition, with reference to human knowledge of God, scripture speaks both of humans "knowing God" and "knowing *that* God . . ." While a *clear* and *objective* distinction would be ideal, meaning is dependent on a particular *use* within a context and a term's semantic domain. Thus, to press a distinction in every case would be less than accurate. In some instances, however, there appears to be distinguishable characteristics that differentiate the two (e.g., where a command to know *that* God is powerful or omniscient does not connote knowing God in intimate fellowship, as with the Egyptian in Exod. 7:5), whereas in other cases, the distinction cannot be easily determined (e.g., where knowing *that* God is Lord implies or expects a *responsive* and *obedient* relational commitment, as with the people of Israel in Exod. 31:13). Even then, a great deal of overlapping of concepts may be present and not strictly distinguishable (e.g., where recognizing the authority or covenantal love of God *expects* a positive inclination to *fellowship* from those who have been privileged to "know" such truths, as with Deut. 4:1). In the case of "doing justice" and "loving mercy," for instance, the foundation for such beneficent activities would appear to include some level of awareness or "knowledge" of God or God's will/commands. In these instances, *behavior* can be viewed as "knowing God," or *demonstrating* "knowledge of God." 3) Salvific or Saving Knowledge of God—relates to the concepts of one's (or a community's) knowledge of God issuing in redemption, whether through Jesus Christ or some other means (e.g., response to general revelation [Rom. 1:18ff.]). As stated above, *ultimately* God alone determines the constitution of "saving knowledge." Therefore, it should *not* be assumed in this book that the use of *any* of the terms and phrases denoted here *necessarily* carries with it a sense of

responding directly with the primary thrust of this work: contemporary evangelical theological epistemology. (In a later section, we will consider each of these shifts in relation to approaches to theological knowledge.)

The twenty-first century is proving to be an important—even revolutionary—testing ground for reforming evangelical theology. Robert Webber notes that we have entered into a "new cultural condition": one that calls for continuing the historical process of deconstructing and reconstructing evangelical theology. His book *The Younger Evangelicals* deserves the careful attention of evangelical theologians and philosophers.[18] Webber claims that the moves being made by "younger evangelicals" are a positive development, at once connecting with both the postmodern culture and premodern Christianity.

> The younger evangelical wants to release the historic substance of faith from its twentieth-century enculturation in the Enlightenment and recontextualize it with the new cultural condition of the twenty-first century. This contextual methodology is no different than the method the Reformers used to deconstruct the church's reliance on the medievally culturalized form of Christianity in order to release the faith to be contextualized into the cultural situation of the emerging English and European culture. Evangelicals have carried out this process of deconstruction and reconstruction repeatedly throughout history. Those who resist this process in the current debate deny the evangelical commitment to a changeless faith indigenized into various cultures.[19]

Especially since the mainstreaming of postconservative thought over a decade ago,[20] younger evangelical thinkers from diverse theological backgrounds are envisioning evangelical theology in some ways dissimilar from their mainly traditionalist and fundamentalist predecessors. Consequently, such "post-fundamentalist" scholars are stimulating significant changes within the spectrum of evangelical thought and praxis, and will receive our deliberate attention throughout this study.

---

certainty with respect to salvific knowledge—only insofar as explicit declaration of such exists in scripture ought such conjectures be made (e.g., as in John 17:3).

18. Webber, *The Younger Evangelicals*. Another equally important book that chronicles major developments occurring within evangelicalism, along with its future prospects, is McGrath, *The Future of Christianity*.

19. Webber, *Younger Evangelicals*, 17.

20. I am roughly correlating "the mainstreaming of postconservative thought" with Olson's article, "Postconservative Evangelicals," 480–83.

Design and Goals of This Study

Summary
of
Book

Before proceeding further with our exploration of postconservative evangelical theology, we will first need to summarize the overall strategy and organization of this project. To begin with, we will seek to identify, in somewhat general terms, evangelical postconservatism. Then, we will attempt to exposit the basic epistemological issues underlying Olson's manifesto. Next, we will trace the emergence of postconservative theological epistemology via the intellectual journey of evangelical scholar Clark Pinnock, explaining the various ways in which Pinnock, through the outcome of his own theological evolution, comes to endorse Olson's postconservative themes.

From there, we move to an analysis of epistemological notions that have significantly contributed to the emergence of postconservative approaches to theological knowledge. Here we will examine modern foundationalism and its exploitation within evangelical theology. We will also focus our attention on potential alternative nonfoundationalist epistemologies being suggested by certain Christian scholars.

Next, we consider the essence and continuing development of postconservative theological epistemology. We begin by concentrating on primarily younger evangelical scholars, who, drawing on the work of the father of postconservative evangelical theology (i.e., Pinnock) are seeking alternative philosophical and theological resources for evangelical thought—including postmodern philosophy—as they attempt to find what they view as a more holistic, communal understanding of the knowledge of God.

Next, we introduce the so-called Wesleyan Quadrilateral, where we will attend first to the content of scripture in connection with theological knowledge. Following our survey of what the biblical data reveals, we will be looking at the entire Quadrilateral as a potential model for moving beyond a restrictive view of *sola scriptura* in our quest to capture more ways of envisioning theological knowledge from a biblical basis. Upon finding even the Quadrilateral inadequate for expressing the many ways for understanding the knowledge of God, and given the emerging missional, cultural, and ecumenical challenges, we will then introduce and assess the approach of Lesslie Newbigin, whose position both echoes and expands upon the ideas being explored among postconservative thinkers, yet in a context quite distinct from theirs.

Finally, we will offer a critique of postconservative thought and Newbigin's perspective via a comparative account of their methods. As part of this critique, we will also be suggesting a constructive approach to the knowledge of God for contemporary evangelical thought within the early twenty-first-century context.

In general, then, we will move from a somewhat broad introduction and overview of postconservative evangelical theology to a more focused analysis and assessment of contemporary evangelical approaches to theological knowledge, concluding with a modest proposal for revitalizing theological epistemology.

Having delineated the outline of this study, we will now begin by searching for a helpful understanding of the essential shape of postconservative evangelical theology, a movement that now appears to be shaping much of contemporary evangelical scholarship.

Defining Postconservative Evangelical Theology

An attempt is underway by a variety of evangelical thinkers to label something that in certain ways does not fit comfortably—according to standards of these same thinkers—within the conservative evangelical theological guild. The labels these primarily younger evangelical scholars employ are rather diverse: "postconservative," "postmodern," "nonfoundationalist," "postfoundationalist," "new conservative," "progressive," "revisionist," and "reformist," with some of these thinkers employing several of these labels in theological strains spelling out their perspectives.

In spite of this variation in labeling, it is not difficult to construct at least a general definition of who postconservative evangelical theologians are, and what they believe. Basically, they compose a loose coalition of thinkers who are seeking to facilitate a number of *beyond* moves, theologically: beyond the agenda of the modernist/fundamentalist dichotomy toward what they see as a more holistic theology; beyond classical foundationalist epistemology toward alternative concepts of knowledge; beyond concentration on rationalism toward incorporating additional ways of knowing; beyond inerrancy debates and concerns toward an instrumental use of scripture; beyond academy-centered theologizing toward ecclesial and community-oriented thinking; beyond gatekeeping or boundary-setting doctrinalism toward a generous orthodoxy with a pietistic emphasis; and finally, beyond what they view as a fixation on the concerns of modernity, often motivated by a fear of liberalism, toward a more positive view and selective appropriation of postmodern insights.[21]

However, in moving *beyond* much of what conservative evangelical theology has attached itself to, it is appropriate to ask what the movement's *toward* trajectory looks like in greater detail.

Fundamental Characteristics and Concerns of Postconservative Evangelical Theology

Olson presents what he sees as some key markers that characterize a postconservative approach to theology, serving to "indicate progress in reforming evangelical theology in a non-fundamentalist, non-liberal, postconservative direction."[22] First, postconservative evangelical theology lacks an obsessive fear of liberal theology. Olson perceives that the intended outcome of conservative evangelicalism was to protect evangelical theology from the modernists (especially of the 1920s through 1950s), yet the captivity of this conservatism to the basic motifs of modernity was an unfortunate "accommodation of the biblical witness and the gospel of Jesus Christ to a secular spirit."[23] Olson considers "reformists" as "those evangelicals with a postconservative spirit . . . committed evangelical theologians who are determined to break free with bold confidence from captivity to categories of 'right' and 'left' and develop a liberated evangelical theology that is more and not less biblical because it is open to radical challenges from the word of God in Scripture."[24]

Second, the evangelical identity of postconservative theology is not defined by "rigid boundaries and 'gatekeeping.'"[25] On this point, Olson appreciates David Bebbington's four general characteristics of evangelical-

---

21. In Olson's thinking, "a truly evangelical theology can move along a trajectory away from fundamentalism and even conservatism (i.e., traditionalism, rigid preservation of the 'received evangelical tradition') and toward a more biblically faithful, more culturally relevant, and therefore more evangelical theology" (see Olson, "Reforming Evangelical Theology," 201).

22. Olson, "Reforming Evangelical Theology," 202. Although Olson is specifically referring to the essays in *Evangelical Futures*, it seems neither inappropriate nor misleading to view his assessment as characterizing postconservative evangelical theology in general.

23. Ibid.

24. Ibid., 203.

25. Ibid.

ism (activism, biblicism, conversionism, and cruci-centrism),[26] as well as John G. Stackhouse's addition of *transdenominationalism*.[27] He also echoes Stackhouse's biting assessment of "would-be self-appointed conservative gatekeepers of 'authentic evangelicalism,'" agreeing with Stackhouse that "we simply can't afford the luxury of continual heresy hunting and the division that it produces. . . . Such intra-evangelical wars are actually anti-evangelical."[28]

Third, postconservative evangelical theology promotes liberation from Enlightenment realism and rationalism, combined with a preservation of objective truth and coherence. Olson believes that "for many conservative evangelicals . . . this move is impossible."[29]

Fourth, postconservative evangelical theology retains a "respect for doctrinal heritage without rigid traditionalism."[30] While noting that Alister McGrath may not unproblematically be labeled as postconservative, Olson says that McGrath

> correctly affirms and asserts that any part of the great tradition of Christian teaching could be in need of correction by better understanding of Scripture. This is a postconservative move. So is McGrath's hearty acceptance and endorsement of evangelical diversity.[31]

However, Olson also notes that

> if McGrath really wishes to recognize evangelical diversity, he should include in a more positive light the heroes of non-Reformed evangelicals, such as Menno Simons and Balthasar Hubmaier, Jacob Arminius and John Wesley, Philipp Spener and August Hermann Franke. And Clark Pinnock.[32]

Fifth, postconservative evangelical theology reveals a "fusion of the practical-spiritual with the theoretical-intellectual in evangelical theologi-

---

26. See Bebbington, *Evangelicalism in Modern Britain*.

27. Stackhouse, "Evangelical Theology Should Be Evangelical," 42.

28. Olson, "Reforming Evangelical Theology," 203, citing Stackhouse, "Evangelical Theology Should Be Evangelical," 58.

29. Olson, "Reforming Evangelical Theology," 204.

30. Ibid., 205.

31. Ibid.

32. Ibid., 206.

cal methodology. That is to say, theology cannot be divorced from concrete experience."[33]

Other observers besides Olson have also sought to provide a definition of postconservative evangelical thought. For instance, Gary Dorrien (not himself an evangelical) maintains that the theologies being advanced by these generally younger evangelical leaders are a possible coming to pass of Hans Frei's wish to witness the emergence of "a kind of generous orthodoxy" that couples and transcends elements of both evangelicalism and liberalism, thus raising "a voice that reconnects modern evangelicalism to the polyphonic orthodox tradition of Irenaeus, Augustine, Chrysostom, Aquinas, Luther, Calvin, Hooker, Wesley, and Barth."[34]

Theologian Kevin Vanhoozer claims his own method as

> *post*conservative theology because it transcends the debilitating dichotomies between referring and expressing, between propositional and personal revelation, between God saying and God doing, precisely by focusing on the Bible as a set of divine communication acts. God in Scripture is doing many things with words, not simply conveying information, nor even revealing himself. The approach is *post*conservative in that it maintains there is something in the text that is both indispensable and authoritative, namely the divinely intended meaning.[35]

While the preceding perspectives are helpful in gaining insight into several aspects of postconservative evangelical theology, returning to Olson's *Christian Century* article opens up a broader panorama of this theological landscape. In his influential piece, Olson describes the movement's *ethos* in what may be divided into sixteen primary characteristics:

1. Retention of the four defining features of evangelicalism (defined by Bebbington as activism, biblicism, conversionism, and cruci-centrism).

2. Dethronement of the chief place of apologetics—especially the Reformed scholastic version.

---

33. Ibid.

34. Dorrien, *The Remaking of Evangelical Theology*, 209.

35. Vanhoozer, "The Voice and the Actor," 76. Vanhoozer is a leading postconservative voice from whom more theological and epistemological insights will be culled later in this work.

3. Movement away from modernist/fundamentalist categories and related preoccupation with rationalism.

4. Dialogue with non-evangelical theologians (e.g., postliberals).

5. Concern for social location and ethnic diversity in evangelical scholarship.

6. Biblical equality and egalitarianism.

7. Broadening of sources for theology beyond *sola scriptura* (e.g., narrative-shaped experience, tradition, culture).

8. Theology as second-order reflection on first-order narrative-shaped word of God in scripture.

9. Discontent with evangelical theology's connections to modernity and Enlightenment epistemology.

10. Holistic or canonical approaches to scripture's inspiration and authority.

11. Movement away from classical Christian theism toward God as self-limiting, vulnerable, and passable (e.g., "free will theism").

12. Openness to a dynamic relationship view of nature and grace.

13. Abandonment of exclusivism for inclusivism relative to salvation, while rejecting pluralism.

14. Emphasis on Christ's humanity, with openness toward reconceiving Jesus' divinity in more relational terms (i.e., relational unity with the Father).

15. Resurgence of synergism concerning the God-human relationship in salvation.

16. Rejection of triumphalism, especially those elements influenced by fundamentalism and the accompanying hubris relative to truth-claims, epistemological certainty, and theological systems.[36]

Olson's outline of postconservative evangelical theology has provided observers with an important framework from which to discuss and critique the movement. More difficult is determining *who* in fact postconservative thinkers are. As might be expected, it depends greatly on who does

36. Olson, "Postconservative Evangelicals," 480–83.

the defining and categorizing. To date, not many evangelical thinkers are self-confessed postconservatives: Pinnock and Vanhoozer would be two. And the boundaries between postliberals and postconservatives are, for some writers, very fluid, while for others, fairly rigid. Some like Nancey Murphy (who has been classified in various "post" categories) think the term "postconservative" is "not a suitable description since conservatism (favoring the past in a contest between traditional formulations and contemporary relevance) will continue to characterize one end of the [theological] spectrum."[37]

Rather than giving too much attention to what potential designations fit best with particular thinkers, we can simply offer a listing of thinkers who consider themselves—or are considered by their peers—as being in agreement with a majority of postconservative theology characteristics. So included, to varying degrees, are William J. Abraham, David Basinger, Bruce Ellis Benson, Donald Bloesch, Gregory Boyd, Robert Brow, Barry Callen, Tony Campolo, Rodney Clapp, Jack Cottrell, William Dyrness, Gabriel Fackre, John R. Franke, Stanley J. Grenz, Rebecca M. Groothuis, Trevor Hart, William Hasker, Veli-Matti Kärkkäinen, Henry H. Knight III, Richard Middleton, Nancey Murphy, James Wm. McClendon Jr., Alister E. McGrath, Brian McLaren, Lesslie Newbigin, Thomas Oden, Dennis L. Okholm, Roger E. Olson, Tim. R. Phillips, Clark H. Pinnock, Keith Putt, Bernard Ramm, Richard Rice, John Sanders, John G. Stackhouse, John E. Thiel, Kevin J. Vanhoozer, Miroslav Volf, Brian J. Walsh, Robert E. Webber, Merold Westphal, Stephen Williams, W. Jay Wood, and Amos Yong.

New movements often encompass some combination of response to the status quo and renewed desire for practical relevance: postconservative evangelicalism shares this same activist attitude and pragmatic vision. Clearly, postconservatism did not begin *de novo*, but rather has been deeply influenced—even shaped and molded to a great extent—by its theological and cultural context. Whether viewed as a necessary correction, radical over-correction, or contagious corruption, this broad-based and increasingly visible movement, with its growing coalition of thinkers, sees itself as emerging out of the milieu of a dying modernism and a rising "after modernity" spirit.

While the critique of modernity has been ongoing since at least Nietzsche, the full-orbed mainstream rejection of much of what character-

---

37. Murphy, *Beyond Liberalism and Fundamentalism*, 90.

izes it is probably only now reaching its pinnacle. Today, evangelical think-ers are interacting with, not two, but *three worlds*: modern, postmodern, and biblical. The question of how theology engages these worlds looms large on the postconservative agenda. As Stanley Grenz observes concern-ing the evangelical response to the contemporary postmodern context, "Nancey Murphy and other observers are surely correct in suggesting that any parting of ways evident in theology today, whether evangelical or mainline, arises largely from how thinkers engage the postmodern condi-tion."[38] If Murphy is correct, then it would seem imperative for evangelical philosophers and theologians to ask themselves some vital questions about the use of modern and postmodern theories of knowledge—particularly *theological* epistemologies—in philosophical and theological constructions for evangelical thought. We think such considerations are of tremendous importance to the future of evangelical theology. Thus, for the balance of this discourse, we will be giving primary attention to the subject of theo-logical epistemology as understood and articulated by evangelical thinkers, especially those of the postconservative variety—keeping in mind the wide spectrum between those embracing much, and those affirming much less, of what may be considered postconservative.[39] We begin this analysis and evaluation with a look at the current state of affairs in intellectual evangeli-calism having to do with means of approaching theological knowledge.

38. Grenz, *Renewing the Center*, 184–85.

39. An imagined postconservative spectrum might encompass something suggestive of scholars on one end of the scale who agree with several of the aforementioned char-acteristics, to those on the other end who accept virtually all of them. Perhaps a better model would be more web-like and emblematic of a *centered* set rather than *bounded* set configuration.

2

The Emergence of Postconservative
Theological Epistemology

Introduction and Overview: The Current State of
Evangelical Approaches to the Knowledge of God

MAINSTREAM CONSERVATIVE EVANGELICAL THEOLOGY IN THE MODERN
period has traditionally approached epistemological questions with definitive—and allegedly indubitable—answers generally based on a modern
foundationalist method of biblical interpretation: a system characterized
by an unwavering belief in the ability of reason and evidence, primarily in
the form of conservative Christian apologetics, to provide the church and
the world with certain knowledge and truth. Many evangelical scholars,
however, are intent on shedding the dominant Enlightenment approach
to knowledge and its characteristic foundationalist search for indubitable
certainty.[1] Of course, this is having—and will continue to have—profound implications for evangelical theological method. It seems appropriate to consider why many of these thinkers are abandoning the quest for
objectivity—or in its strongest form, absoluteness—in favor of alternative
models of knowing: in rare cases, moving beyond epistemological concerns altogether.

Why is this happening? What historical, philosophical, and theological developments have led to the disillusionment with foundationalism?
Is it even acceptable for evangelicalism to abandon the presumed solid
foundation upon which much nineteenth and twentieth-century conser-

---

1. Later we will discuss modern foundationalism—its rise, characteristics, and rejection—at some length under the heading, "The Rise of Cartesian Foundationalism and the
Fall of *Opinio*."

vative theology was built? Shall we seek yet another foundation, or should evangelical thinkers be looking to incorporate alternative epistemologies for theology? How might postconservatism answer these questions?

Has the postmodern critique thoroughly devastated the categories of knowledge and truth? Is this a matter of sellout to the culture—a capitulation to the spirit of the times? Could there be other considerations driving hundreds of evangelical leaders to revision, re-imagine, or reform evangelical theology and its claims to knowledge? Is there perhaps something for evangelicals to learn from postmodern philosophical critiques of Western culture? Do evangelicals have a mandate to engage with such apparent radical thinking, or is postmodernism nothing more than godless deconstruction of Christianity to be avoided like modern pagan rituals and goddess worship? If evangelical theologians *are* to be reconsidering epistemological claims beyond classical foundationalism—even in *non*-foundationalist terms—does it necessarily follow that *all* knowledge and truth claims are to be abandoned as well? Does this, therefore, include claims to inerrancy, infallibility, or even inspiration of scripture? And what about the *meta* nature of the gospel narrative itself?

These are obviously crucial questions evangelical theology must face in this new millennium. Postconservative scholars appear committed to the task of standing in all three worlds—modern, postmodern, and biblical—endeavoring to address the epistemological concerns of each earnestly and adequately.

As part of this analysis, factors contributing to postconservative evangelical epistemology will receive special consideration. It will also be asked whether a postconservative theory of knowledge is correct in accepting and appropriating certain postmodern criticism and convictions, whether it undermines and abandons its conservative theological heritage for postliberalism, or even liberalism, and whether it can be maintained conscientiously by theologians desiring to remain within the bounds of evangelicalism. Hence, in order to more fully analyze and comprehend *post*conservatism—which need not imply *anti*conservatism—particular aspects of other so-called "posts" in contemporary Western culture that have significantly impacted postconservative theology (e.g., the postmodern communitarian orientation) will be considered alongside our main focus of this section: helping to clarify the what's and why's associated with moves beyond conservative and modern.[2]

2. While this book is mainly focused on the problem of theological knowledge within

The method we have selected in analyzing postconservative responses to major epistemological shifts and the correlative upshot for evangelical theology begins with tracing the theological and epistemological moves made by Clark Pinnock; we look at several of his most important writings, beginning in the 1960s and continuing through to the present day. Considering Pinnock's theological journey will help provide us with a sense of the distinctions between traditionalist and reformist evangelical approaches to theology and theological knowledge, and will also set the stage for careful analysis of recent developments in postconservative thought. Hence, following our exposition of Pinnock, we move to an examination of the work of his theological successors, looking at their theological and epistemological emphases, discussing some of the newer ideas set forth concerning approaches to the knowledge of God. We begin, then, with the intellectual journey of Clark Pinnock.

Tracing the Emergence of Postconservative Theological Epistemology through the Intellectual Journey of Clark Pinnock

Introduction

Clark Pinnock is widely held to be one of the most controversial thinkers in recent evangelical theology.[3] Perhaps no other single evangelical theologian has elicited more critical response in the past few decades.[4] He continues to turn out a significant amount of work, and with each new book or article, Pinnock seems eager to break new ground, causing fellow evangelicals and others to reflect and report on his latest permutation.

---

an epistemological framework, it should become obvious that related theoretical and practical concerns will inevitably come into view (e.g., specific questions concerning the nature of truth), demonstrating the connectivity that pervades and overlaps disciplines sometimes treated compartmentally—as if neat, simple, self-contained, conclusive systems could be designed and maintained without outside interference or interaction. Stephen Toulmin has gone a great distance in deconstructing such compartmentalized thinking in *Cosmopolis*.

3. Randy Maddox, for instance, states that "Clark Pinnock has been one of the most prominent and provocative theological voices in North Atlantic evangelical Christianity since the 1960s," in his foreword to Callen, *Clark H. Pinnock*, xiii.

4. Two other younger evangelical scholars, John Sanders and Greg Boyd, have begun to share the weight of criticisms generally leveled against Pinnock.

Not everyone has been happy with his revisionist efforts.[5] However, a growing number of younger evangelical theologians have expressed sympathy for his explorations, with more than a few joining him in his revisionist project.

As we prepare for a further analysis of postconservative thought, it will be helpful to look at the pattern of Pinnock's theological journey, since he has provided much of the impetus for the movement's reflection on theological epistemology. Thus, a central concern here is to provide description and critical analysis of Pinnock's various positions held throughout his theological journey, especially regarding theories concerning the knowledge of God.

In order to get at his position, the methodology chosen herein considers Pinnock's epistemological views primarily via his theological and apologetical writings. This will also include a consideration of the influences on his theological epistemology, the discussion arranged chronologically, according to significant transitional periods in Pinnock's broader intellectual and theological journey: his earliest academic years, characterized by a commitment to classical Calvinist theology and rationalistic apologetics; his middle years, as he comes to embrace Arminian theology and a "softer" rationalism; and finally, his later years, with his adoption of an open (or free will) theism, incorporating an assortment of theological and epistemological ideas from various Christian traditions, including some outside historic evangelicalism.

Our focus here will be on the way Pinnock's epistemological shifts result primarily from his broader theological methods adopted at various stages in his overall intellectual journey. Pinnock's desire to have a relevant evangelical framework for contemporary culture also contributes to his epistemic moves; it would be inaccurate to claim that his model arises merely from a desire for a more biblical, rather than systematic, approach to the treatment of scripture. A supporting contention is that Pinnock's theological epistemology may be viewed as a move from *bibliocentrism* to *christocentrism* to *pneumacentrism*—roughly corresponding to the *early*, *middle*, and *late* stages of his theological journey (although his most recent work appears to find more grounding in christocentric and trinitarian, rather than pneumacentric, themes).

---

5. For example, see Ware, "Defining Evangelicalism's Boundaries Theologically."

The Theological Journey Begins

Following a very diverse church and parachurch formative background, including growing up in the context of the liberal Park Road Baptist Church in Toronto, Pinnock was converted to personal faith in Christ in 1950.[6] Thirteen years later, he would complete his dissertation at the University of Manchester (1963), previously having begun teaching and writing as president of InterVarsity Christian Fellowship at the University of Toronto (1960).[7] Thus, Pinnock's primary context in these early years was *post-World War II fundamentalism* in North America—a context that would definitively shape his earliest theological positions. By 1960, Pinnock had been profoundly shaped and immersed in the theological writings of the Reformed wing of evangelicalism.

The Early Years (1960s–1974)

Pinnock is candid about his earlier full-orbed absorption within the Calvinistic theology vein of evangelicalism, convinced at the time that "sound" theology and Reformed writings were strictly synonymous.[8] Somewhat paradoxically, Pinnock's Christian community experiences were within various other Christian traditions such as the holiness-oriented Canadian Keswick Bible Conference—which undoubtedly contributed to the self-confessed psychological tensions and theological antinomies he was experiencing at the time.[9]

Pinnock's epistemology in the 1960s was based on a classical *foundationalism* model. He was primarily committed to a Cartesian-like quest

6. For a detailed biographical account of Pinnock's formative contexts, see Callen, *Journey Toward Renewal*, 15–39, whose work I am deeply indebted to as it concerns Pinnock's intellectual journey.

7. Pinnock's connection with InterVarsity has continued via the publication of several of his books by InterVarsity Press, the book-publishing division of InterVarsity Christian Fellowship (e.g., *Flame of Love*).

8. See Callen, *Journey Toward Renewal*, 20. Pinnock indoctrinated himself with the writings of Carl F. H. Henry, J. I. Packer, John Murray, Cornelius Van Til, and a number of other conservative Reformed thinkers, to the apparent exclusion of scholars within other traditions of evangelicalism (not to mention those outside of conservative evangelical circles). As will be seen later, this situation dramatically changes with Pinnock's developing intellectual journey.

9. Pinnock also credits the role of parachurch organizations in his spiritual and intellectual development. Most influential was InterVarsity Christian Fellowship, proving to be critical to his developing Christian identity within the evangelical community.

for epistemic certainty, coupled with an empiricist approach to Christian evidences. His general technique was to employ modern scientific methods in order to *prove* the truth of Christianity, thus obtaining *indubitable* theological knowledge. At the time, in step with many other apologists of that era (C. S. Lewis being one exception), he simply accepted the notions of knowledge and truth that have come to be associated with modernity. Pinnock attributes his reading of B. B. Warfield to making himself "a theological rationalist in addition to being a pietist."[10] Moreover, Francis Schaeffer provided him with a cultural apologetic within which he could incorporate his rationalism.[11] Thus, Pinnock's earliest concerns were evangelism and apologetics, and along with these concerns, the utilizing of rationalist methods that would remove intellectual obstacles to evangelism and pave the way for proclaiming the truth of Christianity with utter certainty. Evidentialist apologetics could provide historical and factual certainty of Christianity's claims.[12] Reason and logic would demonstrate the veracity of central doctrines of the scriptures (e.g., the bodily resurrection of Jesus Christ), utilizing probability in order to eliminate alternative interpretations (e.g., that the body of Jesus had been stolen).

Three of Pinnock's earliest books demonstrate his commitment to Christian apologetics, and these helped to quickly establish him as a key spokesperson in defense of conservative evangelical theology. A brief consideration of each of these works will give some perspective on the epistemology of Pinnock's early years, while also aiding us in comprehending traditionalist approaches to theological knowledge still evident within much contemporary evangelicalism.

A Defense of Biblical Infallibility (1967)

It was in the opening sentence of Pinnock's first apologetics book that he defined what he saw as the crux of the theological issue of the day: "The central problem for twentieth-century theology is its own epistemological basis."[13] Thus, Pinnock focuses at this stage on attempting to demonstrate the necessity of having an inspired Bible—also inerrant and infallible—in

10. Callen, *Journey Toward Renewal*, 28.

11. Ibid.

12. It would seem that John Warwick Montgomery, a staunch evidentialist and colleague of Pinnock at Trinity Evangelical Divinity School, may have had some influence on Pinnock's apologetical method.

13. Pinnock, *Defense of Biblical Infallibility*, 1.

order to avoid the demise of historic biblical Christianity. Rather than scientific discovery threatening the doctrine of inspiration, the real pressure is modernity's *a priori* dismissal of the doctrine. Pinnock also takes to task the so-called new view of revelation and truth (he has in mind here the existential theology as seen in Bultmann) as being an epistemological sellout to the contemporary ethos of the culture:

> This shift is an attempt to make peace with the philosophical mood of the twentieth century. But having forfeited its right to appeal to Scripture for truth, modern theology has surrendered its right to speak at all. . . . Existential theology capitalizes on the blur created by negative criticism around the Bible and attempts a salvage operation amidst the wreckage. The result however is the rescue of nothing Christian.[14]

Pinnock's rebuke is even harsher when speaking of experiential- and existential-centered claims to theological knowledge, as when he states:

> The wider we allow the gap to grow between the existential or theological "truth" of the Bible and the historical, factual, and doctrinal truth of it, the more vulnerable our theology becomes to the charge of meaninglessness. Inspiration and errancy are unequally yoked together in modern theology. The two are incompatible. If the historical material is inaccurate, the theological statements are uncertain too, and inspiration has no meaning. Falling back on experience alone leaves the person in the never-never land of untestable feelings.[15]

In contrast with some of the newer philosophical approaches to truth being advanced (e.g., coherence theory), Pinnock contends for the correspondence theory, noting that the doctrine of infallibility relies on it: "the divine intention behind the language is not hidden; it is discernible in the plain sense of the text. . . . The divine intention is revealed precisely *in* the language of Scripture."[16]

---

14. Ibid., 6–7.

15. Ibid., 8–9.

16. Ibid., 13–14. The coherence theory of truth is one of a number of alternative theories proposed to replace the correspondence theory. The former views truth as holistic—a belief being verified when it is part of a consistent and harmonious total system of beliefs, while the latter holds that a belief (proposition, statement, etc.) is true provided that a fact corresponding to it exists. See Audi, *Cambridge Dictionary of Philosophy*, 930–31, for a compendium of theories of truth.

Following Pinnock's development and propounding of a rational defense of infallibility and inerrancy of the Bible—essential in his mind for maintaining a biblically sound orthodoxy—his final paragraph closes with a reiteration of its connection to epistemology:

> Evangelicalism is called to maintain a pure testimony. It must insist that it is impossible to sustain the *sola scriptura* principle without infallibility. Denial of it brings into serious jeopardy the entire epistemological base of Christianity.[17]

Set Forth Your Case (1967)

Published the same year as *A Defense of Biblical Infallibility*, the purpose of *Set Forth Your Case* is essentially the same as the former, although broader in scope. The book focuses on Christian apologetics, primarily with making a rational defense of the historic Christian faith in light of the challenges of secularization in Western society via the growing acceptance of existential philosophy, and the encroachment of modern theology[18] within the Christian church. Concerning this encroachment, Pinnock places blame for the inability of orthodoxy to "bridge the gap" with modern agnosticism squarely on "the sheer laziness of evangelicals to relate their treasure with intellectual courage to the questions being asked," noting that the situation calls for "rugged conviction and boldness."[19]

Epistemologically, Pinnock is concerned with what he sees as the growing separation between faith and fact, resulting from defective modern theology. He views the theological problem through the metaphors of "upper story" (the field of intuition, faith, and conjecture of the new theology) and "lower story" (where the Bible is placed as a victim of scientific criticism, alleging biblical fallibility and errancy) created by contemporary theology. Pinnock fixes the blame for this perilous development on historical figures like Kant and Kierkegaard and their modern progeny. He speaks directly about the new theology's inability to address the contemporary problem of existentialism:

17. Pinnock, *Defense of Biblical Infallibility*, 31–32.

18. For Pinnock, at this stage, "modern theology" is a synonym for contemporary liberal or neo-orthodox theologies and is not to be equated with contemporary conservative theology, which he sees as synonymous with a strict Calvinist theological system.

19. Pinnock, *Set Forth Your Case*, 8. Included among Pinnock's contextual concerns are particularly influential theological movements (e.g., "Death of God" and "neo-orthodoxy") and cultural trends (e.g., mystical experience and anti-establishmentarianism).

> The single greatest tragedy in modern theology is the failure to challenge this secular shift to irrationalism at its foundations. Instead, theology has largely moved in the same direction. It too has accepted the unthinkable, namely, a divided field of knowledge with mystical intuition as the clue to reality. . . . Instead of challenging our culture with the distinctive feature of the gospel, namely its objective historical base (Jn. 1:14), modern theology has jumped on the bandwagon on its way to a fool's paradise. . . . The Bible believing Christian has never been confronted by so clever a device before. But if he will take the time to master this divided field of knowledge trick, he will find himself in a good position to counter it.[20]

Within the first fifteen pages of *Set Forth Your Case*, Pinnock has, in rather dramatic fashion, characterized modern theology as inimical to true Christianity—using terms like counterfeit of the gospel, solipsism, insanity—because of its denial of the importance of, and in certain cases the reality of, historical facts and evidences for historic Christian faith. Moreover, modern theology has dispensed with biblical infallibility and inerrancy, settling for *subjective* experience regarding faith and reserving *objective* truth for brute facts void of all religious content. As Pinnock puts it, this involved three steps toward the abyss of the complete destruction of apologetics and evidences: subjectivism, relativism, and agnosticism.[21]

Pinnock turns to the important principle of *sola scriptura* for the definitive epistemic structure for Christianity. Here, he pursues a foundationalist approach to theological knowledge—an epistemology resting on the reliability of the teachings of Jesus Christ and the apostles in its written (and primarily propositional) form: i.e., scripture,[22] providing an indubitable foundation for theological knowledge. Pinnock arranges his argument as follows:

> The Christian message is historical to the core. All of its doctrines arise from God's self-disclosure in history. Its doctrine of authority, therefore, is given in the disclosure situations of redemptive histo-

---

20. Pinnock, *Set Forth Your Case*, 10–11, 13.

21. Ibid., 15.

22. It is important to mention that while Pinnock refuses at this stage to grant that *errors* exist in the Bible, he does maintain that *difficulties* therein are real. However, these difficulties "do not overthrow the infallibility principle," but are rather "mountains yet to be scaled and lands yet to be conquered . . . really only *masquerading as errors*" (ibid., 71–73). He writes at some length of the numerous "errors" that had already been cleared away via "further reflection and new discoveries."

ry; that is, the nature of Scripture is determined from the teachings of divinely authenticated messengers, Jesus Christ and his apostles. *The entire edifice of theology is built upon this epistemological foundation.* Without the propositional revelation in Scripture, theology is an impossible endeavor.[23]

Hence, while Pinnock believes knowledge of God to be more often than not propositional in nature, he acknowledges that in scripture "the existence of God is both a historical truth (God acted in history), and an existential truth (God reveals himself to every soul). His existence is both objectively and subjectively evident."[24]

With reference to the influence of "the Linguistic Turn" in philosophy, and its implications relative to truth-claims, Pinnock only briefly mentions the problem, assuming that its rise means the demise of philosophy, when he writes:

In philosophy . . . serious grappling with ultimate questions of life and death has almost vanished, replaced by word-games and language analysis. With the loss of absolutes since Hegel, in which the distinction between true and false, right and wrong, breaks down, the philosopher is virtually out of a job.[25]

Thus, regarding the definition of truth, Pinnock apparently dismisses out of hand any concept involving its interrelatedness to meaning systems based on social contexts and fixed by convention (a later Wittgensteinian concept). Rather than philosophy of language contributing to understanding human categories of truth, he would say that it testifies to individuals "losing a grip on their humanity, and finding themselves unable to operate in the real world."[26]

---

23. Ibid., 69. Emphasis mine.

24. Ibid., 76–77. Upon closer observation, Pinnock appears to be mixing the categories of "belief" and "knowledge," assuming that adherence to the former equates with a certain grasp of the latter. In addition, he seems adamant about achieving *certainty* of such knowing. Unfortunately for Pinnock's epistemology, such alleged certainty is now widely recognized as a myth perpetuated in the failed quest of modernity to obtain god-like ahistorical knowledge—a sort of Archimedean vantage point. Failure to acknowledge the shaping of one's historical context evidently leads Pinnock to making some rather pretentious statements that he categorically abandons years later. For instance, "according to the Bible, the nonChristian positions are deceptive and self-defeating," and "moralism without the Christian base is a one way ticket to hell" (see ibid., 28, 85).

25. Ibid., 29.

26. Ibid.

For Pinnock, at this stage, *historical evidence* is indispensable to the Christian faith, and without such a structure to undergird the theological and epistemological claims of Christianity, all sorts of insurmountable problems ensue. The following statement reveals the importance of historical facts to Pinnock's early epistemology:

> If the gospel cannot be sustained by historical data, it cannot be sustained at all. . . . The fact is that we can come to know Jesus Christ historically before we know him personally. Indeed we *must*. Otherwise the Christ we know personally is the mirror of our own visage.[27]

His elaboration continues on what he sees as the public and evidential basis of the Christian faith:

> It is a matter of public *fact*, not of unreflecting *faith*, that the historical foundations underneath the Christian message are exceedingly secure. . . . Faith is the resting of the heart in the sufficiency of the evidences. . . . The existential cart must remain *behind* the historical horse and not intrude in front.[28]

BIBLICAL REVELATION (1971)

No ambiguity arises for the readers of Pinnock's *Biblical Revelation* as to the central concern of the moment for theology—epistemology is clearly of utmost importance:

> The central problem for theology is *its own epistemological base*. From what fountainhead does theology acquire the information from which she forms her doctrinal models and tests her hypotheses? What is the *principium theologiae* which measures and authenticates the subject matter for theology and preaching? No endeavor in theology can *begin* until some kind of answer is given. . . . All issues pale before this one. It is the continental divide in Christian theology. Everything hangs on our solution to it.[29]

For Pinnock, commitment to biblical revelation is *the* answer. One need not look any further than the Bible for epistemological certainty:

> Scripture is not only relevant to the need in theology of a proper epistemological base, and to the need in philosophy of an empirical anchor to resolve the truth question, it is a particularly com-

27. Ibid., 55.
28. Ibid., 43, 48, 52.
29. Pinnock, *Biblical Revelation*, 11.

pelling solution to man's *existential* dilemmas. The metaphysical wasteland in which man is presently languishing was created by the tragic loss of God's reality and His sure Word.[30]

Pinnock's definition of Christian theology in this phase is instructive, including its relationship to *plenary inspiration*:

> The time is ripe for a fresh examination from an orthodox Protestant perspective which will sharpen and improve the case for plenary inspiration. . . . *Christian theology is the articulation of the truth content implicit in divine revelation mediated in Scripture.* . . . The high doctrine of Scripture is not an a priori dogma, assumed arbitrarily to suit a particular view of God and truth. It is the conclusion of an examination of what revelation *is*, a divine self-disclosure which generates a documentary residue, inspired by the Spirit.[31]

Engagement with *neo-orthodoxy* is of particular importance to Pinnock, especially to demonstrate its epistemological problems relative to inspiration, revelation, and scripture. While he expresses some appreciation for certain thinkers (for instance, Karl Barth with respect to his commitment to the Bible as the *sole* authoritative witness to revelation), Pinnock laments the movement's disassociating revelation from doctrine—especially the doctrine of God—saying that "in the entire neoorthodox movement there is a strong depreciation of the noetic content of revelation, without an apparent awareness of the nihilistic implications of this for theology. There is a *crisis of content* here."[32]

The concepts that "theology and the Bible represent the human response to revelation," and that it represents "a religious interpretation [which is] superimposed upon the ambiguous data of history by the act of faith" are to Pinnock nothing short of fatal to theology in that they "surrender the objective biblical authority of God speaking."[33] Fideistic approaches to revelation are devoid of substantial content, and the gospel cannot be sustained if not by historical data.[34] He comments that "the validity of Christian theism rests on its *historical credentials*," and "any disengagement from history is docetic in direction and deeply hereti-

---

30. Ibid., 14.
31. Ibid., 15–16.
32. Ibid., 24.
33. Ibid., 26, 28.
34. Ibid., 46.

cal."[35] Still, Pinnock concedes that historical facts cannot be considered to be definitely assured when he writes, "factual, empirical knowledge falls somewhat short of absolute certainty. When we enter the realm of fact, we deal in probability. . . . Probability is the guide to life; it is the guide to religious truth too."[36]

Another major feature of *Biblical Revelation* is its unequivocal stance concerning the Bible as necessarily being fully inerrant and infallible.[37] His attack on the idea of *limited inerrancy* is pronounced—a position that he himself would soon come to embrace.[38] At this earlier time, however, Pinnock felt strongly that a compromise on inerrancy would mean disastrous consequences to follow for theology, declaring,

> The result of denying inerrancy, as skeptics well know, is the loss of a trustworthy Bible. Limited inerrancy is a slope, not a platform. . . . What is lost when errors are admitted is divine *truthfulness*. Evangelicals confess inerrancy because it is biblical to do so.[39]

Under the heading "authority" in *Biblical Revelation*, Pinnock concentrates on the epistemological foundation of inspiration. There can be little doubt that the early Pinnock substantially interconnected theological knowledge and the doctrine of the inspiration of scripture:

> More than merely an article of faith, the doctrine of inspiration is fundamental, the epistemological foundation of sacred theology, the basis of every article. Scripture is the *causa media* (mediating instrument) of our knowledge of God, the *principium cognoscendi*

35. Ibid., 45.

36. Ibid., 46.

37. In chapter 2, Pinnock devotes more than fifty pages to a classical defense of verbal, plenary inspiration, inerrancy, and infallibility of the Bible (ibid., *Biblical Revelation*, 53–106.) It is dumbfounding to read what Pinnock claims here (with apparently deep conviction) in light of the substantial shift he would make just a few years later, as will be shown shortly. One wonders whether he has ever revisited the arguments posed here since modifying his views, or whether he simply moved on subsequently to embracing material changes in his approach to the subject. The latter scenario would appear to be more likely. Evidently, as will be seen with Pinnock's second phase, the pertinent and challenging writing of Dewey Beegle (1973) and Stephen Davis (1977) become highly influential to Pinnock's thinking as to biblical revelation and inspiration.

38. One of his main targets of criticism is Dewey Beegle, who would soon challenge—and in part, convince—Pinnock, with his consequential book, *Scripture, Tradition, and Infallibility.*

39. Pinnock, *Biblical Revelation*, 80.

(first principle of knowing). The doctrine of Scripture is perennially at the heart of the theological discussion.[40]

For Pinnock at this point, because the Bible is God's word, we have
certainty concerning knowledge of God. While he includes the human element in the production of scripture, Pinnock nonetheless sees the overrid-
ing work of the Spirit in "safeguarding the truth deposit" of the revelation
of the knowledge of God, and thus he can unequivocally affirm inspiration
as the basis of our theological knowledge. (Later, with Pinnock's emphasis
shifting more weight to the human contributions to scripture, knowledge
of God becomes understandably less conspicuous.) While he notes the
importance of other sources for theological knowledge, such as tradition,
Pinnock holds scripture as preeminent, because unlike alternative sources,
"what knowledge we have in Scripture *is* knowledge of *God*."[41]

Compared to Pinnock's earlier writings, *Biblical Revelation* clearly
reveals that he has become more aware of sociological and historicist accounts of human knowledge, and even more willing to admit them into
his overall worldview. Nevertheless, Pinnock is convinced that this cultural
and historical conditioning of human knowledge does *not* disturb an evangelical theological epistemology, since the theological content of scripture
is in effect ahistorical, due to the *divine* nature of the Bible:

> Sociology has shown . . . that human knowledge is relative to the
> culture in which it exists, and that religions are historically con-
> ditioned. If the scriptural revelation were just another man-made
> religion, it would be characterized by 'historicity' at every point;
> as it is, it makes an explicit claim *not* to be. The finality of Jesus
> Christ and the inspiration of Scripture provide an Archimedian
> point in the flux of the human situation against which the flow of
> history may be measured and evaluated.[42]

Pinnock closes his book with a theological call to arms, stating in no
uncertain terms that the very future of theology (and truth itself) rests on
winning the "battle" for the Bible. His tone here, as elsewhere in his early
writings, is combative and inspiring, generating a new enthusiasm among
other evangelical apologists:[43]

40. Ibid., 95.

41. Ibid., 127–28.

42. Ibid., 128.

43. Such enthusiasm led, for instance, to Harold Lindsell entitling his bombshell book,
Battle for the Bible.

> To cast doubt on the complete veracity and authority of Scripture is a criminal act creating a crisis of immense proportions for theology and faith. The cost of losing the battle for the Bible is the loss of all theology and truth. Everything stands in question. . . . We will not admit that the debate over plenary inspiration is an insignificant and out-of-date squabble. It is a matter of life and death. . . . If the church allows her truth base to slip away, she will embark upon a quest for certainty which will never succeed . . . the loss of biblical authority is the cause of the doubt and uncertainty which plague the modern church. . . . The move toward mystical subjectivism will result in the demise of authentic Christianity. . . . If ever an age needed a sure Word from God, it is our own.[44]

The concern expressed for certainty, based on a foundationalist epistemology and focused in turn on the Bible itself, looms large in this phase of Pinnock's theological journey. The next stage of the journey will reveal not only a changing approach to theology, but also a modified, softening epistemology. This consequential move appears to be in its embryonic form by the fall of 1973, reflected in Pinnock's somewhat toned-down and irenic manner visible in a paper delivered at the Conference on the Inspiration and Authority of the Scripture in Ligonier, Pennsylvania.[45] Although unwilling at this point to embrace a limited inerrancy position, the die has been cast for such a subsequent move with his nuanced view of what inerrancy actually concerns. After taking to task those who attempt to retain biblical inerrancy *only* as it concerns the saving or revelatory content of the Bible (his examples include Daniel Fuller and the documents of the Second Vatican Council), Pinnock writes:

> Restricting inerrancy to *the sense intended by the inspired writer* is not, in our judgment, any basis for speaking of limited inerrancy. It simply respects the *meaning which the writer wished to convey* rather than some other. The message of the writer is the message of the Bible, and to that, and that alone, inerrancy refers.[46]

Pinnock's epistemological justification for retaining a plenary view of inerrancy—although limiting it to the *intention* of the inspired writer—is evidently based on *foundationalist* presuppositions. According to Pinnock,

---

44. Pinnock, *Biblical Revelation*, 228–30.

45. Pinnock's paper, "Limited Inerrancy," is subsequently published as one among a number of essays concerning the inerrancy debate in Montgomery, *God's Inerrant Word*.

46. Pinnock, "Limited Inerrancy," 148–49. Emphasis mine.

if non-soteric (let alone soteric) truth is surrendered to errancy or irrelevance, then serious consequences follow for theology:

> We surrender the only sound method of building theology. Since
> our knowledge of things divine derives from Scripture, the whole
> structure of theology is ready to collapse as soon as trustworthiness
> is given up. . . . Surely it is wiser and truer to recognise that the
> Bible is a seamless garment. We are not to pluck out a thread and
> discard a cloth. "*All* Scripture is God-breathed."[47]

Pinnock is doubtlessly concerned about the *base* of proper systematic
theology being undermined, and his own approach continues to reveal an
unequivocal commitment to foundationalism.[48] To abandon it would mean
nothing less than abandoning Christ himself. "It is obvious that the stakes
are very high. Nothing less than the authority of Jesus is on the line."[49]

There can be little doubt that Pinnock's own historical context greatly
factored into his early apologetical and epistemological focus—although
at times he seemed unaware of his modern, ahistorical approach to theological knowledge. A brief synopsis of Pinnock's context and involvements
during this early phase of his journey may shed light as to the primary
influences on his thinking: immersion in Reformed theology to the virtual
exclusion of other theological traditions, practically equating the systematic theology of Calvinism with biblical revelation; in social circles, having
professional and personal relationships that—with a few notable exceptions like C. S. Lewis—were composed of parallel-theological-tradition
evangelicals, reinforcing his then current philosophy; cultural and philosophical trends challenging claims of biblical authority and theological

47. Ibid., 150.

48. Recall that for Pinnock at this stage, the *only* proper systematic theology is *Reformed*
theology, consistently based on modern foundationalism. Pinnock repeatedly uses traditional terms to express this epistemic model (e.g., building, structure, foundation, base). Of
course, exceptions to the foundationalist model within Reformed thought can be found.
See, for instance, Holmes, *Faith Seeks Understanding*.

49. Pinnock, "Limited Inerrancy," 152. Thirty years later, Pinnock would express his
thoughts about the powerful impact foundationalism had had on his formative theological
thinking, noting the degree to which it profoundly influenced his own early writings:
"It did so in a covert way since I was not tuned in to these subtleties. Because religion
appeals to the need for security in life, it is easy to fall into foundationalism as a way of
attaining it. It has a particularly seductive appeal for fundamentalists with their passion
for certainty" (Clark Pinnock, unpublished paper, delivered at the evangelical-process dialogue, Claremont School of Theology, 1997, as cited in Callen, *Journey Toward Renewal*,
57, n.49).

knowledge; new theologies challenging conservative theological and epistemological claims; alternative views concerning the idea of truth being advocated within philosophy of language; conflict within his own Baptist denomination, especially the contentious battle between conservatives and moderates within the Southern Baptist Convention; personal concern for the integrity of the gospel in the light of a perceived erosion of adherence to objective truth and doctrinal propositions; use of a rationalistic methodology that alleged to provide certainty of knowledge and truth; *a priori* commitment to a strict view of biblical inerrancy, seen as elemental for avoiding an assumed logical destruction of both evangelism and apologetics; and love for the lost and commitment to the work of evangelism.

Without a doubt, other contextual factors could be mentioned that influenced Pinnock's thinking during this early stage of his intellectual journey, including the radical political views of John Howard Yoder and Jim Wallis, which captured his attention from the late 1960s through the mid-1970s. It now seems clear that Pinnock's political zigzag through the 1970s involved three primary moves: first, away from a Billy Graham-like commitment to social change through individual conversions; next, embracing and being immersed in "radical politics and Anabaptist hermeneutics," which witnessed his associating the Kingdom of God with a social utopianism; and finally, awakening from his "radical dream," partly due to his coming to admire the work of Michael Novak, which led to genuine appreciation for positive feature of the American experience (e.g., free speech and limited government).[50]

Less conclusive is the overall impact of Pinnock's political diversity upon his theology. The answer appears to be somewhat more complex than that it merely paralleled—perhaps even *caused*—substantive theological changes (such as motivating Pinnock to leave Calvin for Arminius). A more nuanced account is required, for as Callen suggests, "while he was becoming more Wesleyan-Arminian in matters related to salvation and discipleship, Pinnock has followed his brief period of radicalism by becoming more Calvinistic in a political theology featuring Christ as the transformer of culture."[51] What may be safely assumed, then, is that as Pinnock's theology developed throughout the 1970s and beyond, it reflected an increasingly *practical* and *pietistic* emphasis, coinciding with

50. I am indebted to Callen for the political theology discussion of Pinnock's views in *Journey Toward Renewal*, 106–20.

51. Ibid., 116.

his greater involvement in, as well as regard for, social-political issues, regardless of particular "left to right" positions adopted on the political spectrum.

Summary

The historical-cultural milieu of North America that Pinnock found himself a part of during these years helps explain the strategies he used in *setting forth his case* for the gospel—a case that elevated the young Pinnock into the conservative evangelical spotlight, acclaimed as one of the most influential evangelical theologians of the day. But in his later years, Pinnock would view his early rise to prominence in a very different light. For instance, in a 1997 postscript, responding to a book he had written in 1968 directed primarily to Southern Baptists, Pinnock reflected on this stage of his journey,[52] voicing strong self-criticism and penitence for his polemical approach:

> One sees here the bitter root of fundamentalism-evangelicalism manifesting itself: the militancy, the rationalism, and the doctrinalism. . . . How at thirty years of age I fell into it, I am unsure. My own roots spiritually were warmly pietistic and my sympathies charismatic. . . . At any rate, in the late 1960s I found myself heralded as a conservative voice, and I succumbed to the populist adulation. . . . I am embarrassed about the attitude that I expressed here. I did not start out the Christian life in this spirit, and I am sorry for any harm that I did.[53]

As we have seen, the early years of Pinnock's intellectual journey reveal a theology that is deeply rooted in epistemological foundationalism, and that centers on the scriptures as the divinely inspired and authoritative revelation of God to humanity. Because the Bible *is* God's word, Pinnock would say, it provides humanity with an Archimedean vantage point of timeless and unchanging truth; therefore, we possess indubitable certainty as it concerns the knowledge of God. Pinnock supposed that without the propositional revelation in scripture, theology would be an impossible endeavor—its edifice, which is built upon this type of revelation and supporting historical evidences, would be bound to collapse. To undermine this foundation for theological knowledge was, to his mind, unthinkable.

---

52. Pinnock, *New Reformation*.
53. Callen, *Journey Toward Renewal*, 223–24.

Hence, the formative theological period of Clark Pinnock may properly be described in theological terms as *bibliocentric*—the Bible itself being the core source for knowledge of God. As we have seen, he could confidently assert then, "We can come to know Jesus Christ historically before we know him personally. Indeed we *must*."[54] But as will become evident shortly, Pinnock's tone will soon begin to change—at times dramatically—as we move forward to consider the second phase of Pinnock's theological journey and its bearing upon his epistemology, keeping in mind the consequential influence his moves would have upon many younger evangelical theologians following in his wake.

The Middle Years (1974–88)

At least five key developments between 1974 and 1977 motivate us to date this period as the beginning of the second phase (or middle years) of Pinnock's theological journey, including his epistemological direction. First, his move from Trinity Evangelical Divinity School (1969–74) to Regent College in Vancouver, Canada (1974–77), followed by his acceptance of a post in theology at McMaster Divinity College in Ontario, Canada in 1977, which he held for a quarter century. Apparently, both Regent and McMaster (especially) provided settings for greater theological probing than did his earlier academic environments. Second, the appearance of a book—one that he took very seriously—that was critical of his position regarding biblical "difficulties": Dewey N. Beegle's *Scripture, Tradition, and Infallibility*. Third, the way in which scholar Harold Lindsell brought Pinnock into the inerrancy debate by means of his own 1976 provocative book, *The Battle for the Bible*. Fourth, the appearance of another important book: Stephen Davis' *Debate About the Bible: Inerrancy Versus Infallibility*, and its immediate impact on Pinnock relative to biblical inerrancy.[55] Fifth, Pinnock's own intellectual evolution, entailing a move from a particular strain of Reformed theology and its more rationalistic system of thought, to an Arminian theology and its concern for a more experiential and (in Callen's words) "dynamic work of the Spirit in relation to the biblical authors/editors and his thought and life. . . ."[56] This last development led to

---

54. Pinnock, *Set Forth Your Case*, 55.

55. Davis, *Debate About the Bible*.

56. Callen, *Journey Toward Renewal*, 60.

Pinnock's embracing a *progressiveness of revelation*, leading to a new focus on the Spirit and direction of the principles found in the biblical text.

By the arrival of the 1980s, Pinnock had been in theological transition for six or more years. A number of alterations in his thinking became apparent during this middle period, as seen in the content and spirit of what Pinnock was advocating: a modified, nuanced position on inerrancy; a softening of rationalism; openness to modern (i.e., critical) biblical scholarship; repudiation of Calvinism and endorsement of Arminianism; a renewed call to evangelism and social responsibility; a softening critique of Pentecostalism; and finally, an increasing place for piety.

As we consider two of Pinnock's major works written during this middle stage, *Reason Enough* (1980) and *The Scripture Principle* (1984), will we begin to see the evolvement of his theological and epistemological views that will continue through to the later stage of his intellectual journey. And it will be these two latter phases of his theological development that give rise to a *postconservative* evangelicalism, and thus to the growing contingent of younger evangelical scholars seeking to expand upon the program principally initiated by Pinnock.

REASON ENOUGH (1980)

Thirteen years had elapsed between the writings of *Set Forth Your Case* and *Reason Enough*, and through these years, as we have noted, Pinnock had made numerous intellectual and theological adjustments. The cultural climate had also moved from what some have dubbed "the secular sixties" to a period of increasing spiritual interest and a turning toward faith. Rather than faith being "vain superstition" or "cruel illusion," Pinnock (in 1980) "is convinced that the Christian world-view is adequate intellectually, factually and morally," as he sets out to present an *evidential* picture for its *reasonableness* via a program of five interrelated circles of evidence: pragmatism, experientialism, cosmic, historical, and corporate. The work is both apologetical and polemical in purpose.[57]

The overall tone of Pinnock's approach is quite different from his early works. Here, his apologetical shift involves a departure from a dogmatic, combative approach, to a softer, more common-ground method. For instance, rather than continuing to appeal to special knowledge (i.e., scripture) as *the* rationale for attempting to get to the truth of Christian

---

57. Pinnock, *Reason Enough*, preface.

faith, Pinnock begins instead with the following common-ground epistemology:

> We gain our knowledge of reality through our interaction with the external world. . . . Of course, our perceptual knowledge is not flawless or complete. Nevertheless, there is no other comparable avenue for obtaining information about the external world, and it is one I certainly propose to travel along with you. . . . Second, I assume the only way we can draw reliable conclusions from what we perceive is by thinking coherently and consistently about the data we encounter. . . . We could not make any progress in knowing if we refused to accept the significance of the data at hand. . . . I do not want to make any special demands in the area of knowledge. I have no hidden assumptions, no special philosophy. My contention is that the truth claim of the Christian gospel can be checked out in the ordinary ways we verify the things we know.[58]

Furthermore, Pinnock's theological shift from a strict form of Calvinism to Arminianism is markedly evident throughout the book. For example, his chapter dealing with religious experience demonstrates an abandoning of Reformed doctrine concerning humankind's desire for autonomy from God.[59]

Antecedents to Pinnock's later theology of religions are everywhere evident. For instance, he maintains, "All religions emphasize the need to develop and mature in spiritual disciplines that lead to the knowledge of God."[60] On the epistemic question of whether knowledge of God is truly revealed in religions other than Christianity, his response displays a significant shift in thinking from his earlier phase as the following excerpts demonstrate with regard to considering truth in other religions:

> Atheists have to believe all religions are false, and believers often believe they are all false but one. I do not think a Christian is forced to take such a narrow view. . . . Paul's glimpse of the universal sovereignty of God does not limit God's total activity to the knowledge of it we have been given in the Bible. . . . I think we should regard religions of the world as a patchwork quilt, combining light and dark colors in various proportions. . . . There are *elements of truth* and falsehood, *authenticity* and deception alongside each other in the fabric. There is a need for careful discernment.

58. Ibid., 16–17.
59. Ibid., ch. 2.
60. Ibid., 44.

But that is not to deny that in the world religions there are some good and positive features. There is devotion and commitment, often putting Christians to shame. The fundamental questions of life and death are also engaged there, and the quest for salvation pursued. In particular, there is the perception we are speaking of, some sense of the goodness and majesty of God and of our need to depend upon him in life and death.[61]

Hence, by the middle stage of his intellectual journey, Pinnock is viewing the knowledge of God as *not* being found solely through the Christian scriptures, or via a distinctly Christ-confessing experience; rather, theological knowledge may be available to human beings in a variety of religions and experiences. Knowledge of God, then, appears to be a matter of *degree*—the greatest degree experienced within the explicit and settled faith found in Christianity. Thus, non-Christian religious experience in general is not ruled out from the start as demonic or false (as it was with Pinnock's first three apologetics books written in the later sixties and early seventies). Instead, religious experiences demonstrate the activity of God to some degree within the world of faiths, and "any of their experiences can be used by God to bring them closer to knowing him."[62] Most evident in *Reason Enough* is Pinnock's turnabout on the matter of *experience* providing an apologetic for the Christian faith—something he previously viewed as less that suitable for theological epistemology.

Pinnock's third circle looks at natural theology and its role in providing evidence for the truth of the Christian message. His thesis here is that although it "is not an end in itself," it is a *"preparatory step"* toward taking the message of the Incarnation—"what God is like"—seriously, and toward "enquiry after the historical credentials of the good news about Jesus who proclaims God with a human face."[63] Thus, the apologetic role of appealing to the "proofs" of natural theology is simply a supportive one for the knowledge human beings already suspect is reasonable (e.g., that God created the earth), and that Christians affirm as true (e.g., that God loves the world).

61. Ibid., 45. Emphasis mine.

62. Ibid., 46. However, Pinnock does not neglect the potential or real *negative* side of religions, noting that they can also separate people from God and actually "prevent them from meeting him."

63. Ibid., 70–71.

The fourth circle concerns the historical basis for the Christian faith. After developing an extensive argument in favor of the biblical account of the gospel, Pinnock reminds the reader of the *lack of absolute certainty* that comes with historical argumentation:[64]

> Of course the knowledge we arrive at through historical argumentation is only probable. That is true of all the knowledge we gain in an empirical way. . . . But it is the sort of knowledge we are able to operate on in all the affairs of life, and it is adequate to provide us with a sound basis for the trustful certainty of faith.[65]

Is "trustful certainty of faith," then, based on the probability of the evidence being true? If so, then there remains an important place for historical evidence in having a sound basis for faith in something or someone—an element that Pinnock is committed to retaining for his apologetics, albeit in a less rationalistic and more irenic manner than in the first phase of his theological journey. He seems willing, therefore, to accept a *limited yet adequate* rather than *certain* knowledge, due to historical and contextual factors that shape—even distort—our thinking to some degree. Yet, the evidence is decisively in favor of Christian claims being true as to the gospel of Jesus Christ, and that to reject such claims outright would be irrational.

Near the end of the book, Pinnock speaks of the fact that God has not revealed to us all we would like to know, and as a result, Christians are called to an attitude of humility regarding theological knowledge claims, once again reflecting changes in his epistemological method:

> If our knowledge of the things of God and of his ways with us is sufficient but partial, then it follows that we will likely be ignorant or inadequately informed on a number of subjects. Things that fall outside the circle of the light of revelation will remain obscure and may not reveal their secrets even under the closest scrutiny. Clarity on them may not be given until the end of history. . . . There must be a place in our consciousness for *modesty and even reverent agnosticism* on subjects that are just not ours to know.[66]

---

64. Yet Pinnock asserts that mathematics provides absolute certainty (see ibid., 88).

65. Ibid.

66. Ibid., 108. Emphasis mine.

THE SCRIPTURE PRINCIPLE (1984)

Because of the substantial theological moves Pinnock was making in the seventies and early eighties, he seems to have sensed the obligation to write a book clarifying his evolving view of scripture: he accomplished this with *The Scripture Principle*.[67] Although the primary focus of the book is the nature of scripture and biblical authority, Pinnock's writing revealed refinements in his theological and epistemological views, which we will now consider.

With the introduction to *The Scripture Principle*, Pinnock makes clear that what he feels is at stake over the question of scripture's authority is the very "well-being of the church and the effective proclamation of its message to the world," pointing out that

> the church depends upon a sure word of instruction in regard to her gospel foundations. We need to possess *a true knowledge of God and his salvation, and this is what the inspired Scriptures provide for us.* Should they be discredited, we would lack the requisite knowledge of God's Word and the necessary foundations for the life of faith.[68]

Hence, Pinnock maintains that evangelical epistemology is wrapped up with the notion of biblical inspiration, and that it is imperative to affirm belief in the epistemological authority of the Bible in respect of disclosing a "true knowledge of God and his salvation," and as "the primary sacrament of the knowledge of God, his own communication."[69]

Concerning general and special revelation, Pinnock announces his contrasting perspective with the traditional Protestant position. He is open to seeing that *all* people will be given an opportunity to know God in his salvation, seeing that

> God by his grace makes an offer of salvation to them all, in keeping with his stated desire (1 Tim. 2:4). . . . But the revelation remains rather hidden and unclear and calls for further revelation that is definitive and out in the open. This is exactly what we have in special revelation.[70]

67. Pinnock, *Scripture Principle*. All future references will be to the 1998 edition.

68. Ibid., xv. Emphasis mine.

69. Ibid., xv, xix.

70. Ibid., 7.

Pinnock believes that the deeper and salvific orientation of the Old and New Testaments points to God's self-revelation via *acts* that he performs in the midst of humanity, most definitively in the ministry and salvific work of Jesus Christ. True and saving theological knowledge is most effectively obtained through the *experience of God with humanity* as attested to via the inspired scriptures—especially through the self-revelation of God in Jesus Christ.[71]

Pinnock also discusses cognitive revelation and objective knowledge of God. Although typically rejected by recent secular—as well as postmodern—philosophies, Pinnock views these as part of the revelational material found in the scriptures, thus needing to be affirmed by evangelicals since "the New Testament is contentful and intelligible and speaks to human beings about subjects we are able to understand."[72] He offers the following word on the Bible's epistemic role pertaining to God:

> Rather than turning over the gospel truth to fallible human beings in its entirely, as he might have done, God has given the church the canonical Scriptures *to help ensure the integrity of our knowledge of God* and *to prevent the proclamation from being lost or twisted beyond recognition*. It is not that Christianity rests upon the foundation of the Bible[73] (its foundation is Jesus Christ) as much as that Christian truth comes in and through the medium of Scripture and brings a doctrine of inspiration with it.[74]

This passage represents Pinnock's shift during the middle stage of his intellectual journey from a *bibliocentric* to a *christocentric* epistemological foundation for Christianity. In short, it is *Jesus Christ*, the *subject* of scripture, upon whom our *first-order* knowledge of God is dependent. The *Bible*, then, is a *second-order* attestation (or witness) to who God is. This change in Pinnock's epistemological base for theological knowledge also

---

71. Pinnock makes the important point that "the word of God in the New Testament refers primarily to the proclamation of the gospel at work in people's lives when received by faith," and that contemporary Christians need to keep in mind that while we need to "secure for the Bible a place under the category 'word of God' that it deserves, when a person testifies to the saving grace of God, he or she is indeed speaking the word of God" (see ibid., 14).

72. Ibid.

73. This statement is in direct contrast to Pinnock's early apologetical arguments concerning the Bible as *the* foundation of Christianity. For instance, see Pinnock, *Biblical Revelation*, Introduction.

74. Pinnock, *Scripture Principle*, 19. Emphasis mine.

signals a more open attitude toward the possibility of further revelation beyond the pages of the Bible, while preserving the unparalleled revelation of God in Christ:

> If revelation has not been exhausted, even though normatively outlined in the Scriptures, then it is possible to hope that our understanding of the truth will grow and mature over the years. Now that we are in touch with world religions, for example, and in a position to learn what is true in their experience of the God who addresses everyone, it may be possible to sharpen our understanding of what God is intending in the Bible. In the mutual struggle and competition of religions we can all be stimulated and challenged to learn more of the divine mystery. This need not relativize the absolute truth given in Jesus Christ that is, we believe, the definitive revelation of God.[75]

Pinnock views the biblical pattern of revelation inclusive of both *propositional* and *personal* communication, presenting the "acts of God and the response of faith, the words of God and the call to obedience, the objective and the subjective," and that "it tells us about God and brings us to God."[76] Modern theologies that attempt to divorce revelation from biblical doctrine and ethics in an attempt to make revelation a purely subjective matter falsely represent theological epistemology since, as Pinnock notes,

> Revelation, according to the Bible and historic theology, is not merely subjective and existentialist but a meaningful disclosure of the gracious God who acts and speaks. It supplies us with crucial information about the character and purposes of God, given in creaturely modalities we can understand, that enable people to be reconciled to God. It enables us to become acquainted with God so that we might meet him and know him. It is critically important not to lose this conviction. The Bible presupposes that God is able to reveal himself and truth about his plan to us. . . . Not only have countless Christians experienced the Bible to be a special vehicle of the knowledge of God, and the occasion of freshly encountering God and learning from him, but the pattern of revelation as presented in the Bible everywhere assumes that God has communicated to us in human speech, thus rendering the relationship between God and people fully personal.[77]

75. Ibid., 20.
76. Ibid., 27.
77. Ibid., 27–28.

In Pinnock's delineation of what he calls a "Scripture principle," it is possible to see his commitment to an *objective* revelation of God to humankind—albeit through "a creaturely text that is at the same time God's own written Word"—through which "we can consult his Word, which reveals his mind, and seek to know his will in it." Thus, knowledge of God is found in the scriptures:

> God has communicated authoritatively to us on those subjects about which Scripture teaches, whether doctrinal, ethical, or spiritual. . . . [T]he text is not reduced to an expression of human experience and tradition, as in liberalism, but in a contentful language deposit that addresses, as it decides, with the authority of God.[78]

Moreover, the question of how we are to approach the text is centrally important to the question of knowledge of God itself. Does the New Testament, for instance, intend the reader to take an apologetical approach toward reconciling diverse accounts of resurrection appearances of Jesus, or rather, does it primarily call for a *faith commitment* in the risen Lord because through him we know, and are saved, by God's power? Pinnock views this issue as a critical one, noting the related prejudice evident within secular academic circles:

> We must take into account how the Bible wishes us to approach it and for what purpose. It obviously wants us to come to know God in Jesus Christ. Therefore, we are within our epistemic rights as Christians when we insist upon approaching the Bible in the spirit of faith. . . . The secular, academic approach to the Bible is already predisposed to reject the Bible's message. It is not neutral scientific investigation at all but has a debunking character. The whole spirit of the enterprise breathes that human autonomy that wishes to be free of God and not subject to his Word.[79]

Pinnock seems particularly concerned with conservative Christians focusing on issues peripheral to the central message and focus of the New Testament: God as revealed in Jesus Christ for our salvation. He would insist that missing this most important feature of the text is to fail to comprehend the knowledge of God as being revealed in the person of Christ:

> The God who caused light to shine out of darkness is able to send shafts of spiritual light into our hearts to disclose the glory of God

78. Ibid., 62.
79. Ibid., 133.

in the face of Jesus Christ. Here is a subjectivity we must not turn away from. The saving knowledge of God depends upon it.[80]

Thus, in addition to the knowledge of God being revealed *objectively* in the scriptures, Pinnock affirms the complementary aspects of the *subjective* knowing of God by means of the work of the Spirit in conjunction with the Bible:

> By the Spirit, the Scriptures do occasion fresh events of revelation . . . that are more than just the analyzing of propositions. . . . Because of the Spirit, the Bible can be a channel of grace and speech of God to us. . . . God may not be giving foundational Scripture anymore now that this has been done, but he is still engaged in communicating himself and filling our lives with his loving presence. He has not and never will finish illuminating the minds of believers in the truth. . . . [81]

SUMMARY

By the end of the middle period of his intellectual journey, Pinnock's epistemology is undergoing more than a few modifications. Apparently, several factors have led to these revisions, among them Pinnock's increasing acceptance of cultural and historical influences upon the biblical texts, and thus recognition of the absence of an Archimedean vantage point for human beings. Other considerable changes in Pinnock's theology and epistemology were taking place, including his willingness to embrace the progressive character of biblical revelation, considering the important role of linguistics in theology, acknowledging problems inherent within a hard rationalist approach to scriptural authority and biblical interpretation, giving greater recognition to the role of the Holy Spirit in inspiration and illumination, and rediscovering a significant place for piety within evangelical theology.[82] Barry Callen summarizes some of the crucial moves Pinnock was making during this middle period:

> By 1980 he was actively questioning the dominance and appropriateness of the rationalistic epistemology typical of evangelicalism. He was replacing it with a "softer" rationality, a modified "foundationalism," a less militant frame of mind . . . he was now see-

---

80. Ibid., 162.

81. Ibid., 165.

82. Callen, *Journey Toward Renewal,* 75.

ing that, as a biblical Christian, he was not obligated to a view of knowledge that needs a rationally unshakable foundation, like a Bible which is claimed to have an "inerrant" text direct from God's hand. Knowledge, in fact, is more "web-like," requiring the humility of faith, and yields relative and not absolute certainty. While this softening rationality left him with a "post-modern ambiance," he still maintained that truth is *sought* rather than *created*. It relates to more than the "grammar" of the believing community. Christian claims about truth supersede their contextual settings, influential as these settings always are. We who believe have to do with more than ourselves; there is a God and God's truth. It may be apprehended only partially and articulated only tentatively, but divine revelation does exist and enables at least a meaningful apprehension of its essence and intent.[83]

Hence, the middle years of Pinnock's theological journey would signal a return to his pietist roots and a refocusing on the heart of the gospel message and the person of Jesus Christ in place of rational apologetic endeavors to prove the perfection of the Bible and Christian knowledge and truth claims—more faith and less reason. Nevertheless, Pinnock continued to affirm that we could be quite certain that knowledge of God is revealed in the face of Jesus Christ.

Hence, this second phase in Pinnock's intellectual journey can be describe in general terms as a shift from bibliocentrism to *christocentrism* for his theological epistemology. As the third phase of the journey begins, the problems of foundationalism will press Pinnock to again reevaluate his view of theological knowledge.

The Later Years (1989–present)

Pinnock's intellectual journey began to undergo another permutation by the latter half of the 1980s—this time the move would involve a turn toward story-oriented narrative theology. Moreover, Pinnock's own story of his theological journey appeared in a 1989 landmark book he edited (*The Grace of God and the Will of Man*) where he describes his transition from Calvinism to Arminianism, or as his title suggests, from Augustine to Arminius. Serving as the lead essay, this piece also provides a glimpse of the theological pilgrimage Pinnock envisions for intellectual evangelicalism:

83. Ibid., 122–23.

> One thing I am asking people to give up is the myth that evangelicals often hold—that there is such a thing as an orthodox systematic theology, equated with what Calvin, for example, taught and which is said to be in full agreement with the Bible. As if theology itself were an immutable system of concepts not relative at all to the historical context in which they are conceived and framed! Granted, the idea holds great appeal to us, not because it is our experience, but because it delivers such a delicious sense of security and gives us such a great platform from which to assail those dreadful liberals who are such historicists. . . . I guess it is time for evangelicals to grow up and recognize that evangelical theology is not an uncontested body of timeless truth. There are various accounts of it. Augustine got some things right, but not everything. How many evangelicals follow him on the matter of the infallible church or the miraculous sacraments? Like it or not, we are embarked on a pilgrimage in theology and cannot determine exactly where will it [sic] lead and how it will end.[84]

And where this "pilgrimage in theology" led Pinnock in the late 1980s and into the nineties was in the direction of *dismissing* his foundationalist epistemology. A catalyst for this dramatic epistemic move came in the mid-1980s, when Wesleyan scholar Randy Maddox challenged Pinnock's epistemological foundationalism. Callen explains the situation:

> Maddox found cause to judge that Pinnock was still retaining a basic "foundationalist" presupposition, seeming yet to accept the assumption that believers must be able to *prove* that Scripture is reliable knowledge or its authority will be called into question. Was John Calvin not right in teaching that the witness of the Spirit is itself the final ground of the Scripture's perceived authority? By the 1990s, especially with his book *Flame of Love* in 1996, Pinnock increasingly had heeded the concern of Maddox and moved farther from the urge to engage in aggressive and rationalistic apologetics.[85]

As the decade of the nineties arrived, so did Pinnock's theological volume, *Tracking the Maze*, which promptly provided critics with a clear sense of the direction he was moving heading into the new millennium—the way forward he envisioned for evangelical theology. Pinnock would break new theological ground for contemporary evangelical thought as the decade progressed and on into the twenty-first century. We will thus

84. Pinnock, *Grace of God and the Will of Man*, 28.

85. Callen, *Journey Toward Renewal*, 123.

consider several of his pioneering moves, especially regarding theological knowledge, by means of five writings of this later phase of Pinnock's intellectual journey: *Tracking the Maze* (1990), *A Wideness in God's Mercy* (1992), *Unbounded Love* (1994), *Flame of Love* (1996), and *Most Moved Mover* (2001). Additionally, we will examine some of Pinnock's reflections on his earlier writings via his Journey Toward Renewal Postscripts (written between 1997 and 1999) appearing in Callen's *Clark H. Pinnock: Journey toward Renewal* (2000).

Tracking the Maze (1990)

The release of *Tracking the Maze* signaled, at the beginning of a new decade, an apparent continuation of the transitioning of Pinnock's theological epistemology. For instance, speaking of the polarization visible between conservative and progressive theologies, Pinnock points to the basic problem found within each—an unwarranted emphasis on theories of theological knowledge:

> The fact that we have been able to picture contemporary theology by looking at the methods it uses and considering the sources it consults is an indicator of a basic problem in it. It has accepted an agenda dictated to it by the Enlightenment, which sees as important chiefly questions of epistemology. What can we know, and how can we know it? Important though such questions are, the solution to our current impasse will probably involve transcending them and focusing on something more important.[86]

At this early point in the book, Pinnock has yet to reveal the "something more important." Yet, what he argues *against* as an epistemological approach to theology (in this particular case, Barth's method) displays his evident shift away from the Bible—and here, even Jesus Christ himself—as *foundational* to attaining a conclusive knowledge of God. Pinnock says concerning Barth:

> [He] wants to rest everything on the *unsubstantiated claim* that God has revealed himself definitively in Jesus Christ, as attested

86. Pinnock, *Tracking the Maze*, 73–74. The same year Pinnock co-authored another book, this one focusing (as the back cover states) on making a plea for "a constructive liberal/conservative dialogue by demonstrating what such an exchange can be like" (see Pinnock and Brown, *Theological Crossfire*. Although the book is not discussed here, it should be noted that both of the book's authors agree that human knowledge of God is fallible and partial, and therefore modesty is the best approach to dialoguing over theological questions.)

by the Scriptures, and gives the certain knowledge of this revelation to believers. . . . His answer to those for whom the certainty
of Christianity may be fading was to posit a revelation so absolute
as somehow to overwhelm unbelief. Only God can reveal God,
Barth thundered, and God has done so only once, in Jesus Christ.
The revelation in question has been recorded once and for all in
the Bible and made effective by the Spirit. Barth's great brilliance
cannot conceal the weakness of a method that leaves us with an
arbitrary appeal to the Bible as the one and only way to vindicate
revelation.[87]

At the same time, however, Pinnock sees Barth's rejection of the ex-
aggerated claims of human rationality in a positive light with respect to
evangelical theology, for it opens a space for "postmodern orthodoxy." No
longer do theologians have to feel pressured to capitulate to the canons of
human authority resident within modernity now that criticism has disclosed its faulty reasoning and cultural conditioning.

Pinnock's doctrine of revelation in *Tracking the Maze* places theological knowledge squarely on the shoulders of the Christian story of salvation.
Pinnock makes the following claim:

> According to the Christian message, God is making himself known
> to humankind *through historical actions recounted in the salvation
> story*. The revelation of God is *objectively given* in the history of
> salvation culminating in Jesus Christ and is *subjectively appropri-
> ated* by faith as we allow God's light to shine into our hearts. . . .
> Revelation according to the Christian story encompasses historical
> actions, verbal disclosures, and personal encounters. All of these

87. Pinnock, *Tracking the Maze*, 117. Emphasis mine. While Pinnock criticizes Barth
for this move, he himself later asserts that God did "definitively manifest himself" in Jesus
Christ. He even states rather emphatically that "revelation is the only possible basis for us
to know a God who created the world. If God as a person does not disclose himself, God
will not be able to be known by humanity. . . . In Jesus Christ, the God of the universe is
uniquely present and working in history among us, as validated by the Resurrection from
the dead" (ibid., 197–98). Perhaps Pinnock's reaction against the conservative position on
inerrancy has so influenced his thinking that avoiding his older views blinds him to the fact
that he actually affirms much of the same *in practice*, while trying to undermine conservative *a prioris* concerning scripture and its propositional content. (Obviously, his primary
source material for the comments he makes above is the New Testament.) Whatever the
reason, Pinnock ends up in an apparent contradiction in at least this case. Later in the
book, in chapter 14 ("Articulating the Story"), he provides the reader with his comprehensive views on the knowledge of God.

are included in the process whereby God unveils truth about God's character and purposes to the believing community. . . ."[88]

Pinnock emphasizes that "revelation does not remain alone," but that "by its very nature" it actually "generates vehicles of revelation [i.e., 'secondary forms of itself'] that will enable its passage down through history."[89] This belief leads him to appropriate the so-called Wesleyan Quadrilateral, while affirming that revelation itself is the "precondition of them all":

> It occurs and finds itself recorded in the sacred writings, passed down through the generations, all the while eliciting a richness of experiential responses and rational reflections. In this way, revelation empowers a written form (Scripture), a remembering community (tradition), a process of subjective appropriation (experience), and testing for internal consistency (reason).[90]

Pinnock's next move is to acknowledge the Bible's human and culturally-shaped character, even though it retains its authority because of its being the primary witness to the central salvific work of God in Jesus Christ. In fact, he apparently disaffirms his earlier (1984) "scripture principle" when he discusses the state of having a more "historically conditioned witness" (i.e., the Bible) than previously admitted, saying:

> Does this mean that theology is on the brink of collapse? . . . I do not think so, because theology rests, not on a scripture principle as such, but upon Jesus Christ and the Christian story, mediated to us by means of a rich complex of norms.[91]

However, Pinnock then refers the reader to part two of *Scripture Principle* to support his conclusion that it should not count as a negative to have been given this "treasure in earthen vessels" (i.e., these norms) because they are "God's own way of dealing with humankind."[92] One wonders whether Pinnock is trying to have it both ways—a "scripture principle" in conjunction with other norms (e.g., tradition) *in practice*, yet not a "scripture principle" *in theory*. Evidently, his practical *a priori* commitment to a highly nuanced and severely limited biblical inerrancy (i.e., inerrant only as it concerns explicit teaching or affirming) has muddied

88. Ibid., 171–72. Emphasis mine.

89. Ibid., 171.

90. Ibid.

91. Ibid., 180.

92. Ibid.

the quadrilateral waters in ways that Wesley himself probably would not have envisioned.[93]

Since Pinnock views Christian doctrine as a second-order reflection or language and not as absolute truths, *narrative theology* is given center stage. Thus, theological epistemology must primarily seek its understanding via the four-fold gospel narratives rather than by means of the epistles, which are mainly "second level reflections upon what is truly primary—the biblically narrated promise."[94]

At this early point (1990) in the later stage of Pinnock's intellectual journey, his theological epistemology continues to be centered on humanity having been provided with knowledge of God's via God's self-revelation in Jesus Christ:

> In the Incarnation, God gives the answer to the age-old question: How, if God exists beyond the limits of the world and is hidden from us, can mortals know God? How, unless God chooses to reveal himself to us? How better than in human flesh? The knowledge of God who is transcendent obviously depends on God's own will and action, whether or not to reveal himself. Revelation is the only possible basis for us to know a God who created the whole world. If God as a person does not disclose himself, God will not be able to be known by humanity. The astounding claim of the Christian story is that through this man, Jesus of Nazareth, God has definitively manifested himself. In Jesus Christ, the God of the universe is uniquely present and working in history among us, as validated by the Resurrection from the dead.[95]

Concluding *Tracking the Maze* with a section on "Sound and Unsound Doctrine" (chapter 15), Pinnock admits, on the one hand, "some truth" in liberal theology's claim that theological knowledge is subject to the relativity of all human claims to knowledge, and thus something less than certainty exists for our claims to the knowledge of God. But on the other hand, he is not hesitant to reiterate the necessity for Christians to

---

93. John Wesley's own commitment to an infallible (and inerrant) Bible has been well attested. For instance, see Jones, "Rule of Scripture." Perhaps Pinnock's theological journey away from strict inerrancy to a highly nuanced *limited inerrancy* position—along with his attempt to hold a middle-ground position between progressives and conservatives—has resulted in his sometimes abrasive (and at times caustic) critique of allegedly extremist views held on the issue of biblical inspiration and authority.

94. See Pinnock, *Tracking the Maze*, 182–86.

95. Ibid., 197–98.

remain vigilant defenders of the "everlasting gospel," acknowledging that "modesty can go too far":

> Christians are committed to a story of redemption that is not de-void of content and meaning. . . . When they say they fear that certain doctrines ruin the story and threaten the spiritual health of the individuals and communities that believe them, they are not guilty of pride or exceeding their place as historical creatures. They are simply telling the truth that they believe such and such a denial really spoils the good news and threatens to prevent the grace of God from shining through. . . . On many matters we should be open-minded. But when the gospel is at stake, being open-minded is a sign of immaturity, not maturity. Paul calls Christians who cannot make up their minds on matters of substance babies and "children, who are tossed to and fro and carried about by every wind of doctrine" (Eph. 4:14). Opening the mind is not an end in itself. The idea of opening the mind, like opening the mouth, is to close it again on something solid.[96]

We can construe from these statements the point that Pinnock holds the gospel message, as revealed in the scriptures, to be foundational to theological knowledge. Nevertheless, as we will see shortly, he also envisions other means whereby God reaches out to humanity and provides opportunities for people to acquire knowledge of God.

A Wideness in God's Mercy (1992)

With the publication of one of his most controversial books, *A Wideness in God's Mercy*, Pinnock continues the argument for *general revelation* being a vehicle for theological knowledge. He reasons that for many, this is the only means of access available to the knowledge of God, and thus salvation is made possible based on the "presumed generous grace of God in Jesus Christ."[97] God can be known, at least to some extent, in and through other religions as part of general revelation. This is not to say that religions "ordinarily function as paths to salvation" or are "stepping stones to Christ." In fact, says Pinnock, "More often they are paths to hell."[98] Nevertheless, he affirms:

---

96. Ibid., 216–17.

97. Callen, *Journey Toward Renewal*, 168.

98. Pinnock, *Wideness in God's Mercy*, 91.

World religions reflect to some degree general revelation and pre-venient grace. Just as God himself is present in the world, so too is God's reality and revelation. Since God never leaves himself without a witness (Ac 14:16–17), people always have divine light to respond to. . . . Because of the cosmic or general revelation, anyone can find God anywhere at anytime, because he has made himself and his revelation accessible to them. This is the reason we find a degree of truth and goodness in other religions. What an opportunity to engage this truth and to sort out the various claims in the knowledge that God is revealing himself to humankind. He wants people to know him.[99]

As a consequence of God's desire for all people to know him, Pinnock reasons, institutions of religion beyond the Christian church may serve God's purposes of making God known to a "holy pagan," keeping in mind that already "all persons know God precognitively, and must acknowledge him cognitively as well."[100]

Concern for the destiny of the unevangelized deeply influences Pinnock's thinking; consequently, his epistemological focus shifts to the question of *how much knowledge* of God is one required to possess in order to be saved? It seems reasonable to conclude that Pinnock believes God is not concerned with an individual's noetic limitations, but rather *trust and obedience based on the available light* one has is more central. In fact, *objective* religions may—and sometimes do—significantly distort the biblical picture of God, making it virtually impossible for adherents to gain a true knowledge of God. However, *subjective* religious experiences can—and sometimes do—provide individuals with potential or actual saving knowledge of God because of the *relational* component, and so involves a *faith principle*. Pinnock expresses his position on this as follows:

The faith principle is the basis of universal accessibility. According to the Bible, people are saved by faith, not by the content of their theology. Since God has not left anyone without witness, people are judged on the basis of the light they have received and how they have responded to that light. Faith in God is what saves, not possessing certain minimum information.[101]

99. Ibid., 104.

100. Ibid., 102. Concerning this quote, Pinnock references both Norman Geisler and Wolfhart Pannenberg, noting that the latter's theology is rooted in the religious nature of humankind.

101. Ibid., 157–58.

Pinnock expands this line of thought in ways that many evangelicals (particularly, traditionalists) may find very uncomfortable:

> A person is saved by faith, even if the content of belief is deficient (and whose is not?). The Bible does not teach that one must confess the name of Jesus to be saved. . . . One does not have to be conscious of the work of Christ done on one's behalf in order to benefit from that work. The issue God cares about is the direction of the heart, not the content of theology.[102]

Pinnock seems to be searching for a balance between confidence in the truth of the gospel and finality of God's self-revelation in Jesus Christ, and epistemic modesty in the arena of religious plurality or the "contest of the gods." Accepting the notion of *eschatological verification*, Pinnock sees evangelical claims to knowledge and truth as awaiting final confirmation in the future. Until then, we are to trust in Christ rather than our own reasoning, bearing in mind the following:

> One is to avoid being a hard rationalist in pursuing truth. Although we trust in Jesus Christ unreservedly, we admit that we only know in part, in finite, fragile ways. Unlike God's understanding, human understanding is partial and provisional. The full truth of anything will not be divulged until the end of time, when God reveals his glory. John Hick was right to speak of eschatological verification. . . . This does not entail relativism, but it does require epistemological modesty . . . a middle position between relativism and dogmatism. Truth will be resolved eschatologically. This means we will never fully resolve the conversation but patiently await the arrival of full knowledge from God. . . . Jesus is the prolepsis of the end of history, but until then we will not know what all that means.[103]

Near the conclusion of the book, Pinnock opts for a *postmortem encounter* addition to his theological system, affirming that, for some, an *explicit* knowledge of Jesus Christ may come only after death. Among the other reasons given for this position is the empirical reality that a significant portion of the world's population has not heard—and are unlikely to hear—the gospel of Jesus Christ, thus not having an opportunity to respond *in this life* to the knowledge of God as definitively revealed in Christ. Rather than accept a middle knowledge view,[104] and while ad-

---

102. Ibid., 158.

103. Ibid., 146–47.

104. In this context, middle knowledge is the idea that God knows how a person would

mitting the scant biblical evidence for his position, Pinnock prefers an after-death encounter for a variety of reasons, including its provision for epistemic fullness, which he sees as critical to the salvific process:

> The exegetical evidence may not be plentiful, but the theological argument is strong that those who have been seeking God in this life will have their knowledge of God updated when they enter into his presence. They want to know God better, and God wants to know them better. A postmortem encounter applied to this class of human souls means the completing of a faith decision already made on the basis of premessianic revelation and does not in any way diminish in importance the choices made in this life. It would in fact confirm these choices, since these are the ones who decided to move toward God in this life. Now they will meet the God they love in the fullness of his grace after death. For them a postmortem opportunity is firmly established.[105]

Evidently, by 1992 Pinnock has moved far from an exclusivist view of salvation, and no less far from the hard rationalism that characterized the earliest stage of his intellectual journey. His theological epistemology has accompanied his intellectual shift; he also leaves behind an allegedly indubitable, ahistorical, strict foundationalism, for a softer foundationalism characterized by modesty, with the recognition of the significant influence of historical and cultural influences upon one's theology. Turning to Pinnock's next book will help in understanding his further evolving epistemology alongside his intellectual journey.

UNBOUNDED LOVE (1994)

Two years after the appearance of *A Wideness in God's Mercy*, Pinnock would co-author a book focusing on revisioning evangelical theology.[106] The volume's central purpose involves advancing the vision of a *creative love theism*—a model that, from the standpoint of Pinnock and Brow, seeks to replace a "distorted model" that is "marked by a minimizing of divine grace, an exaggeration of the legal dimension of salvation and a misrepresentation of God's sovereignty," with what they view as "a vision

---

have responded to the gospel had they heard its message because God foreknows how everyone will cooperate (or would have cooperated) with grace.

105. Pinnock, *Wideness in God's Mercy*, 172.

106. Pinnock and Brow, *Unbounded Love*.

of God who, having created us to enjoy his love, does everything to enable us to participate in grace to the full."[107]

With *Unbounded Love*, Pinnock begins to give a larger place to God the Spirit in relation to theological knowledge. As previously mentioned, he has doubtlessly left behind his earlier view of the Bible in and of itself being the inerrant and indubitable source for the knowledge of God. But with this book, Pinnock apparently moves even beyond a primary focus on Jesus Christ for theological knowledge, to an emphasis on the following:

> [Revelation] does not refer to the Bible in the first instance but to God's revelation in history. Yet we would not know much about that revelation were it not for the biblical witness. Through this testimony, human as it is, *the Spirit brings about a true knowledge of God*. . . . God's revelation comes to us mediated in human forms; it does not give us direct access to God's essence. *What we know about God surfaces by way of the stories and metaphors* the Bible gives us. Our models are constructed as we organize and interrelate the metaphors. This is a human and an imperfect activity. Problems arise when people assume that their construal of the metaphors is the only possible one and catches the very essence.[108]

Scripture narrative and metaphors, illumined by the Spirit are now viewed as the primary means of accessing theological knowledge. This move is conjoined with Pinnock's view that other religions, as part of general revelation, are also sources for the knowledge of God.

FLAME OF LOVE (1996)

In a book intended to renew thinking about and experiencing the third Person of the Trinity, Pinnock again articulates his view that theological knowledge necessarily goes beyond the rational, yet without negating it. His confidence in and references to theological resources beyond evangelicalism has become increasingly evident:

> I appreciate what Orthodoxy calls the "apophatic." This term is used by St. Basel, for example, to indicate how God surpasses all our thoughts about him and how we know God not by reason alone but by spiritual sensitivity as well. . . . The apophatic does

107. Ibid., 8. That same year Pinnock contributed to another book—one that has generated a great deal of ongoing debate—and in summary fashion, reiterated the main theological positions espoused in *Unbounded* (see Pinnock et al., *Openness of God*).

108. Pinnock and Brow, Unbounded Love, 32–33. Emphases mine.

not imply agnosticism concerning the truth of dogmatic formulations. It surpasses but does not negate the truth.[109]

It is evident that with *Flame of Love*, Pinnock's theological epistemology is now more directly focused on *experience*. For instance, when speaking of the Spirit of God, he states, "knowing the Spirit is experiential, and the topic is oriented toward *transformation* more than *information*."[110]

Concerning human knowledge of the immanent Trinity (God in himself), Pinnock asserts that such is "revealed by the economic Trinity (God in history), from which we learn that God is Father, Son and Spirit." Therefore, theological epistemology is centered in "*a true, though partial, knowledge of God in the economy of salvation.* What has been revealed about the relationship of the Father, Son and Spirit reveals something about the divine relationships." Pinnock concludes that while this is evident in the Gospels, we remain "well aware that our knowledge in these matters is very limited."[111]

In chapter 5 ("Spirit & Union"), Pinnock begins to focus on a *relational* model of salvation that encompasses theological knowledge: through *union* with the Trinity, God is known. "Spirit is leading us to union—to transformation, personal, intimate relationship with the triune God. 'This is eternal life, that they may know you, the only true God, and Jesus Christ whom you have sent (John 17:3).'"[112]

Perhaps the best way to understand Pinnock's theology of the knowledge of God in *Flame of Love* is by means of what may be called his "global church" paradigm. He has tapped into numerous Christian traditions (Eastern Orthodoxy, Roman Catholicism, Wesleyanism, Pentecostalism) and has proceeded to incorporate exegetical, theological, and epistemological ideas from each in a way Pinnock believes best represents an evangelical understanding and experience of God. God can—and wants to be—known through a variety of instrumentalities. Pinnock's theological paradigm envisions God as loving Father, reaching out to draw everyone into relationship and union with the Trinity. God works in multifaceted ways to accomplish this primary goal. Where a Christian witness is not present, the Spirit is still present and works through every facet of life

---

109. Pinnock, *Flame of Love*, 250, n.10.

110. Ibid., 14. Emphasis mine.

111. Ibid., 32. Emphasis mine.

112. Ibid., 149.

(including organized religion) to make God known, even if only partially or in a pre-Christian way, because of God's desire that no one should perish (2 Pet 3:9).

Pinnock's model suggests that *everyone* has or will have opportunity to know—including to know *savingly*—and experience the triune God, whether that be in this life or in a postmortem encounter. What drives his conviction is an overarching vision of the Spirit's universal work, both through the particularity of the gospel message of Jesus Christ *and* where that message is not represented. Pinnock summarizes his perspective:

> God is always reaching out to sinners by the Spirit. There is no general revelation or natural knowledge of God that is not at the same time gracious revelation and a potentially saving knowledge. All revealing and reaching out are rooted in God's grace and are aimed at bringing sinners home. *Access to grace is less of a problem for theology when we consider it from the standpoint of the Spirit, because whereas Jesus bespeaks particularity, Spirit bespeaks universality.*[113]

> Spirit works ceaselessly to persuade human beings to trust and open themselves up to love. Those with eyes to see can discern the Spirit's activity in human culture and religion, as God everywhere draws people to friendship. People can search for him and find him because "he is not far from each one of us" (Acts 17:27). People can shut themselves off from God and refuse the call, but they may also respond to the One who rewards those who diligently seek him (Heb. 11:6). The Spirit's work is not limited to Jews and Christians. God is truly "the Savior of all people, especially of those who believe" (1 Tim. 4:10). Peter says, "God shows no partiality, but in every nation anyone who fears him and does what is right is acceptable to him."[114]

Even pertaining to non-Christian religions, Pinnock reasons that God can be known, asking several provocative questions and referring to the particular situation involving Cornelius as recorded in Acts 10:

> If the Spirit gives life to creation and offers grace to every creature, one would expect him to be present and make himself felt (at least occasionally) in the religious dimension of cultural life. Why would the Spirit be working everywhere else but not here? God is reaching out to all nations and does not leave himself without witness (Acts 14:17). Would this witness not crop up sometimes in the

---

113. Ibid., 187–88. Emphasis in the original.
114. Ibid., 195. Emphasis mine.

religious realm? It seemed to do so for Cornelius, a non-Christian whose moral and spiritual life before conversion is highly praised in Scripture (Acts 10:2). Evidently the Spirit had been at work in his life and faith prior to his conversion. People search for God in religions; are we to say that they never encounter God in religion, in spite of the inadequacies and distortions that are to be found in every religious worldview?[115]

Returning to the idea of God's self-revelation in the gospel, Pinnock affirms that "in revelation God also causes light to shine out of darkness, giving us true if partial knowledge of triune relationality and salvation."[116] *Flame of Love*, then, regarded by the publisher as Pinnock's *magnum opus*, explicitly seeks to incorporate concepts from various Christian traditions and thinkers—many outside contemporary evangelicalism—in order to be faithful to both scripture and tradition as they address the problem of theological knowledge. A consideration of some of his more recent thinking in this arena will continue our study of Pinnock's intellectual journey and associated theological epistemology.

JOURNEY TOWARD RENEWAL POSTSCRIPT (1997–99)

Reflecting in 1999 on the epistemological shift he was making in *Reason Enough* (1980), Pinnock notes it was a move away from a hard to a softer rationality, or "as we might now say, from modernity to postmodernity."[117] Knowledge of God and the truth of the gospel message were to be found not so much intellectually, but rather cumulatively. Pinnock concludes his postscript noting that his "journey has taken him in a softening direction."[118] This confession characterizes his recurring criticism of the hubris he finds prevalent in foundationalist approaches to epistemology.[119] Commenting on this problem, with relevance to belief in the inspiration

115. Ibid., 200–201.

116. Ibid., 224.

117. Pinnock, "Appendixes," 229.

118. Ibid., 229.

119. Perhaps Pinnock's "softening" resulted in part not only from repeated encounters with a pronounced lack of humility within conservative evangelical theology, but also the lack of tolerance for more modest or even nonfoundationalist views of knowledge (for instance, coherentism). Unfortunately, there remains within some of the more fundamentalist-leaning groups within conservative theological circles the false assumption that a nonfoundationalist approach to knowledge *necessitates* a rejection of a high view of scripture (e.g., infallibility or inerrancy). This presupposition is unwarranted. See, for instance, Holmes, *Contours of a World View.*

and authority of the Bible, Pinnock opines that "the desire to have absolute truth is for many evangelicals stronger than their desire to accept the actual biblical witness."[120]

In another postscript, Pinnock is reflecting on *A Wideness in God's Mercy* where he discusses again the issue of people acquiring a salvific knowledge of God, reiterating his position with the question, "How can we possibly say that the God who loves the whole world has chosen to neglect providing any means of access to salvation for the majority of the human race? I cannot imagine it. . . ."[121]

In yet another moment of reflection, Pinnock in his Afterword to Callen's *Journey Toward Renewal*, comments that Christian theology is "a continuing search for the truth of God made known in Jesus Christ." Thus, it is feasible to see his later theological epistemology in part being an ongoing seeking after ways in which "the fuller truth of God's Word" can reveal more knowledge of God and his will in this world.[122]

Finally, Pinnock's full-circle return to pietistic roots, coupled with an incorporation of thought from a rather full spectrum of Christian traditions, reveals a broad conception of theological knowledge—viewed as being primarily experiential: God being and becoming known in multifaceted ways. This supposition emerges largely from Pinnock's "relational and loving" model of God, which demands that we see God reaching out *in every way possible to make himself known* in order to have relationship with humanity, and to bring the same into union with the Trinity. Rather than the Bible revealing to humankind who God is mainly through propositional statements, we know and experience God today as those in biblical times did—via encounter with the living God as he acts in *our* history. The gospel story of Jesus Christ is the consummate expression of God with us, and demonstrates that knowledge of God is based on God's self-revelation, and a willing human response to God's self-disclosure, whether such disclosure be found in Christian form or otherwise (e.g., in general revelation amid other religions).

With the opening of the new millennium, Pinnock unfolds the latest permutations along his intellectual journey. Hence, we turn our attention

---

120. Pinnock, "Appendixes," 237.

121. Callen, *Journey Toward Renewal*, 251.

122. Ibid., 270–72.

to his most recent book, which describes several more of his important theological moves.

MOST MOVED MOVER (2001)

Most Moved Mover focuses primarily on setting forth the "openness of God" model, especially as it relates to the doctrine of God.[123] The opening paragraph clearly sets forth Pinnock's evolving view of evangelical theology, seeing it now as a "research program":

> One's theology is a work of human construction, even when based in divine revelation, and interpretation requires strenuous effort. Our interpretations are provisional and truth is, to some extent, historically conditioned and ultimately eschatological. . . . The truth claims that we make are all open to discussion and we ought to be teachable and ready to learn because none of our work rises to the level of timeless truth. There will always be multiple models and any one of them may be valuable in expressing the richness of the divine mystery.[124]

Theologically, Pinnock is hoping to present a coherent and convincing case for the adoption of an "open theism" among evangelicals, hoping for it to be embraced as another viable option within "big tent" evangelicalism. In a nutshell, he is convinced that this *theology of love* model is both biblically and practically sound: a preferred alternative to "conventional theology"—a classification he equates with strict, conservative forms of the Reformed tradition. Arguing that the open view is a form of Arminianism, Pinnock claims that openness actually improves upon the classical Arminian view, being a more coherent model, while in some ways moving beyond Wesley and Arminius altogether.[125]

Pinnock contends, for instance, that most of Christian history and theology is on his side regarding libertarian free will. He believes that the early church fathers, before Augustine's influence, argued for many of the same positions endorsed by openness theologians today—as have historic Eastern Orthodoxy, Wesleyanism, and Pentecostalism.

---

123. Pinnock, *Most Moved Mover*. The back cover of the book suggests Pinnock's purpose as being "to once again counter the classical, deterministic view of God and defend the relationality and openness of God." This material greatly expands on Pinnock's earlier contributions to the openness model in Pinnock et al., *Openness of God*.

124. Pinnock, *Most Moved Mover*, ix.

125. For instance, in presuming a partly unsettled future (see ibid., 13).

Apologetically, Pinnock sees the open view of God being in a much better position than what critics allege—and practice themselves—since openness

> embraces a modern [i.e., contemporary] understanding of reality as dynamic not static. It invites us to see reality and God's experience of it as open not closed. This affinity with modern thought, however, is based in the Bible and is not an accommodation to philosophy. Ironically, it is our critics who are overly indebted to (ancient) philosophy, which prevents them from being biblical or relevant. The real issue is not the inerrancy of the Bible but the inerrancy of the assumptions that are being used to interpret it.[126]

Consequently, Pinnock wants his theological method to begin with an appeal to the content of scripture—not a philosophical system—in understanding reality and God's role in the world. Echoing the Wesleyan tradition, Pinnock looks to *the Bible* as the *prima* for theology, while also choosing to make full use of the so-called *Wesleyan Quadrilateral*. In fact, he states his position precisely as adhering

> to the rule of Scripture within a trilateral hermeneutic. First, as an evangelical, my primary commitment is to Scripture not to tradition, reason, or experience because I believe that any authentically theological model must have biblical backing and resonance. I hold the Bible to be the primary norm for theology in the midst of the other sources.[127]

As a result, Pinnock repeatedly appeals to the biblical witness to find support for his theology of love, which he sees as parallel with scripture's primary theme: God's suffering love.

As to biblical interpretation and theological knowledge, Pinnock continues to give "particular weight to narrative and to the language of personal relationship in it," arguing,

> The story involves real drama and is a unique vehicle of truth and a powerful witness to the interactivity of God. It lifts up God's self-involvement in history, and, supremely, the decision to become incarnate in Jesus Christ. Too often we have privileged the non-historical and supposedly non-metaphorical propositional material. But we have to take it all into account.[128]

---

126. Ibid., 118.

127. Ibid., 19.

128. Ibid., 20. To the chagrin of more conservative biblical interpreters, Pinnock,

Hence, Pinnock reiterates his rejection of the idea of approaching scripture via any predetermined systematic scheme, opposing what he sees as "the proof-texting method of evangelical rationalism which disregards narrative but plucks texts out of context in support of traditional notions and a system already in hand."[129]

We can see, then, that as it concerns the knowledge of God, Pinnock wants to begin with God's self-revelation in the Old and New Testament narratives—revelation that "takes the form of interpersonal communication and frees us to see the world as created and redeemed by God." Thus, this divine revelation is decidedly personal in nature:

> We get to know God, as we get to know other persons because God voluntarily makes himself known by the things he does and the promises he makes. Thus, God's revelation comes to us through a narrative that discloses God as an agent who acts in the world, revealing his character and purposes. This is the root metaphor. God is a person with a name. God acts and interacts, engages and suffers.[130]

Let us consider in further detail, then, the two ways that, according to Pinnock's later-stage thinking, the knowledge of God is revealed through the biblical narratives—at least for Christians.

First, theological knowledge comes by way of God's self-disclosure in the history of Israel. Pinnock sees this as evident vis-à-vis several examples: "in the promise to Abraham, the revelation of his name to Moses, the deliverance of Israel from bondage, the giving of the law, and the preaching of the prophets."[131] Second, God is made known through his Son, for it is "especially in the life, death, and resurrection of Jesus Christ, who is God's Word incarnate in a human life and through whom, Christians be-

---

rather than seeing the authors of scripture presenting a unified theological picture, accepts "the diversity among the biblical witnesses" and recognizes "the dialogical character of the Bible. . . . The Bible does not speak with a single voice; there is dialogue between the difference voices. The writings contain a long and complex search for the mind of God and in this struggle various points of view compete and interact . . . therefore, it is important to remember that the Bible is a complex work by many authors whose views may vary and . . . the text is open to various plausible interpretations" (ibid., 21).

129. Ibid., 20.

130. Ibid., 26.

131. Ibid.

lieve, God has taken the initiative to freely make his identity and purposes known to all humankind."[132]

In a later section under the topic of "interpreting Scripture," Pinnock turns to a discussion of biblical metaphors, seeing them as a way of understanding "the reality of God's involvement in time and space and the intimacy of his relationship with us" while avoiding what he views as the extremes of literalism and agnosticism.[133] Here, Pinnock wants to disregard approaches to theological knowledge that, at the margins, either assume "a one-to-one correspondence between metaphors and God's being," or presume no real correspondence between them at all.[134] A presumably better way is holding a middle position that accepts all language as anthropomorphic and metaphorical since that "it is all we have to work with."[135] But this truth ought not lead to despair:

> We know God because God has participated in our history and makes use of anthropomorphic language in his self-presentation. God shares the context of our spacio-temporal world and makes himself known as a being in relation with us. The truth about God arises from God's use of metaphor and God's coming to us in embodied ways.[136]

Apparently, part of Pinnock's goal in *Most Moved Mover*, as it pertains to critiquing conventional theological methodologies, is to call into question suspected reliance on foundations other than God's personal self-disclosure. For instance, the tendency to "place God as far away from and as high over us as possible and to prefer abstract categories to biblical ones" (e.g., solitariness) requires that we distance ourselves from these models, and instead

> let God's own self-revelation dominate our thinking rather than what natural reason and tradition tell us that God must be like. Preunderstandings, preconceptions and control beliefs that are part of the biblical-classical synthesis threaten to control our interpretation of the Bible. That grip must be broken.[137]

132. Ibid.
133. See ibid., 59–64.
134. Ibid., 62.
135. Ibid., 63.
136. Ibid.
137. Ibid., 79.

In place of what he views as a model characterized by one-sidedness resulting from the biblical-classical synthesis, Pinnock proposes that we try to achieve "a better understanding of God as a triune, loving person, reliable and flexible, sensitive and resourceful, patient and wise, everlasting and all-knowing."[138] And in response to critical claims that this theological move results in a diminution of God's glory, Pinnock states that

> it is not a question of diminishing the glory of God, which is so well captured in traditional thinking, but of recapturing God's true beauty so often obscured by it. . . . We ought to view God in personal not absolutist terms. The primary category in Christian theism is person not substance. God is a subject who relates to us and has purposes in history. . . . God created humanity in his image, as an analogy of God, and the very basis of speaking of God in human terms. God wants to be thought of as a person who relates with other persons, who loves and suffers, responds and plans.[139]

Carrying this idea further, Pinnock sees the openness model having much greater *contextual footing* than its conventional theology counterparts possess—especially on the subject of God's relationship with humanity. He also imagines the open view being grounded more in scripture than—as critics protest—in the philosophy of contemporary culture. In fact, compared with models employed by openness opponents, Pinnock declares the following:

> The openness model places us in a happy position relative to the modern context because it enjoys biblical support and helps us establish a positive relationship with aspects of modern experience. Although critics try to convert the asset into a liability, by charging that we obtained the model from modernity, the fact is that the open view helps us speak convincingly to contemporary hearers. Its concept of God lacks the disadvantage of feeling like a relic of ancient philosophy and can present itself as a challenging, contemporary option. People do not want and do not need a God distant from the world and untouched by its suffering. But they do need a God who enters into history, becomes incarnate, dies on a cross and rises again. They do need a God who, though he transcends the world, identifies himself with temporality and even with death, and whose truest being lies in his coming and becoming.[140]

138. Ibid.

139. Ibid., 79–80.

140. Ibid., 119–20.

Thus, with *Most Moved Mover*, Pinnock has candidly expressed his concern over traditional (in Pinnock's words, "conventional") evangelical theology's presumed failure to be sufficiently *relational*: theologically or epistemologically. He supposes that a pagan inheritance strongly superimposes the divine-human interpersonal relations observed in the biblical narrative. Therefore, it is mandatory to present evangelical theology with a coherent alternative to the traditional Reformed model. However, even classical Arminian approaches lack the necessary consistency. Hence, Pinnock offers openness theology as an important way forward for intellectual evangelicalism, seeing it as a biblically-sound and contextually-attractive option.

Whether a theology of God's openness can answer the criticisms leveled against it is yet to be seen.[141] A variety of questions has been and will continue to be raised that require serious reflection: What factors have contributed to the open view's disillusion with conventional evangelical theology? What are the major arguments set forth by openness proponents, and which appear to reveal this theological method's greatest strengths/weaknesses? How will openness affect both Calvinist and Arminian thought? Which are the most controversial positions taken by "theology of love" theologians, and why? Who, and what criteria, will determine the validity of the various openness arguments? Will the open view become a sort of "third way" for future evangelical theology? What consequences will the open view of God have for theological epistemology? What level of connectivity exists between openness and postconservative theology—is there a one-to-one correspondence, or can we detect moderate to significant variations between them?

Since our thesis pays primary attention to postconservative evangelical theology—and more particularly, approaches to the knowledge of God—evident overlap between openness and reformist positions throughout the remainder of this study may be evident. This overlap notwithstanding, a general guideline pertaining to the distinction between postconservatives and openness advocates can be upheld: even as open-view scholars embrace a postconservative theological method, it appears that many (if not most) postconservatives do not correspondingly

---

141. Because of the relative recency of openness theology, sustained critique of the movement is somewhat limited to date; nevertheless, the body of literature is growing rapidly. See, for instance, the important nine-article interchange on open theism in *JETS* 45, no. 2 (2002).

admit the openness model—especially regarding the matter of whether the future is partially open even to God. Ostensibly, then, practically all theologians who identify themselves as openness scholars would also label themselves as postconservative, whereas more than a few postconservative thinkers refuse to identify themselves as openness scholars—apparently due in large part to the latter's views of the doctrine of God, particularly on issues of God's unchangeability, eternity, omniscience, and above all, foreknowledge.[142] Consequently, it can be assumed—with these noted exceptions—that postconservative theological and epistemological perspectives are fairly representative of openness thought comprising these areas under discussion.

SUMMARY

For the later Pinnock, human knowing is significantly conditioned (though not determined) by myriad factors, such that a rational/propositional method that assumes an Archimedean point is an impossible chimera, deserving to be replaced by a more dynamic, relational, and modest epistemology. In a 1997 keynote address to the annual meeting of the Wesleyan Theological Society, Pinnock expounds on historicism's impact on theological and epistemological claims:

> The rational/propositional method as practiced at old Princeton and since defended by scholastic evangelicals embodies a view of revelation consisting chiefly of the doctrinal truths of the Bible. The main task of theology was to systematize these truths into a stable and more or less timeless theology. With a verbatim of God's thoughts in hand, this approach could instill a feeling of high confidence, bolstered by apologetics of the hard rationalist variety. The Enlightenment strengthened this orientation by encouraging an epistemology which upheld ideals of rational certainty and unshakable foundations.[143]

Pinnock continues, obviously concerned with what he sees as evangelical neglect of tradition's role in theologizing:

> By ignoring the influence of tradition on our work, we are tempted to claim unwarranted certainties for our conclusions. . . . The historical situatedness of all theology operates whether it is recognized or not. . . . Disregarding tradition does not eliminate its effects

142. See Pinnock, *Most Moved Mover*, 13.
143. Pinnock, "Evangelical Theologians Facing the Future," 13.

but only lets them function under wraps. It frees people to select a strand of the past and privilege it. It makes disciples prisoner to that segment of history and short-circuits growth beyond it. It can even lead us to reject other people affected by some other segment. Traditions can be what is really at stake without either side knowing it. As Charles Kraft has taught us, reality is mediated to us through the grid of world-views, and the essence of faith is always mixed up with historical form. Every theology combines the essence of religion with particular forms. Even evangelical versions of Christianity grow out of particular situations.[144]

Consequently, if historical situatedness conditions all theology, how can Christians be certain that their knowledge of God is genuine rather than a reflection of the self? To begin with, Pinnock thinks it necessary to disavow the "mythical" idea of certainty; instead, all of life is based on probability (including religious knowledge) and this truism necessitates modesty for one's epistemic claims pertaining to theology. But more to the point, his model of God as loving Father, coupled with the goal of the Trinity (reaching out to everyone everywhere so that all may know and grow toward union with God) implies that the witness of scripture testifies to the plan of God's self-revelation to humankind—most explicitly and definitively in Jesus Christ. Therefore, the biblical record is the primary—yet by no means exclusive—*instrument* for communicating the knowledge of God as found above all else in the narrative of Jesus Christ, and also in theological metaphors used in language games evident in the Bible.

However, knowledge of God is regularly being made immediately accessible to all human beings, because Spirit is ever-present and ever-working to bring creation to experience the divine life of God in a sort of celestial "dance." And while this gracious drawing can certainly be refused, God's goal is for all to come to the *knowledge* of salvation (i.e., a "non-rejection" of God's wooing all human beings to himself). Hence, in this later stage, Pinnock seems to have settled on an increasingly *pneumacentric* approach to theological knowledge as compared with the bibliocentric foundationalism indicative of his early stage, and the christocentric focus of his middle phase.

Especially with *Flame of Love*, Pinnock appeals to the Eastern Orthodox ideas of *theosis* and universality of Spirit. And coupled with his open theism, this move essentially recast the question of theological

144. Ibid., 16.

epistemology rather than asking, How do (or can) human beings come to a knowledge of God, we must ask, *Since* all human beings are already perpetually experiencing the knowledge of God in various ways—whether conscious of it or not—how can evangelicals best help everyone to interpret these Trinitarian wooings as a call to union with God?

Nevertheless, five years after the publication of *Flame of Love*, Pinnock seems to have returned to a more *christocentric* theological framework in *Most Moved Mover*, with strong orientation toward the *personal* dimension of theological knowledge, based on the "triune community of love."[145]

Conclusion

Clark Pinnock's theological journey has been fascinating to watch and to engage. Regardless of the particular phase of his walk, he appears to have always been cognizant of the importance of proclaiming the word of God in the world of God's creation, although the *form* that the word may take has been perceived in amended ways over the years. Pinnock's theological epistemology has undergone substantial changes over four decades of teaching and writing—changes that roughly parallel the trajectory of his wider theological journey. With the apparent exception of his recent return to a more Christ-centered and trinitarian framework, Pinnock's approach to the knowledge of God seems to indicate a rough parallel with his transitioning theological systems; while moving from Calvinism to Arminianism to open theism, his theological epistemology moved from a bibliocentric to a christocentric to a pneumacentric principle. Of course, this observation is far from suggesting that one's theological camp is determinative for one's epistemic theories. Nevertheless, Pinnock does recognize the powerful influence that sociological contexts and formative relationships have had on his own theological method and epistemological considerations.

Certainly Pinnock's broadening position on a variety of issues will continue to cause significant and varied responses from evangelicals; his *faith principle*, for instance, is almost certain to engender assiduous debate. Pinnock evidently sees salvation as having little to do with the noetic sphere. Instead, God is interested in faith as expressed by those who are looking to God for salvation—regardless of their religious or sociological context. For Pinnock, what life boils down to is knowing God by faith, which, he avers, will be (or become) a possibility for every human being—

---

145. See Pinnock, *Most Moved Mover*, especially 26–28.

whether before or after death. Hope, as Pinnock envisions it, is grounded in the good news of inclusivism and universal access to the triune God by the Spirit, rather than the bad news of exclusivism and hopelessness for most of the world. Whether this more hopeful theology—as well as the theological epistemology of the broader postconservative movement—can meet head-on critical evangelical analysis is a story yet to be told.

However this narrative ultimately ends, an indelible mark has been left on the face of evangelicalism by postconservative pioneer Clark Pinnock, presenting the evangelical intellectual community with alternative ways of viewing Christian faith and doctrine (as was shown in some detail by way of his intellectual journey from strict Calvinism to Arminianism to an open view of God). Along the path, Pinnock's own trek has represented various positions espoused among evangelical faith traditions. Interestingly, proponents of each tradition seem to eagerly—not to mention selectively—utilize Pinnock's works from the particular period of his journey that best typifies the current views of their own tradition.

The implications of Pinnock's later works for evangelical theology cannot be overstated—his theological trailblazing has been the cause for much reflection among the evangelical guild,[146] while his intellectual pilgrimage—unsettling for some—has proven trend setting for a growing number of younger evangelical thinkers. Shortly, we will consider some of the major developments within postconservative theological epistemology that are continuing to expand on the significant contributions and innovations of self-proclaimed theological pilgrim Clark Pinnock. First, however, to comprehend more fully postconservatism's emergence and direction, a more nuanced account of what has stimulated this movement is called for; namely, the rise, dominance, and downfall of

---

146. A case in point involves the Evangelical Theological Society (ETS), of which Pinnock has been a member for decades. The 2002 Annual Meeting saw his work (as well as the work of John Sanders) publicly criticized with charges of denying inerrancy. The charges were brought by long-time member, Roger Nicole, leading to a year-long executive committee review and recommendation. The committee made its (unanimous) recommendation to full members of the ETS at the 2003 Annual Meeting that Pinnock be acquitted of the charges, but that the charges against Sanders (on a vote of seven to two) be maintained, thus recommending that members vote for the resolution to remove Sanders from the society, which would require a two-thirds majority. The resolutions to remove Pinnock and Sanders both failed, albeit by a slim four-percent margin for the latter, and by a much wider margin for the former. This situation had risen to the level on a par with only a few other major disputes within the ETS over the course of its more than half-century existence.

modernity's premiere epistemology—foundationalism—and how evangelical theology has responded accordingly.

Impetus for the Emergence of Postconservative Theological Epistemology

Introduction

Some of the theological moves made by Pinnock, as well as shifts occurring today among younger postconservatives (as we will see in chapter 4) directly connect with the apparent demise of foundationalism. This leads us to surmise that those questioning traditionalist theological methods view certain elements comprising foundationalism as detrimental to evangelical theology, which they understand as having been excessively intertwined with many Enlightenment assumptions and practices. We will therefore need to explore what has occurred for this mainstream theory of knowledge to lose its three-hundred-year grip on Western thought, and why some evangelical intellectuals find this a *positive* development for contemporary Christian thought and practice.

This section begins by considering the rise of Cartesian foundationalism, along with the fall of *opinio*, and early Protestant responses to this development. We will also look at *modern foundationalism's key characteristics*, including its persistent quest for certainty.[147] The issues at hand will be discussed primarily from the postconservative perspective, emphasizing the rejection of modern foundationalism. Moreover, the chapter will conclude with a brief discussion of the rise and impact of postmodern nonfoundationalist epistemologies, and their influence upon postconservative evangelical thought. First, however, an overview of foundationalism's influence—beyond the philosophical sphere.

Foundationalism: The Rise, Reign, and Demise of Modernity's Foremost Epistemology

INTRODUCTION

In *Beyond Foundationalism*, Grenz and Franke point out the pervasive nature of foundationalism, including its affect upon theology:

147. The following exposition ought to be understood in general as an interpretation by critics of modernity and foundationalism.

> The concerns of Descartes and other Enlightenment thinkers spilled over the boundaries of the philosophical guild. Indeed, the foundationalist problematic challenged traditional viewpoints and reformulated thinking in every area of Western society, including theology and religious belief. Soon theologians, swooning under the foundationalist spell, found themselves refashioning the theological edifice in accordance with the newly devised rationalist method.[148]

This rationalist method was also highly individualistic, moving theologians further away from seriously viewing *opinio* as an indispensable source for knowledge—including knowledge of God. Hence, postconservatives view the modern period as somewhat of *an anomaly*, epistemologically. Evangelical revisionists criticize as naïve and unbiblical modernity's focus on the purported autonomous individual, standing apart from *historico-culturo* factors. Most evangelical traditionalists, they say, have underestimated these shaping factors upon theology and method: a serious mistake. The result has led to frequent separation of theoretical reflection from concrete participation in the mission of the church within the historical-cultural context. This misguided modern supposition holds that trustworthy knowledge and truth could not reside within traditions or communities because of divergences in belief and interpretation. Instead, theology and epistemology must bow to the philosophical method associated with Descartes (which in certain respects actually hearkens back to Plato and Augustine, e.g., *cogito ergo sum*). This method attempts to overcome skepticism and interpretive variation, alleging to provide a way to disengage from particular and local issues by means of purely rational and "neutral" contemplation.

Ideas have consequences; Descartes' had many. His attempted rejection of tradition and authority as a starting point—coupled with exaltation of his own mind in the quest for certainty—perpetuated a reason-centered individualism that ruled the day in Western philosophy for centuries. The rise of Cartesianism (and later, empiricism) meant a radical break with previous ways of knowing. It would be roughly three centuries before the West would begin to see its apparent demise. Understanding this powerful philosophical system and its immense influence upon Christian theology is crucial to comprehending the development and characteristics of evangelical postconservative views.

---

148. Grenz and Franke, *Beyond Foundationalism*, 32.

THE RISE OF CARTESIAN FOUNDATIONALISM
AND THE FALL OF *OPINIO*[149]

René Descartes (1596–1650) is widely viewed as the Founding Father of modern foundationalism, an approach to knowledge developed in response to the uncertainty distinguishing his cultural and religious milieu.[150] D. A. Carson illuminates the situation Descartes was facing:

> [Descartes'] pivotal work, *Discourse on Method*, published in 1637, blazed a trail others followed. But we must not think that it was the result of pure, dispassionate thought. The revival of classical [Greek and Roman] learning during the previous century and a half, the extraordinary social and political ferment of the seventeenth century, the relative freedom from monolithic ecclesiastical control achieved by the magisterial Reformation, and the dislocation caused by the barbarisms of the Thirty Years' War all doubtless contributed to the desire for certainty in shifting times. And Descartes himself, of course, was trying to overthrow the skeptics of his day.[151]

Rodney Clapp picks up on the uncertainty and diversity of that era—ecclesiastical disunity included—something Descartes believed he needed to quash:

> The problem at hand seemed clear: time changes everything, including beliefs. And ideas or identities based on localities—whether cities, cantons or states—are a veritable recipe for interminable fighting. But no longer were philosophers, scientists and politicians answerable to the church. Furthermore, the church was no longer a unified, consolidated authority, the generally accepted conduit of truth eternal, truth from beyond time and place, for all times and places. Thus Descartes sought a secular, or nonecclesial, foundation of knowledge that rested on grounds beyond time and place.[152]

Pursuing epistemological certainty, Descartes believed two major problems required resolution. The first was skepticism, for it was challenging the authenticity of both *scientia* and *opinio*—crucial categories

149. I am indebted to Stout, *Flight from Authority*, for much of this section.

150. More precisely, Descartes *revitalized* and *popularized* classical foundationalism that was typically expressed within ancient Greek and Roman cultures, then rediscovered in the Renaissance period.

151. Carson, *Gagging of God*, 58.

152. Clapp, "How Firm a Foundation," 82–83.

pertaining to knowledge; the second was that of *many authorities*, particularly manifest within the nascent Protestant movement. Some elaboration on each of these problems will show in greater relief the epistemological predicament Descartes sought to answer satisfactorily.

Briefly, *opinio* authorized tradition; that is, theological reflection and argumentation by learned and believing church authorities was viewed as a trustworthy (although not provable) means of arriving at truths/doctrines. Thomas Aquinas (1225–74), for instance, appealed to *opinio*, along with natural theology, in his use of *scientia*. Before Descartes, then, we have a question of what actually qualifies as knowledge. The answer is that only matters involving scientific, deductive proof could meet the criteria for *scientia*. Everything else was *opinio*—a sort of proof, dependent upon appeals to authority.

The challenge to *scientia*, especially pertaining to theology, would come within a few generations following the death of Aquinas, most clearly in the thinking of William Occam (ca. 1285–1347) and his fourteenth-century followers as they began raising doubts about *scientia*. This occurred as their perspective of limitation began to be applied to natural certainty in light of God's omnipotence. Occam held that God is omnipotent and free, and can do anything that is not logically contradictory; furthermore, the world is totally contingent. Therefore, assertions about finite things are conditional truths subject to the will of God.[153]

Other major contributors to the growing pre-Cartesian era of skepticism surrounding *scientia* were the Augustinian doctrines of human nature and fallenness, as expressed primarily by Protestant reformers, and the sixteenth/seventeenth-century discovery and distribution of ancient skeptical writings. (Descartes' move would be to "foundationalize" a long-reigning paradigm, formulating the indubitability of *scientia*.)

Even greater uncertainty and questioning arose over the concept of *opinio* as a central source for theological knowledge and truth. Aquinas had distinguished—and made substantial use of—the Aristotelian categories. For Aquinas, all *scientia* conforms to the deductive model in the domain of demonstration, while *opinio* is based on non-deductive probability. However, probability was not a matter of statistical analysis, which would not arise until centuries later. For both Aquinas and Descartes, probability was a matter of *what the authorities accepted or approved*.

---

153. See Ferguson, Wright, and Packer, *New Dictionary of Theology*, 724.

In addition, there was the distressing quandary of many authorities. This multiplicity of voices alleging authoritative interpretations of the Bible and Christian theology seriously complicated efforts of philosophers and theologians. This problem, however, had been developing long before Descartes "discovered" it. As Jeffrey Stout notes—and in relation to *scientia* and *opinio:*

> [I]f there were difficulties with *scientia*, doubts about its scope and possibility, these would in effect expand the domain of merely probable opinion. And this expansion would in turn place a heavy burden on the notion of authority, in terms of which probability was then construed. What is more, the notion of authority, now asked to shoulder more social and intellectual weight than ever, proved anything but stable. As competing authorities multiplied and began to diverge more and more sharply, conventional means for resolving disputes arising from such competition became less and less effective. *Where probability is a matter of what the authorities approve, and the authorities no longer speak with one voice, it becomes anything but clear which opinions one should accept.* This problem, which we may name "the problem of many authorities," is the central social and intellectual difficulty of the Reformation. The domain of *opinio*, no less than that of *scientia*, had entered the sphere of the doubtful.[154]

Early Protestant Responses to Opinio: Certainty

The problem of many authorities began proliferating with the expansion of the Reformation. A century before Descartes, Martin Luther (1483–1546) sought to justify questioning the *opinio* of his contemporaries. Initially, he appealed to tradition (e.g., papal decrees), but then made substantial changes to his *opinio* criteria, decreasing the number of "recognized authorities." Eventually Luther introduced several more critical modifications: (1) considering scripture *alone* as divinely authoritative, (2) papal decrees having only human authority, and (3) the pope himself possessing no legitimate authority.[155]

Consequently, two major developments occurred within epistemology. First, *sola scriptura* would become not only a Reformation motto, but, more importantly, it would make special revelation (i.e., in this sense, the Bible) the unequaled source of theological knowledge sanctioned by

---

154. Stout, *The Flight from Authority*, 40–41. Emphasis mine.

155. For more details on Luther's moves, see Stout, *Flight from Authority*, 41–43.

Protestant reformers. Questions involving *opinio* as a kind of knowledge became pivotal in the debates and divisions that would come to characterize the period.

Equally revolutionary would be Luther's claim that only *certainty* could suffice for such weighty matters as faith. The fateful step toward radically increasing the problem of many authorities came with his assertion that all Christians *individually* had the power to discern and judge right and wrong in matters of faith.[156] In essence, every believer had the capacity to become their own authority on matters of biblical interpretation, theology, Christian practice, ethics and the like.[157] This move would engender robust polemical rejoinders from Roman Catholic critics challenging the reformers' criticisms of ecclesial authority.[158] However, for many others who welcomed this individualistic autonomy in connection with issues of faith, *opinio* had lost its value—and more importantly, its authority.

John Calvin (1509–64) further expanded on Luther's own view of interpretive autonomy, promoting a move for Protestant epistemology that would provide justification for professions of personal illumination on myriad biblical and theological matters. Calvin, while committed to the principle of *sola scriptura*, taught that it was the Holy Spirit alone who could—and would—provide the necessary illumination to individuals. This *inner persuasion* could be counted on for confirming the *absolute certainty* of scripture alone being the rule of faith, in that scripture is self-validating and faith is self-authenticating.

> [T]hose whom the Holy Spirit has inwardly taught truly rest upon Scripture, and that Scripture indeed is self-authenticated; hence, it is not right to subject it to proof and reasoning. And the certainty it deserves with us it attains by the testimony of the Spirit. For even if it wins reverence for itself by its own majesty, it seriously

156. See, for instance, Luther, *Three Treatises*, 20–22.

157. Still, Luther insisted that "no man can make a Doctor of Holy Scripture except the Holy Spirit from heaven. As Christ says in John 6 . . . 'They must all be taught by God himself'" (Luther, *Three Treatises*, 98).

158. The reaction from Rome came primarily from the Council of Trent (1545–63). Exertion of church authority and conciliar fiat were used to counter the challenge to tradition's authority. A lengthy process ensued involving delineating the differences between the official church position and that of the reformers. One of the horrific and drawn-out consequences of this intellectual and ecclesial battle was the protracted religious wars that followed, fought literally on bloodied battlefields—between brothers with contrasting authorities. This environment would be the formative climate that Descartes would find himself in as he sought answers to the pervasive and divisive problem of many authorities.

affects us only when it is sealed upon our hearts through the Spirit. Therefore, illumined by his power, we believe neither by our own nor by anyone else's judgment that Scripture is from God; but above human judgment we affirm with utter certainty (just as if we were gazing upon the majesty of God himself) that it has flowed to us from the very mouth of God by the ministry of men.[159]

This circularity made both the idea and practice of debate (or even discussion of the issue) practically impossible, since reformers could simply charge critics with not being illuminated by the Spirit, claiming the issue was beyond debate—a matter that was simply in God's hands. Eventually, strong disagreement interrupted the initial Calvinist harmony, inevitably compelling some to revise the reformers' arguments. One such dissenter was Sebastian Castello of Basel, who withdrew from the idea of claiming *absolute* certainty, believing there were too many obscurities relative to religion and scriptural interpretation.[160]

Thus, this early magisterial Protestant appeal to authority as individual conscience and inner persuasion of the Holy Spirit—in place of *scientia* and *opinio*—had exponentially added to the quandary of many authorities. Divorced from the authority of the church, believers could individually become, in essence, their own "authorized version"—every conscience a separate authority. Eventually, each major historic Protestant denomination (i.e., Lutheran, Reformed, and Anglican) would develop its own authoritative tradition by means of confessional statements. Afterward, dissenters came to separate from their authoritative statements, with the same procedure repeating itself time and again.

Because of this escalating diversity of authority and interpretations, Descartes believed trustworthy foundations for knowledge and truth must rest elsewhere. This epistemological crisis was crucial to Descartes' decision to *ignore* tradition in attempting to establish certainty—a move that Jay Wood sees as essential to Descartes' strongly individualistic method:

> He doesn't feel obliged to seek wise council from fellow academics, clerics, friends or a broader intellectual and cultural tradition to quell his doubts about whether we have knowledge of a mind-independent world. Indeed tradition, with its conflicting signals, was part of the problem, an obstacle to be overcome, not a voice to be indulged. Instead Descartes believed he had to free his thoughts

159. Calvin, *Institutes*, I.7.5, 80.

160. For a more detailed account, see Stout, *Flight from Authority*, 44.

from history's influence, endeavoring to accomplish his philosophical tasks alone.[161]

Thus a pioneering epistemology was obligatory. Accordingly, he sought a foundation of certainty for all knowledge, established on *reason*. Descartes' passion for comprehending the truth independently is assumed from his own admission that

> without wishing to say anything of the employment of others I thought that I could not do better than continue in the one in which I found myself engaged, that is to say, in occupying my whole life in cultivating my Reason, and in advancing myself as much as possible in the knowledge of the truth in accordance with the method which I had prescribed myself. I had experienced so much satisfaction since beginning to use this method, that I did not believe that any sweeter or more innocent could in this life be found,—every day discovering by its means some truths which seemed to me sufficiently important, although commonly ignored by other men. The satisfaction which I had so filled my mind that all else seemed of no account.[162]

An *indubitable* foundation had to be constructed and utilized to prevail over skepticism. Hence, this model needed to be impenetrable by (and impervious to) assault. All *doubts* would be considered innocent until proven otherwise.[163] Wood indicates what this method actually entailed:

> Descartes sought to rise above the competing claims of knowledge by using a method that would, as it were, allow him to climb outside his own skull, there achieving a kind of Archimedean standpoint (a God's-eye perspective, if you will) from which to conduct an internal audit of all he believed, ostensibly to settle once and for all the true relation between his claims and a mind-independent reality.[164]

Descartes used his method to prove the existence of God and external reality, claiming in *Discourse on Method* that

161. Wood, *Epistemology*, 87–88.

162. Descartes, *Discourse*, 1:97–98.

163. Richard Rorty judges Descartes' quest for foundational immediacy as tyrannous, in that such a yearning "expects that reality will be 'unveiled to us, not as in a glass darkly, but with some imaginable sort of immediacy which would make discourse and description superfluous'" (as cited in Thiel, *Nonfoundationalism*, 26).

164. Wood, *Epistemology*, 96.

there remains only the idea of God, concerning which we must consider whether it is something which cannot have proceeded from me myself. By the name God I understand a substance that is infinite,[165] independent, all-knowing, all-powerful, and by which I myself and everything else, if anything else does exist, have been created. Now all these characteristics are such that the more diligently I attend to them, the less do they appear capable of proceeding from me alone; hence, from what has already been said, we must conclude that God necessarily exists.[166]

While Descartes was personally convinced of the self-evident truth of his idea of God, his claims to the *objectivity* of knowledge soon drew strong criticism because there was *no method to verify* the correspondence between his ideas and the world. As theologian Amos Yong notes, "Skeptics like Hume questioned the connection between knower and known as well as the notion of *cogito* itself, and others like Nietzsche objected to the idea of a universal rationality."[167]

Founded on an *individualistic* rather than a scripture- or tradition-centered approach, dissimilar and contradictory knowledge claims by diverse *subjects* unavoidably raised serious queries over Descartes' allegations of impartiality. Carson further illustrates this unpredicted consequence:

> Not that Descartes himself envisaged such an outcome—but such an outcome is precisely what occurred. This is quite different from a view that holds that there is an omniscient God (who by definition truly knows everything), so that from his perspective all human beings are "objects," and all their true knowing is but a subset of his knowing. In other words, the Cartesian subject/object disjunction, by disallowing God at this foundational step, unwittingly set the stage for a later rising skepticism.[168]

Carson adds that "Descartes' dictum generated a trajectory of thought, the *Cartesian subject/object gap*, that continues to this day as a fundamental problem in Western epistemology" and that as this quest for certainty manifested itself in new disciplines, it increasingly became typified by greater hubris than rationality.[169]

165. An alternative reading for "infinite" in the first French translation is "eternal, immutable," not found in the Latin.

166. Descartes, *Meditations*, 1:165.

167. Yong, "Demise of Foundationalism," 566.

168. Carson, *Gagging of God*, 59.

169. Ibid., 59–60.

With the Cartesian method in place,[170] the epistemological starting place was not only moved from *opinio* to *scientia*, but also from belief to doubting. Stout explains the historic repercussions:

> [E]ven the most sweeping forms of doubt are . . . declared innocent until proven guilty, and implicitly skeptical standards of judgment have therefore been assumed from the start. The category of *scientia* is the only available notion retaining strong enough connections with certainty to be at all useful to Descartes once he has granted this much.[171]

Hence, the certainty necessary to justify beliefs would have to emerge from *scientia*, leading Descartes to look to arithmetic and geometry for answers;[172] tradition and community had lost considerable authority, providing only subjective illumination. But an unanticipated paradox would soon arise. Descartes' *goal* had been to create a firm foundation *for* belief, yet profound questions materialized over his postulations of "objective certainty," and shortly his epistemological foundationalism would be used to lead many into skepticism—*away from* rather than *toward* belief.

Since Descartes' time, many modifications to foundationalism have appeared: most notably, John Locke's empiricist version,[173] Thomas Reid's modest foundationalism,[174] and more recently Alvin Plantinga and Nicholas Wolterstorff's "Reformed Epistemology."[175] Regardless of the differences—

---

170. Pinnock says of Descartes and his method, "His very name now symbolizes the ideal of a human thinker who can bring forth from his unaided human mind a complete rational system that could explain everything, including God. The Cartesian thinker could do it all on the basis of nothing more than the individualized self-conscious serving as the final criterion of truth and the source of clear and certain knowledge" (Pinnock, *Tracking the Maze*, 90).

171. Stout, *Flight from Authority*, 49.

172. See Stout, *Flight from Authority*, 49.

173. Locke argued partly against Descartes, attempting to prove that the foundation for human knowledge lies in sense experience (i.e., empiricism).

174. Reid pointed out that "our psychological constitution draws us irresistibly to accept certain first principles as self-evident. Because we have no reason to suspect that these psychological processes are misleading . . . we are epistemically entitled to accept and employ these first principles" (as cited in Grenz, *Renewing the Center*, 188.) Grenz notes that Reid's proposal came to be known as "soft" or "modest" foundationalism, and played a significant role in nineteenth-century conservative theology.

175. See, for example, Plantinga, *Warranted Christian Belief*, especially Part III. The approach offered by Plantinga (and Wolterstorff) is sometimes characterized as partly soft foundationalism, as it pertains to first principles, and partly nonfoundationalism, based on its community-centered embeddedness.

some quite significant—each model harkens back to Descartes with respect to sharing a commitment to certain foundational beliefs or principles (from which humans derive nonbasic beliefs or principles), seeking to provide a knowledge base for all who search for universal foundations. Nevertheless, several crucial questions in connection with the foundationalist method call for deliberation: What are the characteristics of classical foundationalism from which refinements arise? Is agreement widespread as to the constituent parts of the foundation? And what are the main arguments that postconservatives and others present against foundationalism?

Characteristics of Classical Foundationalism

Classical foundationalism rests on several key assumptions. Grenz presents a useful synopsis of "strong program" foundationalism, often termed classical or Cartesian, summarized here in numerical form: 1) desire to overcome uncertainty of human error and disagreements; 2) grounding all human knowledge on something indubitably certain; 3) drawing from a "building" metaphor to show how knowledge arises and moves in one direction (upward), built on a sure foundation; 4) the foundation consists of an alleged set of incontestable beliefs or unassailable first principles; 5) foundational beliefs or principles are presumed universal, context-free, and (theoretically) available to all rational persons.[176]

Grenz assist us in understanding the foundationalist's initial task: "establishing an epistemological foundation for the constructing of the human knowing project by determining, and perhaps even demonstrating, the foundational beliefs or principles upon which knowledge rests."[177] He maintains that the three primary aspects of the foundationalist depiction of knowledge are a) basic or immediate first principles (or beliefs); b) mediate or nonbasic beliefs derived from these; and c) the basing relation, or the connection between the basic and nonbasic beliefs or principles which tell how epistemic certainty of the former can be transferred to the latter.[178] Moreover, certainty is only transferred via deductive reasoning, i.e., inferring other truths from innate ideas (*pace* Descartes), or inductive

---

176. Grenz, *Renewing the Center*, 185–86.

177. Grenz describes how foundationalists normally place religious beliefs in the "nonbasic" category, thus moving the program beyond description to prescription (dictating what sorts of beliefs are "properly basic"), then moving into the overall system, questioning what systems of beliefs are correct, acceptable, or properly structured (ibid., 186–87).

178. Ibid.

reasoning, i.e., deriving truth from sense impressions by the material world (*pace* Locke). Jay Wood elaborates further on the basic characteristics of strong foundationalism models:

> There are . . . three components to any foundational picture of knowledge. First . . . there is what are called "basic" or "immediate" beliefs; these form the bedrock of all that we believe, undergirding everything else we are justified in believing. All of our "mediate" or "nonbasic beliefs" (everything else we believe) constitute the second element of the foundationalist model. Basic beliefs function like Aristotelian "unmoved movers." They are the epistemic engines of our noetic structures, imparting justification to all of our nonbasic beliefs while not themselves requiring justification from any other beliefs—the support goes just one way. Finally, there is some sort of connection between our epistemological starting points, our basic beliefs, and all that is based on them. This connection is generally referred to as the "basing relation"; it specifies how the epistemic merit of our basic beliefs is to be transferred to our nonbasic beliefs.[179]

The classical foundationalist model certainly held out hope in the battle against skepticism and multiple authorities. Nonetheless, its cadre was vulnerable to attack for several reasons, eventually leading to sustained criticisms and outright rejection by many philosophers and theologians. Whereas many (if not most) traditionalist thinkers have been slow to shelve foundationalism as a basis for evangelical theology and its claims for theological knowledge, postconservative scholars have essentially abandoned modernity's premiere epistemology for alternative frameworks for knowledge. What are the causes for this occurrence? Are there good theological and/or philosophical reasons for it? Is the postconservative position merely mirroring general postmodern reactions against knowledge claims, merely reflecting a transitional historical-cultural move rather than a genuinely biblical or theologically-informed (re)turn to a sounder basis for knowledge? Briefly considering the *raison d'être* for the current widespread rejection of foundationalism and its principle of certainty will help us find a substantial response to these questions.

179. Wood, *Epistemology*, 84. Wood also notes that for strong foundationalists, three conditions (and the satisfaction of any one of them) will qualify as properly basic: a belief is 1) self-evidently true (immediately), often seen as logical axioms or mathematics; 2) incorrigible, a belief that is impossible to believe and be mistaken about (e.g., I exist); and 3) evident to the senses, truths we have as a result of our immediate commerce with the world of objects (e.g., a hand in front of my face). See ibid., 85–86.

REJECTION OF FOUNDATIONALISM AND THE ILLUSION OF CERTAINTY

In *Beyond Foundationalism*, Grenz and Franke assess the current situation pertaining to foundationalism:

> In the postmodern context . . . foundationalism is in dramatic retreat, as its assertions about the objectivity, certainty, and universality of knowledge have come under withering critique. The demise of foundationalism carries fundamental and far-reaching implications for theological method.[180]

This verdict is echoed by philosopher Merold Westphal, "That it [foundationalism] is philosophically indefensible is so widely agreed that its demise is the closest thing to a philosophical consensus in decades."[181] Westphal's emphatic pronouncement demonstrates the endemic rejection of foundationalist epistemology. Alister McGrath also agrees that foundationalism has had its day, stating pointedly, "Foundationalism of any kind—whether philosophical or religious—has been widely discredited."[182]

Countless thinkers point to the irony that, for a theory claiming the existence of unmediated foundational beliefs or first principles, upon which all other beliefs or principles are mediated, such vast disagreement exists over what particulars actually *compose* the foundation of this Enlightenment model. One attempt to remedy this and other foundationalist problems is the move made by some scholars to a *modest* or *soft* version, which will be discussed in a later section.[183]

Wood outlines the besetting *multiple versions* problem faced by foundationalists: "It is the hallmark of foundationalism to affirm that the ideal logical ordering of our cognitive lives begins with foundationally basic beliefs," yet there is a real problem in that "there are multiple versions of foundationalism on the market. Just what beliefs are reckoned as properly basic, by what criteria they can be identified and just how they lend support to the other things we believe are . . . matters of significant dispute." Thus, *lack of consensus* as to what the basic beliefs or principles are has generated

---

180. Grenz and Franke, *Beyond Foundationalism*, 24.

181. Westphal, "Reader's Guide to 'Reformed Epistemology'," 11.

182. McGrath, "Evangelical Evaluation of Postliberalism," 24.

183. See the discussion under the heading, "Soft or Modest Foundationalism," on page 112. Because this author generally sides with critics of soft foundationalism (especially Louis Pojman's assessment), only the strong version will be viewed herein as actually representing foundationalism, unless otherwise noted, and thus will receive primary focus as it pertains to foundationalist epistemology.

considerable debate and criticism. Wood poignantly adds, "It may not be an exaggeration to say that there are as many different versions of foundationalism as there are foundationalists who have written on the subject."[184]

Discussing the many problems present within a strong foundationalist program, Wood clarifies some of the more critical concerns: First, a failure to see that all perceptions (even colors) are theory-laden, "embedded in larger theoretical and linguistic frameworks ('language games')."[185] Strong foundationalism apparently disregards our conceptual schemes—subject to revision—that inform our perceptions. A second problem is failure to recognize that basic beliefs cannot be invincibly certain because they are set within "larger frameworks of belief."[186] Another problem directly connected with the second is strong foundationalism's unrealistic access requirements; if retained, an infinite regress occurs when attempting to justify proper foundations for knowledge.[187] Finally, a strong program entails an improper focus on independence of beliefs, rather than a "concurrence" or "coherence" between beliefs. In other words, it fails to comprehend the web-like interrelatedness of belief support, which is "not always from the bottom up."[188]

Concerning the demise of *empiricist* foundationalism, Nancey Murphy points out that the death knell was recognition of the theory-ladenness of scientific facts. She points to Thomas Kuhn's demonstration that "the construction of the experimental apparatus with which the observations are made will require theoretical knowledge. . . . For this reason, if we are to hold to the picture of knowledge as a building, we now have to imagine the foundation partially suspended from a top-floor balcony!"[189] Relative to the demise of the Cartesian method, "Descartes's strategy has been rejected by most philosophers simply because, in the passage of time, it has turned out that what is indubitable in one intellectual context is all too questionable in another . . ."[190] Finally, Murphy believes that although some thinkers have chosen to remain "chastened" foundationalists—add-

184. Wood, *Epistemology*, 85.

185. Ibid., 91.

186. Ibid., 93.

187. Ibid., 91.

188. Ibid., 93.

189. Murphy, *Beyond Liberalism and Fundamentalism*, 91.

190. Ibid.

ing "a long list of qualifications to the theory"—the best option is simply to reject the model entirely:

> There is good reason for abandoning the foundationalist picture altogether. There is no way, using this model, to represent the fact that the "foundations" are partially supported from above. . . . For this reason, if for no other, we need a new picture, a new model, that will more adequately represent what we now know to be the case about knowledge."[191]

In addition to Murphy, McGrath, and Wood, Grenz cites several other important Christian thinkers who agree that foundationalism is dead or dying: Westphal, van Huyssteen, and Wolterstorff.[192] He notes van Huyssteen's concurrence with this theme: "All postmodern thinkers see the modernist quest for certainty, and the accompanying program of laying foundations for our knowledge, as a dream for the impossible, a contemporary version of the quest for the Holy Grail."[193] In like manner, Stephen Toulmin notes that

> critics of Modernity proclaim or regret (it is not clear which) the absence of any established foundations for contemporary thought. Their observation is accurate: the dream of *foundationalism*—i.e., the search for a permanent and unique set of authoritative principles for human knowledge—proves to be just a dream, which has its appeal in moments of intellectual crisis, but fades away when matters are viewed under a calmer and clearer light.[194]

Added to this dirge is the now somewhat famous statement by Wolterstorff some years ago: "*On all fronts foundationalism is in bad shape.* It seems to me that there is nothing to do but give it up for mortally ill and learn to live in its absence. Theorizing is without a foundation of indubitables."[195]

THE EVANGELICAL THEOLOGY CONNECTION WITH FOUNDATIONALISM

As we have seen, then, postconservative thinkers, along with some other evangelical scholars,[196] have chosen to reject the modern foundationalist

191. Ibid., 93.

192. Grenz, *Renewing the Center*, 190.

193. van Huyssteen, "Tradition and the Task of Theology," 190.

194. Toulmin, *Cosmopolis*, 174.

195. Wolterstorff, *Reason Within the Bounds of Religion*, 56.

196. For instance, Arthur Holmes points to the mistake of foundationalism being its

method that has helped to shape evangelical thought from the seventeenth to the twentieth century (and beyond). This move has entailed a variety of significant consequences, some of which we will discuss in the next chapter; namely, new or renewed approaches to history (from ahistorical to tradition), theology (from propositionalism to narrative), and apologetics (from rationalism to embodiment).

It seems important to press for an answer to one further question of direct relevance to such substantial transitions: Can the strong reaction, among certain evangelical scholars, against the use of this method be attributed to the utilization of foundationalism by particular theologians or theological communities—especially concerning theological knowledge? If so, we will need to understand who the theologians and what the issues were. This inquiry will perhaps reveal answers as to why the ongoing distinctions between postconservative and traditionalist theological methods persist.

Many revisionist evangelicals argue that the general way mainstream evangelical theology has been envisioned and propagated is according to the pattern laid down by the intellectuals of nineteenth and early-twentieth-century Princeton Seminary. And since postconservatives more often than not claim that contemporary traditionalists generally derive their approach to theology from ideas carried out at Old Princeton, surveying the methodology of its foremost scholars ought to give us insight into what reformists deem as problematic therewith for evangelical theology, especially respecting its understanding of theological knowledge.

We must ask, therefore, What are the alleged faults with Old Princeton theological methods, according to postconservatives? Are these issues central or peripheral to Christian faith and the knowledge of God? Could dialogue feasibly provide agreement on at least some areas of division? The following section will take up these and related questions connected with postconservative critiques of Old Princeton thought.

---

mechanistic approach (relative to the knowledge of God): "Enlightenment philosophy . . . did not abandon natural theology. Mechanistic science substitutes for Aristotelian science as the metaphysical model, so that theistic proofs begin with concepts drawn from the mechanistic view of nature, and the logic used is that of mathematical reasoning. . . . Critics of enlightenment natural theology such as Hume and Kant were in principle correct when they concluded that its problem is epistemological, that religious knowledge modeled on mechanistic science is precarious, and that the knowledge of God has more of a personal than of a scientific basis" (Holmes, *Faith Seeks Understanding*, 142).

Postconservative Concerns with Traditionalist Theological Epistemology: A Case Study of Old Princeton Theology and its Use of Scottish Common Sense Realism

INTRODUCTION

Determining the validity of the postconservative assessment will be one primary goal of this section. The conflict is widespread over matters of theological method held by traditionalists and reformists, contributing to apparently growing division within the evangelical academic community. It is important, therefore, to explore the possibilities for greater understanding and appreciation of disparate theological methods offered by the evangelical scholarly community.

To better comprehend and work constructively toward transcending the present gulf between postconservative and traditionalist thinkers, particularly regarding the question of theological knowledge, this section will analyze a representative model of the traditionalist position—Old Princeton Theology (OPT), along with the philosophical structure undergirding its theological method: Scottish Common Sense Realism (SCSR).[197]

OLD PRINCETON THEOLOGY AND ITS INCORPORATION OF SCOTTISH COMMON SENSE PHILOSOPHY[198]

Brief Overview of Scottish Philosophy and its Reception in America

The influence of SCSR in America is noted by historian George Marsden: "Until after the Civil War almost all American evangelical theologians built their discussions of faith and reason on principles drawn, at least in part, from the Scottish 'Common Sense' school of philosophy."[199]

SCSR was developed in an effort to refute three significant and distinct eighteenth-century philosophical innovations: the skepticism of David Hume, the idealism of George Berkeley, and the radical social view-

197. This essay will utilize several terms as synonyms for Scottish Common Sense Realism: Scottish Common Sense Philosophy, Scottish Philosophy, Scottish Realism, Scottish Common Sense, Common Sense, and Common Sense Realism.

198. This section is deeply indebted to Ahlstrom, "Scottish Philosophy and American Theology."

199. Marsden, "American Evangelical Academia," 224.

points of the French Enlightenment.[200] Mark Noll summarizes its general method and main assertions:

> It argued that normal people, using responsibly the information provided by their senses, actually grasped thereby the real world. Furthermore, an exercise of the "moral sense," a faculty analogous in all important ways to physical senses, gave humans immediate knowledge about the nature of their own minds. And because all humans, humanity in *common*, were able to grasp the truth of the world in this way—in fact, could not live unless they took for granted that truth was available in this way—this *common sense* could provide the basis for a full-scale philosophy as well.[201]

The Scottish philosophers themselves both "modified and defended the great traditions of modern English thought,"[202] and moreover

> regarded truth as a static entity, open equally to all people wherever they lived, in the present or past. They placed a high premium on scientific investigation. They were deeply committed to an empirical method that made much of gathering relevant facts into logical wholes. They abhorred "speculation" and "metaphysics" as unconscionable flights from the basic realities of the physical world and the human mind. And at least some of them assumed that this approach could be used to convince all rational souls of the truth of Christianity, the necessity of traditional social order, and the capability of scientific methods to reveal whatever may be learned about the world.[203]

These emphases are clearly displayed in the writings of Thomas Reid, a Scottish Philosopher who influenced many of the prominent theologians of the Old Princeton School of the nineteenth and early twentieth centuries.[204] Reid's own views are encapsulated in four central assump-

---

200. Noll, *Princeton Theology*, 31.

201. Ibid.

202. E.g., the empiricism of Bacon, Locke, and Newton.

203. Noll, *The Princeton Theology*, 31.

204. The skepticism and radicalism, especially evident within continental forms of Enlightenment thought, were virtually absent from this *evangelical* version. For instance, David Hume's skeptical approach was due in large measure to Enlightenment empiricism that questioned, among other things, Christian claims to theological knowledge. Mark Noll points out that Henry May's *The Enlightenment in America* demonstrates that there were actually "several Enlightenments" perceived by eighteenth-century Americans: *moderate*, represented by Newton and Locke (which Americans respected but held at arms-length); *skeptical* and *revolutionary*, represented by Voltaire and Hume, and Paine, Rousseau, and

tions, briefly summarized here as follows: scientific observation is key to philosophy, and self-consciousness is the primary object of this scrutiny; certain first principles are established by such observations, anterior to and independent of experience, some necessary and some contingent; only an intelligent being can be an efficient cause (matter being only instrumental), and self-consciousness revealing such agency; and self-evident intuitions are the first principles of morality.[205]

While Reid may properly be considered the key articulator of Scottish Philosophy, John Witherspoon's powerful influence as president of the College of New Jersey in Princeton most directly contributed to its rising popularity in America.[206] Just *why* Witherspoon and ensuing generations at Princeton (and elsewhere) thought it essential to employ the tools of Scottish Realism will be the concern of our next section. Before turning there, however, understanding the *use* of this philosophy at other academic institutions may shed more light on its prevalence and diverse applications in American higher education.

At primarily Unitarian Harvard College and Divinity School (c. 1810–89), Scottish Philosophy was advocated in "an unbroken succession" via liberal theology.[207] For instance, James Walker's moralistic sermons include the "Scottish imprint" on the subjects of "virtue, conscience,

---

William Godwin, respectively (both types of which were repudiated by evangelicals); and *didactic*, represented by Hutcheson, Reid, Adam Smith, and Dugald Stewart, which deeply shaped and governed academic life in the United States during its early history. This last variety (didactic) has continued to strongly affect evangelical thought, while receiving significant criticism from postconservative intellectuals. Furthermore, leaders of this Scottish-produced Enlightenment were successful in achieving their goals of restoring "intellectual confidence and social cohesion to the Enlightenment ideal" by contending that "all humans possessed, by nature, a common set of capacities—both epistemological and ethical—through which they could grasp the basic realities of nature and morality. Moreover, these human capacities could be studied as scientifically as Newton studied the physical world. Such rigorous study, especially of conscience, would yield laws for human behavior and ethics every bit as scientific as Newton's conclusions about nature" (Noll, *Scandal of the Evangelical Mind*, 84–85).

205. See Ahlstrom, "Scottish Philosophy and American Theology," 261. "One of the firmest commitment of Reid and his American followers [D. Stewart, J. Beattie, T. Brown, and W. Hamilton] was to the British inductive-empirical school of thought associated with Francis Bacon and Isaac Newton (and more generally with John Locke) concerned above all else to establish a firm base for inductive scientific investigation" (Marsden, "American Evangelical Academia," 224).

206. See Ahlstrom, "Scottish Philosophy and American Theology," 261–62.

207. Ibid., 262–63.

natural theology, and the role of reason."²⁰⁸ Even more influential was the Scottish Common Sense tradition promoted via both (more moderate) Yale and (more conservative) Andover.²⁰⁹ Whether the theology was liberal, moderate, or conservative, Scottish Philosophy reigned as the choice methodology in most nineteenth-century American academies.²¹⁰ This was no exception at Princeton.

Historical Background of the Utilization of Scottish Common Sense Philosophy within Old Princeton Theology

As much as Harvard and Yale employed Scottish Realism in their endeavors to advocate alternatives to conservative theology, Princeton found this philosophical method essential to its own polemical quest—faithfully defending historic Christian doctrine and orthodoxy.²¹¹ Old Princeton's historical-cultural contexts seem to have played at least as significant a part in this novel apologetical system as did the theological pedigree of the Princetonian academics.²¹² Moreover, this new confidence in human moral powers meant not only a foundation for biblical and theological orthodoxy, but for political and sociological justification as well.²¹³ Several other factors could also be cited as evidence for the readiness to integrate Scottish Philosophy with evangelical theology: perhaps chief among them, desire for a "traditionless" and non-external authoritative foundation in

208. Ibid., 263.

209. For instance at Yale, by president and grandson of Jonathan Edwards, Timothy Dwight, and his pupil, professor of Theology at Yale, Nathaniel William Taylor; and of Andover, by Abbot Professor of Theology, Leonard Woods, and his selected successor, Edwards Amasa Park (see ibid., 263–65).

210. However, before the latter quarter of the eighteenth century, it appears that among Reformed thinkers, human nature was viewed as virtually incapable of such Enlightenment-granting abilities, since the effects of sin and evil were all pervasive, quashing the idea of humans possessing a natural sense of morality. The works of Jonathan Edwards and other evangelical intellectuals and practitioners, in and before the mid-seventeen hundreds, illustrate this point (see Noll, *Scandal of the Evangelical Mind*, 86).

211. Charles Hodge's academic title is enough to evidence this focus: Professor of Polemical Theology.

212. For instance, the political forces of the post-American Revolution era, and the intellectual (and theological) need to justify America's break with its Mother Country.

213. Perhaps this is most clearly illustrated in the view expressed in 1787 by then Princeton President, Samuel Stanhope Smith, in his defense of "the unity of humanity." Beginning with his *a priori* confidence in the ability of the fresh moral philosophy, Smith reasons from an "examination of one's own heart to universally valid principles of social order" (Noll, *Scandal of the Evangelical Mind*, 89).

the wake of a society questioning all types of alleged verities and authorities[214] that had previously been widely accepted.

Within theological and apologetical arenas, the influence of this version of the Enlightenment was profound. A strong amalgamation of faith in God and faith in *reason* ensued in an effort to defend the faith against detractors.[215] Along with a logic-oriented Christianity expressed in varying degrees of rationalism and empiricism, intuitionism (i.e., Common Sense) served to secure reliable knowledge. Noll points out that, among evangelicals, including Princetonian academics, commitment to such a model was practically exhaustive:

> So basic did this reasoning become that even self-consciously orthodox evangelicals had no qualms about resting the entire edifice of the faith on the principles of the Scottish Enlightenment. . . . In a word, the basic principle of the Scottish philosophy—that people could reason naturally from the evidence of their own consciousness to the existence of God and the validity of traditional morality—had become very widespread by the early nineteenth century.[216]

Many of the Old Princeton seminal professors learned and embraced Scottish Realism, as did more than a few of their contemporaries of the nineteenth century.[217] In an era confident of the possibilities for a universal and comprehensive knowledge, it is not surprising to discover Charles Hodge referring to the Bible as "a store-house of facts," wherein the Christian theologian's responsibility is to "ascertain, collect, and combine all the facts which God has revealed concerning himself and our relation to him;"[218] the rather transparent scientific method used by Hodge influenced practically every discipline in the dominant "encyclopedia" era.[219]

214. E.g., divine revelation, denominations.

215. See Noll, *Scandal of the Evangelical Mind*, 90–91. At first, apologists like William Paley were called upon to support the reasonableness of Christianity, but by the second decade of the nineteenth century, focus on use of the scientific method and evidentialism became commonplace among evangelical thinkers.

216. Ibid., 93.

217. Although much commonality regarding Reformed theological commitments was shared between Princetonian scholars and Dutch Reformed intellectuals (for instance, Abraham Kuyper), a "great gulf" was fixed between them respecting apologetical approaches: the latter's method being presuppositional, and the former, evidential. See Noll, *Princeton Theology*, 42.

218. Hodge, *Systematic Theology*, 1:10–11.

219. See MacIntyre, *Three Rival Versions*, for a thorough historical discussion and inci-

Many contemporary thinkers depict the Old Princeton academics as walking a theological tightrope, strung between a particular Reformed version of the Christian faith and doctrine, and the philosophical scaffolding of Scottish Realism. The introduction of the scientific method, based on the idea of a universally-recognized intuition and its ability to "prove" the great truths of the Christian faith (e.g., the existence of God), meant a shift toward greater confidence in the human capacity to know—somewhat revisionist of historic Calvinism, not to mention reflective of a strong endorsement of nineteenth-century Scottish Philosophy.

While the most *general* tenets of Calvinism were retained throughout the life of Old Princeton theology, the *emphases* of each of the major thinkers from Archibald Alexander to Machen differed rather substantially at times, in large part due to the immediate historical and contextual concerns each thinker was engaging.[220] To imagine that all of them were simply carrying forward an entirely unchanging tradition would be naïve, despite Charles Hodge's claim that no novelties of thought could be found originating in Princeton seminary.[221]

Nevertheless, the balancing act worked at Princeton Seminary for almost a century, with the end coming only with the fundamentalist-modernist controversy of the early twentieth century. Ahlstrom offers an explanation of the problem Hodge and his fellow Princeton scholars faced:

> The profound commitment of orthodox theology to the apologetical keeping of the Scottish Philosophy made traditional doctrines so lifeless and static that a new theological turn was virtually inevitable. Certainly there is no mystery as to why end-of [nineteenth]-century theology in America turned with such enthusiasm to evolutionary idealism, the social gospel, and the "religion of feeling." It was in search of the relevant and the dynamic.[222]

Though technically ceasing to exist with this major breach, Old Princeton theology continued (and still continues) to live on in differing

---

sive analysis of the *encyclopedia* worldview.

220. For instance, criticism of biblical authority was addressed differently by Alexander, who was faced with challenges from deists and Catholics, than by Warfield, whose context included higher criticism and "enthusiast" interpretations (see Noll, *Princeton Theology*, 40).

221. Noll refers to the recollection of such thinking as evidenced in A. A. Hodge's *Life of Charles Hodge*, in *Princeton Theology*, 38.

222. Ahlstrom, "Scottish Philosophy and American Theology," 269.

degrees among conservative evangelicals—unsurprisingly and most nota-bly within particular modern conservative forms of Reformed/Calvinist traditions, as well as within certain fundamentalist faith communities. Discussion of the distinctiveness of this theological stream within the con-temporary Christian academia and the church must be left to the work of others. The heart of this analysis and evaluation centers on determining *why* postconservative evangelicals consider traditionalist approaches to theological method to be in error (or at least problematic), and how Old Princeton's use of SCSR represents for them this unsatisfactory methodol-ogy. The strategy selected in order to delve deeper into accomplishing this task involves considering the moderate to severe criticisms launched by postconservative scholars against what they see as four central ingredients found in such traditionalist approaches, particularly with reference to theological knowledge.[223]

The strategic focus will consider Old Princeton as *representative* of the general purview of traditionalist viewpoints.[224] One further necessary constriction involves focusing mainly (though not exclusively) on just one of the Old Princeton intellectuals—someone who symbolized the views of the whole.[225] While virtually any of these articulate thinkers could well serve to represent the consensus view, considering his comprehensive and influential systematic theology, along with his prominent utilization of Scottish Philosophy (as will be shown in our study), this appointment goes to Charles Hodge. We now turn attention to analysis of specific postconservative concerns with the traditionalist theological method, and more particularly, theological knowledge.

---

223. As anticipated, there will be considerable overlap between these aspects since they seem to have been deeply integrated and interdependently employed by Old Princetonians. Yet, it seems beneficial to roughly divide them for analytical and evaluative purposes.

224. Obviously, it stands to reason that minor theological variation will inevitably exist between traditionalists—no less regarding approaches to theological knowledge—and the methods and ideas espoused by Alexander to Warfield/Machen Princetonians. Nevertheless, there still remains a large amount of consensus on the most general areas to be discussed, and therefore sufficient commonality by which we may proceed.

225. In *The Princeton Theology*, Noll has convincingly shown that a solid consensus existed at Old Princeton with regard to most important theological and philosophical questions (evolution being one exception). General unanimity also prevailed with reference to its unswerving commitment to Scottish Philosophy.

FOUR POSTCONSERVATIVE CRITICISMS OF THE TRADITIONALIST APPROACH TO THEOLOGICAL METHOD AND EPISTEMOLOGY AS EXHIBITED WITHIN OLD PRINCETON THOUGHT

While postconservatives raise more issues over traditionalist theological method than will be discussed here, this presentation will engage four areas of concern—matters that may influence evangelical thought in the present postmodern context and into the foreseeable future (i.e., perhaps in the terms used by Millard Erickson, a *post*postmodern period, which some feel began in connection with the tragic events of 9/11).[226] In keeping with the theme of representation, four scholars typifying the postconservative perspective will be called on to describe and critique the selected problems associated with the traditionalist theological method—especially pertaining to theological knowledge—as exemplified in the work of Old Princeton scholars, particularly Charles Hodge. Stanley Grenz, Robert Webber, Kevin Vanhoozer, and Clark Pinnock in varying ways reflect a post-Enlightenment evangelical methodology—important in that a primary catalyst for postconservative criticism leveled against traditionalists is their deep drawing from the well of modernity, presumably pervading their theological method and epistemology.[227] Said in another way, postconservative scholars view such an approach as practically obsolete since it is essentially founded on an increasingly discredited modern philosophical system.

We turn now to the first of four major reformist criticisms of traditionalist *modi operandi*, keeping in mind that each of these criticisms begins with the expression, "questionable confidence"—something postconservatives charge as being an inherent part of the problem with Old Princetonian thought, and consequently with traditionalist methodology.

Questionable Confidence in a Theological Method Rooted in Modernity and Scottish Common Sense Philosophy

More than fifty years ago, the impending demise of Scottish Common Sense Philosophy was well underway, according to Ahlstrom:

226. Predominantly focusing on the epistemological arena ought not be misconstrued as connoting that other areas having theological interest (e.g., linguistics) are unimportant to the future of evangelical reflection—on the contrary, they are important. Nonetheless, in light of the scope of this book and the formidable epistemological issues facing evangelical scholarship on a global scale, a more concentrated focus is in order.

227. In addition to these four theologians, two first-class Christian historians, Mark Noll and George Marsden, will be asked throughout this segment to provide further description and analysis of traditionalist methodology.

The Scottish Philosophy is no longer in good repute despite its proud reign in another day. Indeed, few, if any, schools of philosophy have been given such disdainful treatment by historians as Common Sense Realism; and few, if any, philosophers have had to suffer such ignominious re-evaluation as Thomas Reid and Dugald Stewart, who were once lionized as the founders of a great and enduring philosophical synthesis.[228]

If only one thing were to be learned by evangelicals from postmodern philosophy, it would be the wisdom of approaching practically every subject with appropriate tentativeness and humility—something postconservatives are quick to point out is wholly lacking with traditionalist methodology. A case in point involves the general equating—whether implicit or explicit—of Old Princeton's theological method with both biblical and "self-evident" truth, primarily founded on a general acceptance of Scottish Philosophy principles. Part of the problem stems from an assumption of *complete universality* and *objectivity* of their own thinking; this was in contrast to the assumed *bias* or *contradiction* of virtually every other alternative scheme. As Marsden asserts,

> The evangelical apologists, of course, recognized bias. Bias, however, was something other people had. "Tell me what a man's philosophy is," said Hodge, "and I will ask him no questions about his theology." They, on the other hand, considered themselves to hold no special philosophy.[229]

While postconservative scholars appear genuinely confident of their own theological positions, greater recognition of the *fiduciary* character of knowledge seems to prevail among them than among traditionalists like Hodge; therefore a more open stance toward modification and plurality of methods. For instance, Vanhoozer writes of the character of theology as *phronesis*; he also speaks of the goal of practical reason and "looking along the text" with the understanding that there are different theological traditions that "refer to a certain trajectory of biblical interpretation."

228. Ahlstrom, "Scottish Philosophy and American Theology," 257.

229. Marsden, "American Evangelical Academia," 242. Not only Princetonians, but other nineteenth and early-twentieth-century scholars (liberal and conservative, Reformed and otherwise) thought along the same epistemological lines: Common Sense Philosophy served these academic communities in their attempts to present indubitable truth via the empirical route.

These insights ought to make us mindful of an important—and properly humbling—point:

> While the truth about what God has done in Christ may transcend the particular interpretive perspectives, interpreters cannot. While it is true "that God was in Christ reconciling the world to Himself" (2 Cor. 5:19 NASB), we may need more than one interpretive framework to articulate fully its meaning and significance, just as it took four Gospels to articulate the truth of Jesus Christ.[230]

Traditionalists, however, are evidently more likely to envision their model as largely unalterable. This seeming inflexibility may be based upon several factors: for instance, commitment to previous statements of faith or confessions assumed to be highly accurate reflections of true Christian faith.[231] In Hodge's case, there exists a strong commitment to "the veracity of consciousness, or the trustworthiness of the laws of belief which God has impressed upon our nature," with this doctrine serving as "the foundation of all science and of all faith."[232] But this immovable attitude is problematic to reformists, reflecting what has been described in theatrical terms as "the deadly theatre."[233] The relationship of this "epic theology" approach to the theatrical style is vividly described by Vanhoozer:

> The deadly theatre is dull. This is the theater of repetition, the theater of set scenes, cliché, and stock effects. In deadly theatre there is no real connection between actor and audience, only a hollow spectacle. One approaches the classics from the viewpoint that "somewhere someone has found out and defined how the play should be done." This is the theatrical equivalent of . . . epic theology, in which the role of the theologian is simply to repeat the same formulaic confessions. The question that needs to be asked at this point . . . is "Why theatre at all?" Indeed, why theology at all, if we already have the definite interpretation for all times and places. Tradition is an important source for theology, but *tradi-*

---

230. Vanhoozer, "Voice and the Actor," 78.

231. One example of such an allegedly highly accurate confession would be the Westminster Confession, although there seems to be growing unrest among some within more moderately Reformed communities with attributing what amounts to something approaching canonical status to this (or any other) post-Reformation confession.

232. Hodge, *Systematic Theology*, 1:340.

233. See Vanhoozer, "Voice and the Actor," 101–2. Vanhoozer is citing and modifying ideas from Peter Brook, *Empty Space*.

tionalism—the excessive regard for tradition—is the enemy of vital theology.[234]

Consider further that Hodge returns repeatedly to the theme of the "universality" of rational thought, believing this to be an invincible foundation for his theological arguments, including human knowledge of God. Interestingly, biblical revelation is given but one page out of the thirty in Hodge's fourth chapter of Systematic Theology, Volume I, "The Knowledge of God."[235] The emphasis of his section, "Necessity of a Supernatural Revelation," centers on scripture giving us real knowledge and a certainty about the "facts" that it reveals. Hodge's appeal lacks any reference to the personal or relational component of theological knowledge as communicated and evidenced in the scriptures.[236] Instead, the mind plays the central role in the process of knowing the facts of the Bible. But in good Scottish Philosophy fashion, Hodge adds, "The testimony of God is not only to, but also *within* the mind."[237]

No less emphatic is Hodge's belief that his method, with its correspondence theory of truth, provides for objective and unquestioned certainty of theological knowledge:

> If the testimony of men can give us clear and certain knowledge of facts beyond our experience, surely the testimony of God is greater. What He reveals is made known. We apprehend it as it truly is. The conviction that what God reveals is made known in its true nature, is the very essence of faith in the divine testimony. We are certain, therefore, that our ideas of God, founded on the testimony of his Word, corresponds to what He really is, and constitute true knowledge.[238]

234. Vanhoozer, "Voice and the Actor," 101–2. Emphasis mine.

235. Hodge, *Systematic Theology*, 1:335–65.

236. This is not to imply that in *other* writings (or in teaching or preaching) Hodge fails to consider or explicate the personal or relational aspect of the knowledge of God. In fact, Hoffecker supplies ample evidence that he does not fail to do so (see Hoffecker, *Piety and the Princeton Theologians*). Nonetheless, in the chapter of his *Systematic Theology* dedicated to the knowledge of God, Hodge refrains from making such a case for piety, and probably because of his concern with the growing "enthusiasm" and "experientialism" of his cultural context, he opts to concentrate on what he views as arguments that are more objective. Emphasis mine.

237. Hodge, *Systematic Theology*, 1:364.

238. Ibid.

Common sense and reason are viewed by Hodge as separate, authoritative, and stand-alone entities, consummate with his perception of their pure "objectivity," rather than as being alongside one's tradition, context, and culture. Hence, the scriptures are practically granted a *supportive* role for the already "clear" testimony of the universal human conscience relative to theological knowledge:

> It [the revelation contained in scripture] harmonizes with our whole nature. It supplements all our other knowledge, and authenticates itself by harmonizing the testimony of *enlightened* consciousness with the testimony of God in his Word.
>
> The conclusion, therefore, of the whole matter is, that we know God in the same sense in which we know ourselves and things out of ourselves. . . . Our subjective idea corresponds to the objective reality. This knowledge of God is the foundation of all religion; and therefore to deny that God can be known, is really to deny that rational religion is possible.[239]

The "enlightened" that Hodge has in mind here is to be found in a mind that attends to that which is available to common sense. As Marsden explains,

> Hodge (following Reid) remarked in stating his assumptions, common-sense truths were "given in the constitution of our nature." Having been so purposely designed, they could be relied on with perfect security. Moreover, the design of nature was assumed to involve the creation of a single universal human nature. Hence, the presumption was that common-sense principles were universal and unalterable.[240]

By the end of the nineteenth century, Hodge's appeals to "irresistible intuition," coupled with utilization of the arguments from natural theology of William Paley and Joseph Butler, had become, Marsden observes, "futile as far as the Western intellectual community was concerned." The reason was rather simple:

> Hodge could *claim* that the conviction of intelligent design in nature was irresistible and universal, but large parts of the next generation demonstrated that in fact the belief was quite resistible and far from universal. Common-Sense philosophy, claiming to be objective, claiming to rest on no prior assumptions, had no

239. Hodge, *Systematic Theology*, 1:364–65. Emphasis mine.
240. Ibid., 242–43.

adequate response to such an attack on one of its fundamental principles. The supposed objectivism of the system suffered from a fatal flaw. Common sense could not settle a dispute over what was a matter of common sense.[241]

This suggests that there are significant challenges in applying the SCSR model to a global, postmodern culture. Its cultural biases raise problems for its claims to universality—an important factor in a world wherein evangelical theology must address global as well as local realities. Marsden rightly notes this problem with Old Princeton's assumptions:

> The phenomenon that people almost always find themselves trusting common-sense faculties and principles, and even that for the sake of argument they may be obliged to trust them, does not yield a strong presumption that these faculties and principles are especially reliable. Certainly it does not yield any presumption that these are universal throughout the race or unalterable, or that there is one set of assumptions that, in principle, everyone should agree to.[242]

Hodge's confidence in the alleged—and now widely questioned—objectivity and certainty of his amalgamated Scottish Realism and strict Calvinism represents more than a few contemporary traditionalists. And as we will see later in this study, negative reaction among postconservative scholars has generated declarations of the demise of what is seen as an ahistorical, acultural, acontextual approach to evangelical theology, along with its corresponding hubris, particularly in relation to knowledge of its Subject.[243] Reformists are calling evangelicals to move beyond what they see as an antiquated theological method and a restrictive gatekeeping mentality to embrace more appropriate and useful approaches in the postmodern cultural context.

241. Ibid., 244. Emphasis mine.

242. Marsden, "American Evangelical Academia," 243.

243. On the other hand, it must be noted that thinkers like Thomas Reid, Jonathan Edwards, and Blaise Pascal clearly demonstrated restraint in their epistemological claims. Hence, one must be careful not to caricature *all* modern thinkers as excessively dogmatic in their approaches or attitudes. This too easily distorts the variety and depth of thinking in the modern period. Nevertheless, the general *temper* by most accounts is one of unbalanced dogmatism and hubris, bred at least partially by an over-zealous commitment to the supposed objectivity of the scientific method, and the alleged universality of human concepts and religious experience. It appears now that at least some of these misconceptions were due to cultural and ethnocentric myopia. A clearly theological answer gets to the point much more quickly: the sins of idolatry, pride and partiality.

However, the negative postconservative assessment of Old Princeton thought is not shared by everyone. For instance, in contrast to critical evaluations of Hodge and other Princetonians regarding their alleged full reliance upon Scottish Philosophy, Peter Hicks argues that distinct from many of his contemporary intellectuals, Hodge

> was widely read in German philosophy and theology, and, while generally adhering to the Scottish position rather than to the Kantian in epistemology, he never indulged in the extravagant praise of the Scottish school which was common in the first half of the nineteenth century . . . Though many of his ideas and much of his language was drawn from the teaching of Reid and his followers, he would have resisted strongly the suggestion that the Scottish philosophy was the sole foundation of his own epistemology.

> For while he shared with the Scottish school, and indeed with Hume and Kant, the conviction that, despite scepticism, our beliefs and knowledge about the external world are to be treated as reliable and as a sufficient basis for action, he differed significantly from them, and so from many of his contemporaries, in one key point: he recognized that the basis of epistemological realism had to be theological rather than philosophical; philosophical scepticism on its own grounds is unassailable; if we are to accept the dependability of our experience on the external world it cannot be on the grounds of a rationally proved argument, but rather on the grounds of the nature of God, and especially of his relationship with the world; in other words *the doctrine of divine providence.* While Hodge was able to agree with the Scottish philosophers that "it is universally admitted that we have no foundation for knowledge or faith, but the veracity of consciousness" his own conviction went one step deeper: "The ultimate ground of faith and knowledge is confidence in God."[244]

Furthermore, as influenced as they were by Scottish Realism, Hodge and other Old Princetonians "still retained the fidelity to Scripture and Reformed tradition which kept them from being entirely at the mercy of their philosophy."[245] In addition, while not deeply pervading their formal theology, Hodge and his fellow Princeton theologians "supported and

---

244. Hicks, *Philosophy of Charles Hodge*, 166. Emphasis mine. Internal quotes are from Hodge, *Systematic Theology*, 1:214, 1:52, respectively.

245. Noll, *Princeton Theology*, 33.

practiced an active piety."[246] In fact, Andrew Hoffecker is rather enthusiastic in his assessment of their devoutness as it concerns internal evidence:

> The Princeton men could have just parroted Scottish philosophy and made faith little more than knowledge of assent based on evidence. But they continually insisted that faith, while founded on an observed trustworthiness in its object, contains emotional aspects which make it man's act of loving trust. And it was specifically *religious* faith that best exemplified the fiducial aspects.[247]

Still, it seems evident (even to Hoffecker) that the philosophical commitments of the Princetonians had a serious shaping effect on the *focus* of their work—retaining the strong presumption of objectivity, thus de-emphasizing the subjective side of the knowledge (i.e., experience) of God.[248] Hence, as Hoffecker rightly states, despite the "intention of the Princeton men to hold the constituent elements of religious experience in tension, they were more successful in theory than in practice."[249]

Questionable Confidence in the Scientific Method, Reason and Self-Attestation of the Human Mind

Vanhoozer's synopsis of the move from *opinio* to *scientia* captures the strong epistemological emphasis of the modern period (beginning with Descartes):

> What justifies one's knowledge claims is no longer an appeal to authoritative sources but rather an account of how this information has been processed. In this regard the success of the natural sciences is paradigmatic; the scientific method became the envy of other disciplines too. What matters for moderns is being able to justify one's beliefs. Henceforth it's method over matter, epistemology over metaphysics.[250]

The epistemological shift from faith to knowledge persuaded many nineteenth and twentieth-century theologians. The tendency to grant *carte*

---

246. Ibid. In support of this view, see the arguments and evidence advanced in Hoffecker, *Piety and the Princeton Theologians*.

247. Ibid., 157.

248. No doubt, one of the major contributions to Hodge's reactionary method was the experientially-grounded theological method of Schleiermacher (see Schleiermacher, *Christian Faith*).

249. Hoffecker, *Piety and the Princeton Theologians*, 159.

250. Vanhoozer, *First Theology*, 17.

blanche approval to the empirical method was everywhere evident—no less with Old Princeton theologians. It was stated with utter confidence that in the same way scientists approach their subjects, theologians are called to approach the Bible since it contains a bevy of facts that needs unearthing in order that the truth of its contents may be ascertained and consequently embraced by all true believers. Any distinction made between the faith of the scientist and that of the theologian seemed virtually irrelevant, since facts were *neutral* and spoke for themselves. The idea that such facts are unavoidably *interpreted facts* has practically no play in Hodge's theology. Truth is simply truth, regardless of the influence of one's milieu. Hence, by definition, truth comes to us as entirely *a*historical, *a*cultural, and *a*contextual.[251] Combined with the presumption in Scottish Philosophy of immediate and intuitive theological knowledge, one finds that knowledge of God assumes both a universal and an exclusive reality. This might seem at first glance a rather paradoxical posture in that "universal" entails that everyone, everywhere, and at all times will necessarily comprehend the knowledge of God in the same way, whereas exclusive implies that only via the Christian scriptures can one gain correct facts concerning theological knowledge.

Evangelical reformists make the postmodern point that moderns are mistaken in their theory (and sometimes quest) concerning an alleged universal human nature—something most theologians of Hodge's day took for granted. Postconservatives also insist that this educated, male-dominated, Eurocentric, and largely Protestant and Reformed view of human nature has less in common with disparate cultures, ethnicities, traditions, or genders than once imagined. Reformists are cognizant of the dominance this type of scholarship has had upon evangelical theology (at least until recently), and have repeatedly repudiated the modernity-immersed conception of what it is to be human, to know, and to believe.[252]

Nevertheless, postconservatives insist that their reassessment of human character does not entail something less orthodox than their tradi-

251. Vanhoozer reminds us, though, "It is one thing to affirm the history of Jesus Christ as the definitive revelation of God, quite another to enshrine any one telling or interpretation of that event as the definitive interpretation. Alister McGrath has rightly warned of the danger of 'uncritical repetition' in Christian theology" (Vanhoozer, "Voice and the Actor," 98).

252. For example, see Robert Webber's presentation of the major revolutions in scientific, philosophical, and communication arenas respecting the paradigm shift from modern to postmodern thought, and his call for a Classical/Evangelical response, in *Ancient-Future Faith*.

tionalist counterpart when it comes to accepting the universality of the sinful condition of humanity before a holy God, although certain reformist academics seek to reframe the question in terms of an alternative controlling paradigm, emphasizing the *love* of God rather than the *justice* or *holiness* of God.[253]

Since the twentieth century, science has begun to lose its perceived luster as the sole *objective* locus of authority, and as Thomas Kuhn, Michael Polanyi, and others have convincingly argued, *trust* of authority is at the heart of not only religious, but also scientific communities.[254] Therefore, Hodge is viewed by postconservatives as having a misplaced confidence in the authority of the scientific method and its allegedly unbiased and indisputable findings—a confidence that bode well for evangelical theology so long as the scientific "evidence" appeared to *support* the theological framework. However, once the evidence began to be viewed as weighing *against* the Bible and in favor of the growing number of academics within non- or anti-Christian scientific communities, the allegedly perfect "marriage" set in motion a rather uncivil "divorce."

In addition, modern propensities toward *de-personalizing* knowledge affected Hodge's theological method and epistemology. While the personal piety of Hodge and his fellow Old Princeton academics is well documented,[255] merging the seemingly neutral and objective scientific approach with their particular version of conservative Reformed theology diminished the *relational* aspects of theological knowledge. Dogmatic claims appear with regard to belief in specific Reformed doctrine *preceding* the possibility of having knowledge of God. Hence, the order of controlling authority did not appear to be relationship with, or personal knowledge of, God in Christ, but rather assent to certain doctrines deemed essential to belief—*after* this could come personal faith in Christ. Said differently, the formal writings of Hodge insinuate that claiming to know God is an unsubstantiated claim unless one first attends to and embraces a series of doctrinal affirmations—affirmations viewed by Hodge as essential to Christian faith. Of course, strong confidence in the alleged *certainty* of reaching sure conclusions partly shaped the perspective that the suppo-

253. See, for instance, Pinnock, *Flame of Love.*

254. See Kuhn, *The Structure of Scientific Revolutions.*

255. See Hoffecker, *Piety and the Princeton Theologians.*

sitions would be "compelling to any unbiased observer, in almost every aspect of human inquiry."[256]

Hodge could not have foreseen the philosophical revolutions to sweep European and North American thought throughout the twentieth century. Movements away from modern toward post-Enlightenment visions of knowledge, truth, and value would entail the supplanting of individualism, universal reason, and objectivism with alternative schemes incorporating holism, interpreted facts, and plurality of methods. Revolutions in communication, science, and philosophy would diminish the alleged indubitability of evidentialist approaches to Christianity.[257]

Some evangelical scholars became convinced that the Enlightenment foundation (working to support Christian theology and theological knowledge claims) was beginning to crumble. For them, a *post*foundational apologetic—emphasizing the primacy of the gospel metanarrative—would be the best and possibly only recourse.[258] The knowledge of God, rather than primarily a matter for scientific and evidentialist argumentation, must now be envisioned in holistic, communal, and personal terms.[259]

George Marsden sees a very different strand of nineteenth-century Calvinism as pointing to important emphases in contemporary thought. Marsden observes that Dutch theologian Abraham Kuyper rightly saw

> that science cannot be regarded as a sovereign domain that sets its own rules to which Christians and everyone else must conform if they are to retain their intellectual respectability. As philosophers of science now [ca. 1983] are also recognizing, science itself is controlled to substantial degrees by assumptions and commitments. Christians, then, should be free frankly to state their metaphysical starting points and their assumptions and to introduce these into their scientific work in all areas of human inquiry; they should

256. See Marsden, "American Evangelical Academia," 241–42.

257. Several leading evangelical scholars, trained in evidentialist apologetics, were seeing—more than two decades ago—the problems developing for evidentialism. See, for instance, Pinnock, *Reason Enough*, and Ramm, *After Fundamentalism*. It is also important to note that, among his fellow Princetonians, Hodge was perhaps the least inclined toward evidential apologetics, preferring a more inductive rather than deductive approach (see Noll, *Princeton Theology*, 107–8, 130–31).

258. See Pinnock, *Tracking the Maze*.

259. Certain Christian scholars and practitioners have embraced Michael Polanyi's approach in *Personal Knowledge*, adopting his model for their theological epistemology. See, for example, Newbigin, *Proper Confidence*.

employ underlying control beliefs that differ widely from those of non-Christians.[260]

Representative of much traditionalist evangelical thought, Hodge places great emphasis on the use of the mind and its reasoning powers as the means whereby we achieve *certain* knowledge of God. Postconservatives see this focus as largely due to an accentuation of false modern dualisms arising from Cartesian rationalism and carried forward by scientific empiricism—befriended and undergirded by Scottish Philosophy. Hodge's commitment to this philosophical system led to belief in the abilities of the human mind that, in retrospect, seemed to be in tension with his Calvinist view of total depravity (at least with reference to capacity for knowledge). Noll speaks of this tension within Old Princeton theology:

> While it self-consciously taught traditional Calvinism, it did so without smoothing out the various strands of Reformed faith which may not have been so consistent with each other as Princetonians thought. While their theology was rooted in Scripture and the Trinitarian orthodoxy of the early church, it also participated fully in modern philosophical movements—often without fully considering if the religious and secular sources were compatible.[261]

Commitment to Scottish Philosophy moved Hodge to assert that the natural capacity of reason given to all human beings meant that all except the "biased" would have to agree that "neutral" reason leads inescapably to the truth, given the evidence, of historical events (e.g., the resurrection of Jesus Christ). There was one way to reason "properly" from the "facts." The mind—universal in its nature and ability to comprehend reality—must either be reasonable, and thus embrace the veracity so clearly demonstrated, or be unreasonable and reject the "obvious" conclusions of logic and evidence. With such a model, faith arises *after* mental assent to the "facts," since one must *first* see the evidence before believing it.

Generally, postconservatives reject what they see as the radical dualisms averred by Hodge and evangelical traditionalists, who, by focusing intensely on human reasoning capacities, discount individuals as whole beings and as persons-in-community.[262]

260. Marsden, "American Evangelical Academia," 256.

261. Noll, *Princeton Theology*, 25.

262. This is not to imply that Hodge and his fellow Princetonians had no conception of the holistic nature of human beings, only that their *emphasis* on the mind and rational thought proved to be unbalanced and thus unintentionally presented a somewhat distorted

*Questionable Confidence in the Ability to Verify Scripture as the Sole
Inerrant External Authority for Theological Knowledge*

While the Reformation doctrine of *sola scriptura* sought to replace the
authority of the medieval church with the authority of the Bible, Hodge
invoked *exclusiveness* of the scriptures—the written word of God being the
sole external authority for theological knowledge. This may seem to be at
odds with the fact that, along with most other Christian theologians in
his tradition, he also affirmed the testimony of nature as another "book"
of God. Yet, Hodge's *purpose* in appealing to the visible world was rooted
in his view that the Bible itself was the true authority for what we find
in nature, and that the two—since both were "written by God"—cannot possibly contradict one another. Again, this viewpoint was based on
Hodge's insistence that the "facts" of the Bible prove the "facts" of nature,
both being theological excavations waiting to happen.

Apologetical problems arose for Hodge—and even more so for his
successors—with the rise of biblical criticism, Darwinism, and the growing secularization of America. The task of defending the authority and inerrancy of scripture, along with its presentation of theological knowledge,
was given to the scientific method, which was employed by practically
all of the Princetonians. Although they appeared extremely confident of
their abilities to empirically demonstrate the Bible's perfection, Pinnock
points out problems inherent in this reason-driven approach, especially
with reference to defense of scripture's inerrancy:

> In sharp contrast to the Dutch Calvinism of their day, these theo-
> logians thought it was possible to argue evidentially to the author-
> ity of the Bible as an empirical conclusion. By appealing to history,
> logic, and even religious experience, they thought they could dem-
> onstrate the Bible's final authority and not be guilty of begging
> the question. Their basic plan was to prove the Bible as divine
> revelation through evidential apologetics. . . . Of course, there is a
> risk hidden in this strategy, too. Its very empirical openness could
> come back to haunt it. What if it could not be proved that Christ
> taught the inerrancy of the whole Christian Bible, which was, after
> all, not yet even in existence? What if the same empirical method
> were used to justify criticisms of the text that would prove embar-
> rassing to conservative theology? So it is that the empirical ap-
> proach, which is appealing in principle because it posits common
> intellectual ground and appears to be open to honest critical and

---

portrait of the composition of human persons.

scientific enquiry, loses some of its appeal in practice because it might initiate lines of thinking that would not result in a vindication of the Bible in the desired conservative sense. The problem in a nutshell: If reason is given its head, will it reliably lead to orthodox conclusions? Progressives certainly do not believe that it will. Evidently, Van Til, Henry, and Barth do not think it will either. But old Princeton theologians did not doubt that the facts would show anything other than what they already believed in their tradition.[263]

Reformists are reacting to what they view as modern categories born out of traditionalist overconfidence in rationalism and empiricism[264] to provide indubitable certainty (e.g., concerning inerrancy). Scientific standards are inappropriately imposed upon the ancient biblical text—standards foreign to the human authors of scripture.[265] Postconservatives point to, for instance, fallacies associated with many modern word study approaches to the meaning of scripture, including the tendency to bypass the "thick" message for the alleged meanings hidden in the atomic units of the language.

Questionable Confidence in the Reformed/Calvinist Tradition Uniquely Possessing the True Theological Method and Epistemology

If practical consensus existed on any single issue within contemporary evangelical scholarship, perhaps it would be that since the Reformation the intellectual armament has belonged to followers of Calvin—more generally, to the historic Reformed theological tradition.[266] More recently, though, this Reformed dominance has met with an increasing number of challenges to certain philosophical and theological notions associated with Reformed thought, both from within and without. From within, many rising and prominent Calvinists are considered "moderate," "mild,"

263. Pinnock, *Tracking the Maze*, 47–48.

264. Murphy notes, "What finally brought an empiricist foundationalism to an end was the recognition that scientific facts are 'theory-laden'" (Murphy, *Beyond Liberalism and Fundamentalism*, 91).

265. For example, some reformists point to the extent to which fundamentalists will go in order to harmonize diverse accounts of an event within the text, whereby faith in the harmonization (or the method itself) becomes the greater fiduciary act.

266. This is not to dismiss or discount the substantial amount of work done by many outside the Reformed tradition. See Roger Olson's important assessment in *The Story of Christian Theology*.

or "revisionist" in their theological methodology, unwilling to embrace all of the finer points of highly confessional Calvinism.[267]

From beyond the Reformed tradition, something of a new birth of scholarship is taking place among Arminian, Wesleyan, Anabaptist, Charismatic, Pentecostal, and other non-Reformed evangelical academic communities. These intellectuals are exerting significant pressure upon traditionalists (and fundamentalists), offering challenges to long-standing versions of church history, Protestant and evangelical theology, biblical interpretation, philosophy, and epistemology. This apparent shift in authorities is significant, deeply influencing the thought and praxis of the contemporary evangelical church—principally its intellectual and spiritual leaders.

Among the dissatisfactions expressed by reformists regarding traditionalist attitudes is the perceived ready dismissal of virtually *all* other evangelical approaches to theology and theological knowledge. Postconservatives point to what they view as a continuation of Benjamin Warfield's overconfident outlook, wherein he forthrightly dismissed all other perspectives saying, "Calvinism is just religion in its purity," and that "we have only, therefore, to conceive of religion in its purity, and that is Calvinism."[268]

Noll identifies the paradoxical nature of this type of thinking, pointing out that "one of the things that makes study of Old Princeton so easy is its consistent advocacy of the Reformed faith; one of the things that makes it so difficult is their persistent unwillingness to perceive diversity within Reformed Protestantism."[269] So, in effect, alternative voices within the Reformed tradition were viewed as either non-existent or entirely irrelevant for Old Princetonian thought. Only their own method could conceivably represent truly pure religion.

No wonder many see the OPT method involving highly selective utilization of various facets of a rather diffuse "family of theologies," yet treating these chosen aspects as if they constituted "a unified whole."[270] Hence, reformists remain critical of a theological method whereby other

267. Millard Erickson's work seems to exemplify a more moderate form of Calvinism (see, for instance, *Truth or Consequences*).

268. Warfield, "What is Calvinism?," SSWW, I: 389, cited in Noll, *Princeton Theology*, 27.

269. Noll, *The Princeton Theology*, 27.

270. See Noll, *The Princeton Theology*, 28.

"voices" outside traditionalist scholarly communities are categorically rejected or summarily dismissed.

Conclusion

Postconservative scholars appear to be disturbed or distressed about traditionalist theological methodology, especially as it employs many of the same ideas and trajectories as those advocated by Old Princeton theologians. Most disconcerting, perhaps, are traditionalist appeals to doing theology via a method rooted in modernity and Scottish Philosophy: an approach that is resolved to the scientific method and strong confidence in reason and human mental capacities; a structure that confides in its alleged ability to verify scripture as the solely inerrant source for theological knowledge; and finally, a program that views the Reformed/Calvinist tradition as uniquely possessing the true theological method for evangelical theology.

Reformists are calling attention to problems associated with such apparent binding of theological method to the reigning contemporary philosophical movement, which, as they see it, fails to give primary weight to the gospel metanarrative, along with doctrinal developments imparting a distinctly Christian worldview.[271] Robert Webber describes what he sees as several results from meshing modern philosophy with conservative evangelical theology in the nineteenth century—in ways reflective of what transpired at Old Princeton:

> Conservatives responded to the liberal notion of "myth" with what came to be known as "evidential apologetics." Conservatives followed the Enlightenment emphasis on individualism, reason, and objective truth to build edifices of certainty drawing from the internal consistency of the Bible, the doctrine of inerrancy, the apologetic use of archaeology, critical defense of the biblical text, and other such attempts at rational proof. These attempts became inseparable from the modern notions of individualism, reason, and objective truth. In this way evangelical thought became enmeshed with modernity.[272]

Postconservatives are instead looking for fresh approaches to doing theology from an evangelical perspective in early twenty-first-century context. Hence, several current alternative epistemologies have seized their

271. For instance, early Christian statements of belief like the Nicene Creed.
272. Webber, *Ancient-Future Faith*, 19.

attention. What are these other knowledge theories? Are any or all of them compatible with evangelical theology? What might adopting one of these models entail for evangelical thought? Our study will briefly consider these methods while attempting to be cognizant of what potential benefits—as well as disadvantages—may be offered to evangelical theology.

Alternatives to Foundationalism:
Epistemological Options for Evangelical Theology

Modern foundationalism began to come under especially harsh censure within the field of philosophy—especially philosophy of religion—with the arrival of Wittgenstein's *Philosophical Investigations*,[273] and the onset of the "Linguistic Turn."[274] Growing awareness of the historical and social embeddedness of all human knowledge has destabilized theories of objective universal human rationality, truth as correspondence to the real world, and certainty as an attainable reality. Foundationalism's once commanding presence is clearly waning as modernity's favored epistemology continues to experience assiduous censure.

Criticisms leveled against foundationalism from within the Christian theological guild were comparatively rare throughout the first three-quarters of the twentieth century; high regard for foundationalism persisted—especially among conservative evangelicals—into the final quarter. Much of evangelical theology continued to cling to the modern quest for certainty, and in certain cases (e.g., among fundamentalists), the quest continues unabated. As we have witnessed, however, foundationalism has been rapidly losing its nearly incontestable governance over evangelical epistemology, even more so since the emergence of postconservatism.

Consequently, a significant turn to epistemological alternatives is underway. Postconservative evangelicals are expressing the need for evangelical theology to look at nonfoundational models, especially those being referred to as postmodern or postliberal. Traditionalists, on the other hand, seem to be dismissive of most postmodern insights, hence the divide

---

273. *Philosophical Investigations* is widely held to represent perspectives of the "later" Wittgenstein.

274. This perspective follows the account given by Murphy in *Theology in the Age of Scientific Reasoning*, 110–14. Richard Rorty speaks of the Linguistic Turn as the appraisal that philosophical problems are most successfully handled in the arena of language, thus supplanting the modern period turn to epistemology. See Rorty, *The Linguistic Turn*.

between evangelical scholars is widening over the question of adopting certain nonfoundationalist ideas for theology.

While there have been a variety of epistemological models suggested for evangelical thought,[275] at least six major alternatives to modern foundationalist approaches are being widely discussed, and which deserve some examining here. These include modest or soft foundationalism,[276] coherentism,[277] pragmatism,[278] fideism,[279] virtue,[280] and holism,[281] the last two of which we will treat in our examination as postliberal or postmodern theories of knowledge.

Perhaps it should be noted that while these epistemologies clearly diverge—at some points significantly—there is some overlap as well; in certain instances, distinctions may even become infinitesimal. (For instance, all of them share common distrust of certain strong foundationalist assumptions.) To differing degrees, these nonfoundationalist approaches have piqued the interest of postconservative and other evangelical scholars—those who are seeking an alternative framework for theology.

Before proceeding to outline each of these theories of knowledge, it seems advisable to present a basic comparison/contrast between foundationalist and nonfoundationalist ways of viewing knowledge, including *theological* knowledge. Although this distinguishing is merely meant to be a general overview, and therefore is sure to entail a somewhat sweeping assessment, nevertheless it may aid us in determining why apparently substantial disagreement exists between evangelical intellectuals preferring one epistemological method to the other.

---

275. For instance, Amos Yong designates postliberal or postmodern epistemologies as the most frequently chosen alternatives toward which evangelicals have been moving. However, he also notes that the first has an elusiveness-of-truth problem, and the second moves toward pluralism. Uncomfortable with either of these programs, Yong sets out to provide evangelical theology with a third alternative: utilizing Peircean pragmaticism, as we will see under the heading, "Peirce and Pragmatism," in this section.

276. See, for example, Plantinga, *Warranted Christian Belief.*

277. For instance, see the discussion in Grenz, *Renewing the Center,* 191–93, 196–97.

278. See the important discussion of Charles Peirce's methodology in Yong, "Demise of Foundationalism and the Retention of Truth." Yong calls for developing a fallibilistic evangelical epistemology that retains a robust doctrine of truth.

279. Karl Barth is often seen as representative of this epistemological framework.

280. See Vanhoozer, "Voice and the Actor," and Wood, *Epistemology.*

281. See, Lindbeck, *Nature of Doctrine,* and Murphy, *Beyond Liberalism and Fundamentalism.*

A GENERAL CONTRAST OF FOUNDATIONALIST
AND NONFOUNDATIONALIST PERSPECTIVES

- Whereas foundationalists presuppose the existence of basic beliefs or first principles, most nonfoundationalists presuppose the absence of such principles or beliefs.

- Whereas foundationalists within the field of theology have generally sided with either theological liberalism (universal human experience and religious or moral aspirations) or conservatism (especially appeal to an inerrant Bible), nonfoundationalists usually hold to multiple paths to theological knowledge (holism) and openness to so-called Wesleyan Quadrilateralism (scripture, tradition, reason, experience).

- Whereas foundationalists seek absolute or objective certainty, nonfoundationalists accept practical certainty, perspectivalism, and varying degrees of relativism.

- Whereas foundationalists generally disregard the influence of historical and cultural context, as well as human diversity, nonfoundationalists affirm the contribution of these factors, often rejecting objectivity of knowledge claims.

- Whereas foundationalists allege knowledge as a primarily individualistic, rationalistic, or empirical development, not subject to tradition or community, nonfoundationalists assert the embeddedness of all human knowledge in social contexts.

- Whereas foundationalists generally conceive of truth as correspondence to external reality, nonfoundationalists prefer to view truth as contextually-based and language-based, opting for non-correspondence theories (e.g., coherentism or holism).

- Whereas foundationalists generally view knowledge as (at least potentially) *comprehende*, nonfoundationalists see it as *cognosci* (and if ever *comprehende*, eschatologically).

- Whereas evangelical foundationalists generally view theology and evidence as based upon propositions, nonfoundationalists locate theology within the believing community, and evidence via various forms.

- Whereas foundationalists have often viewed theology as an academy-centered pursuit, nonfoundationalists see theology as an activity primarily of and for a particular community or faith tradition.

- Whereas foundationalist approaches have generally been highly rationalistic and logical, nonfoundationalist models seek to integrate additional ways of knowing, while retaining the important role of reason.

- Whereas foundationalists tend toward a "bare facts" view of knowledge and meaning, nonfoundationalists point out that all perceptions (even colors) are theory-laden, embedded in larger theoretical and linguistic frameworks ("language games").

- Whereas foundationalists envision beliefs as moving in only one direction (up from the foundation), nonfoundationalists note that support is relational (not always bottom up), like a "web" or "net".

- Whereas many strong foundationalists have an access requirement for beliefs, nonfoundationalists dismiss this as idealistic.

- Whereas foundationalists have traditionally relied on the presumed objectivity of scientific facts and models, nonfoundationalists point out the theory-ladenness of all such facts and paradigms (*pace* Kuhn).

- Whereas evangelical foundationalists (especially since the modernist-fundamentalist debates) have generally chosen scripture as *the* authoritative foundation in and of itself, nonfoundationalist evangelicals have chosen Jesus Christ as authoritative and the scriptures derivatively so because of their *witness* to Christ.

- Whereas foundationalists appear to leave little room for human sin or limitations with regard to knowledge or truth claims, nonfoundationalists evidently make more space for such limiting realities.

- Whereas foundationalists fail to consider the variety of interpretations of facts that make indubitable and universal knowledge incoherent, nonfoundationalists comprehend interpretive variations and their implications.

- Whereas foundationalists hold to a (potentially) universal language of meaning and knowledge, nonfoundationalists reject this idea.

- Whereas foundationalist evangelicals equate infallible or self-evident knowledge with the integrity of the gospel itself, nonfoundationalist evangelicals generally acknowledge the fallibilistic nature
  of knowledge and the relative or contextual form of all interpretation (though without surrendering to a skeptical or nihilistic
  relativism regarding truth).

While, on the one hand, this contrast conceivably mischaracterizes
and almost certainly overstates particular features of both foundationalism and nonfoundationalism, on the other hand it provides a window
on the significant differences between the two epistemological paradigms.
Considering the material distinctions, is it any wonder that an ever-widen-
ing divide exists between evangelical theologians holding to a *rationalistic
foundationalism* and those espousing a *holistic nonfoundationalism*—between those finding space within their theologies for incorporating particular postmodern philosophical insights, and those opposing this move?

Having concluded a general comparison/contrast of foundationalist
and nonfoundationalist models, we turn now to a brief examination of the
aforementioned five nonfoundational theories of knowledge, seeing what
these models offer to contemporary evangelical theology.

SOFT OR MODEST FOUNDATIONALISM

Modest foundationalism has gained more of a hearing among philosophers and theologians in recent decades, as support for strong foundationalism has waned. The softer version shares with the strong the concept
of first principles or basic beliefs, yet with significant modifications. For
instance, Stanley Grenz points out that Reformed epistemologists like
Alvin Plantinga and Nicholas Wolterstorff hold certain beliefs to be basic,
yet deny the Enlightenment foundationalist restriction on *which* beliefs
count. Belief in God at times is to be viewed as "properly basic," according
to Plantinga. This approach follows Thomas Reid in asserting the following four points: since foundational beliefs are not immune to doubt and
can be overridden, we can affirm only *prima facie* certainty; humans are
epistemically entitled to first principles without having to provide justification; basic beliefs do not require our reflective awareness; and foundational principles are rooted in our psychological natures.

While some like Plantinga see noetic foundations as part of the
"design plan" for human being, critics view soft foundationalism as un-

derestimating the reality of sincere disagreement as to first principles, as well as misjudging human passion and interests—including hidden agendas—relative to the power and distortion of introspective analysis. Philosopher Louis Pojman, for instance, views soft foundationalism as tending to become "indistinguishable from moderate coherentism."[282] However, supporters of moderate foundationalism find several reasons for preferring it to coherentism and other epistemological frameworks.[283] Robert Audi seems to argue in favor of modest foundationalism, stating that with a proper presentation of its "eliminative regress argument," it may "show forth as one of the most compelling accounts of the structure of knowledge and justification."[284]

COHERENTISM

Coherentism matured in the twentieth century—nearly concurrent with pragmatism—as a challenge to foundationalism, and is perhaps best illustrated by way of Otto Neurath's image of a *raft*, in place of foundationalism's *building* metaphor.[285] The central thesis of coherentism assumes that all beliefs representing knowledge are part of an *interconnecting system*. The entire system, rather than its individual elements, is primary, each belief supporting every other belief and the whole, providing justification for the system.[286] Coherentists differ over what actually makes a system of belief

282. For more on this discussion, see Grenz, *Renewing the Center*, 200–201; Plantinga, *Warranted Christian Belief*; Pojman, *What Can We Know?*, 107; and Wood, *Epistemology*, 98–104.

283. For instance, see Audi, *Epistemology*, 205–8, 310.

284. Audi, *Cambridge Dictionary of Philosophy*, 323. Audi also notes that "foundationalism has been very prominent historically and is still widely held in contemporary epistemology."

285. Ibid., 154. The raft, representative of a coherence theory of knowledge, had its roots in nineteenth-century idealism.

286. Demonstrating *interconnectedness* of beliefs as well as *noncontradiction* conceivably adds further substantiation to coherentism's claim to epistemic system validity. A computer software database program may help illustrate the importance of interconnectedness and noncontradiction. In using a relational database program, it becomes imperative to maintain what is known as "referential integrity" so that records in one table continue to retain their integrity with related records in other tables. If not, the database user ends up with "orphaned" or "widowed" records, with the accuracy and integrity of the entire database becoming suspect. For instance, if the record containing the general information on Jane Doe in the "Client" table gets deleted, the medical treatment information relative to Jane Doe in the "Treatment" table becomes "orphaned," and the former integrity and interconnectedness of these two related tables has been damaged (externally), whether

coherent; perspectives include explanatory power, logical implication, the notion of competition, and interest in gaining the truth.[287]

While many modern coherentists remain committed to the quest for epistemic certainty, some have acknowledged this goal to be *ideal*, rather than a present reality. Furthermore, the move away from foundationalism means a shift from the individual part to the *whole system*: from the actual to the ideal.[288]

While in some ways coherentism may surpass foundationalism as an epistemic theory, it *loses power* by requiring persons to be consciously aware of and actively involved with every belief decision, choosing which beliefs to discard, which to retain, and which to add. Thus, when used solely as a *conceptual scheme*, coherentism appears lacking, no less as it pertains to theology. This may not necessarily entail abandoning the theory, but some modifications appear necessary. Imre Lakatos' "Research Program" and Thomas Kuhn's "Paradigm Shifts" provide two examples of adjustments to coherentism that some Christian scholars find useful for evangelical thought.[289]

PEIRCE AND PRAGMATISM

John Thiel explains the concern philosopher and mathematician Charles Sanders Peirce (1839–1914) expressed in 1868 regarding Cartesian epistemology:

> The "spirit of Cartesianism" attempted to advance beyond scholasticism's essentially religious commitment to the mysteries of faith by claiming that the "ultimate test of certainty is to be found in the individual consciousness" that has successfully run the gauntlet of radical doubt and reached the assurance of its own first principles. The expected consequences of such certainty, however, prove wanting in actual practice. Philosophers of reputation disagree, even vehemently, about the definition of first principles, to say

---

or not it is realized (internally). So, in this case, as in the case of the coherence model, without maintaining interconnectedness, the idea of consistency is nonsensical. That is, as the tables in the database must be connected relationally and consistently in order for the program to function properly, so must beliefs in a web model be connected relationally and consistently in order for there to be genuine coherence.

287. See Wood, *Epistemology*, 117.

288. Grenz, *Renewing The Center*, 192.

289. For example, see Murphy, *Theology in the Age of Scientific Reasoning*, passim, especially 51–87.

nothing of the inferences that might be drawn from them. The fact of philosophical disagreement about what should produce un-questioning assent shows the folly of Descartes' confidence in the purifying powers of doubt.[290]

The problem for Peirce regarding foundationalism is its *suppositions*, which he views as nothing more than imaginary. Cartesian doubt is "mere self-deception, and not real doubt" since it too quickly asserts the cer-tainty of first principles where none exists.[291] Conversely, pragmatism is a method that

> seeks to establish firm beliefs about reality from the inferences of perceptual experience. The pragmatic elucidation of truth asks the question: what can be expected to follow from a true hypothesis? The logic of pragmatism is that the vagueness of perception and perceptual judgment lead us to formulate equally general infer-ences (abductions), from which more specific predictions are made (deductions), which are in turn finally tested in a variety of ways (induction). If confirmed, inductive experience is shaped into pro-visional habits that inform our action.[292]

Still, Peirce is regarded as a foundationalist by some since he ap-parently holds that truth is exclusively propositional and that there are indubitables (e.g., perceptual judgments), showing appreciation for Reid's version of Common Sense on the latter matter. On the other hand, as scholar Amos Yong points out:

> Where Peirce differed from Reid, the classical foundationalists, and the Reformed epistemologists . . . was in denying immunity to and positively criticizing these "basic beliefs." He called his own philosophy "Critical-Commonsensism" . . . by which he meant to distance himself from Kant's unknowable *Ding an sich* . . . and from Reid's and Dugald Stewart's Common-Sensism. His quarrel with the latter was that it did not develop a means by which to address the emergence and resolution of doubts which arise from experience.[293]

---

290. Thiel, *Nonfoundationalism*, 7. The internal quotations are from Charles Sanders Peirce, "Some Consequences of Four Incapacities," in *Collection of Papers of Charles Sanders Peirce*, vol. 5 (Cambridge, Mass.: Harvard Univ. Press, 1978), 156.

291. Thiel, *Nonfoundationalism*, 7. The internal quotations are from Peirce, "Some Consequences of Four Incapacities," 5:156.

292. Yong, "Demise of Foundationalism and the Retention of Truth," 575.

293. Ibid., 570, n. 22.

Even so, Peirce assumes that maintaining a *fallibilistic* epistemology is the only legitimate option since all knowledge is liable to be erroneous, and thus even perceptual judgments must be open to revision. But at the same time, this does not necessitate either skepticism or relativism since, as Yong avers, "our knowledge aims at an accurate and truthful engagement with the world."[294]

For Peirce, as well as for subsequent pragmatists,[295] *truth is a coherent system of meaningful beliefs validated by practice.* Thus, he settles on a *practical certainty* model of truth, relying on "the accumulated wisdom of human experience and the consensus of the community of inquirers to establish both truth and reality."[296] And while maintaining a truth-as-correspondence theory, he also acknowledges that the "strongest form can be understood literally only in an eschatological sense."[297]

According to Yong's thinking, then, evangelicals ought to embrace a number of important ideas generated from Peirce's pragmatism: first, a community-centeredness rather than isolated individualism in attempting to establish both truth and reality; second, humility in recognition of the fallibility of human interpretation; and third, a fallibilistic epistemology that need not sacrifice the category of truth or truthfulness.[298] These insights focus attention on three elements crucial to a post-Enlightenment evangelical theological epistemology: community, humility, and truth.[299]

Barth and Theocentric Fideism

Criticisms of foundationalism within the Christian theological guild were not very prominent throughout the first three-quarters of the twentieth century; high regard for foundationalism persisted—especially among conservative evangelicals—into the latter quarter century. However, one early-to-mid-century theologian who took exception to

294. Ibid., 586.

295. Thiel, *Nonfoundationalism*, 7–9. Thiel adds that William James and John Dewey were fellow pragmatics that followed Peirce, yet James denied that truth was inherent in the nature of things, but instead viewed truth as a process through which an idea is verified by event, whereas Dewey spoke more of meaningfulness of experience, saying that "things gain meaning when they are used as means to bring about consequences." Thiel's quotation of Dewey is from John Dewey, *How We Think*, in *John Dewey: The Later Works*, 233.

296. Yong, "Demise of Foundationalism and the Retention of Truth," 577.

297. Ibid., 580.

298. See Yong, "Demise of Foundationalism and the Retention of Truth."

299. More will be said regarding each of these factors in later sections.

the dominant foundationalist approach to theology was neoorthodox theologian Karl Barth (1886–1968). Barth anticipated the *theological* turn from strong foundationalism, concentrating on a theocentric rather than anthropocentric approach concerning knowledge of God. This important theological shift also sought to restore the ecclesial-centered task of theology in place of its mediating or apologetical role consonant with much modern theology.

For Barth, theology since Schleiermacher has been committed to the erroneous task of attempting to satisfy modernity's expectation of proper scientific knowledge, and has thus undermined the true work of theology in the service of the church in compromising the integrity of theological interpretation. Rather than considering the fallenness of humanity and thus the limitations of human knowledge, foundationalism sought to exalt human words over the word of God. Thus for Barth, liberalism is bankrupt in its attempt to subject revelation to experience and the infinite to the finite. Thiel concisely summarizes Barth's views of modern theology and its epistemic status:

> The liberal tradition's subjectivist point of departure is, in Barth's estimation, but a theological expression of the exaggerated claims on behalf of human knowledge and achievement that have flourished since the rise of individualism in Western culture. Barth thematizes this historical diagnosis by decrying the "Modernist view" that "goes back to the Renaissance and especially to the Renaissance philosopher Descartes with his proof of God from human self-certainty." "Christian Cartesianism" tries to establish the possibility of an encounter with God's revelation within the natural capacities of humanity, in some mediating principle or foundation on which the possibility of theological knowledge is believed to rest. In this Cartesian style of theologizing, the act of acknowledging the veracity of God's Word "becomes man's own, a predicate of his existence, a content of his consciousness, his possession."[300]

As a result, Barth sees the epistemology of modern theology as really a sinful human rejection of the word of God, due to its attempt to seek the possibility of knowledge of God *a priori* apart from the revelation of God.[301] And by "accepting human knowledge as the criterion for

300. Thiel, *Nonfoundationalism*, 49, with internal quotations from Barth, *Church Dogmatics*, I/1, 195, 214.

301. Barth's particular presentation against the goal of modernity to attain episte-

divine revelation, the 'Modernist' or 'Cartesian' theologian mistakenly
concedes that the Word of God stands in need before the claims of noetic
expectations, ready to be shaped to the ever-shifting lines of relevance."[302]
However, according to Barth, the knowledge of God cannot be judged
from outside the word of God:

> The question [whether God is known] cannot . . . be posed *in ab-
> stracto* but only *in concreto*; not *a priori* but only *a posteriori*. This *in
> abstracto* and *a priori* question of the possibility of the knowledge
> of God obviously presupposes the existence of a place outside the
> knowledge of God itself from which this knowledge can be judged.
> It presupposes a place where, no doubt, the possibility of knowl-
> edge in general and then of the knowledge of God in particular can
> be judged and decided in one way or another. It presupposes the
> existence of a theory of knowledge as a hinterland where consider-
> ation of the truth, worth and competence of the Word of God, on
> which the knowledge of God is grounded, can for a time at least
> be suspended. But this is the very thing which, from the point of
> view of its possibility, must not happen. . . . the possibility of the
> knowledge of God and therefore the knowability of God cannot be
> questioned *in vacuo*, or by means of a general criteria of knowledge
> delimiting the knowledge of God from without, but only from
> within this real knowledge itself.[303]

Modern theology's attempt to locate knowledge of God *in any way*
outside of the revelation of God is, according to Barth, simply a reflection
of the quest for certainty via methodological first principles—a quest that
ought to be summarily rejected as a spurious epistemic tradition. Hence,
all theological knowledge is based on the revelation of God in Jesus Christ

---

mological indubitability echoes philosophical nonfoundationalist critiques of Cartesian
foundationalism, although the latter would normally dispense with the former's theological
convictions. However, some have charged Barth, along with various conservative theologians, with a form of foundationalism based on their viewing the Bible (or for Barth, his
broader usage of the "word of God") as an indubitable divine revelation. For an example
of this criticism, see Murphy, *Anglo-American Postmodernity*, 88–94. It may be plausible
instead to consider such religious conviction to be more on the order of a *control belief* (i.e.,
a certain belief about what constitutes an adequate sort of theory on a particular matter),
if the conviction is functioning in order to select theories consistent with its values, rather
than in an effort to control religious beliefs via either a rationalist or empiricist version of
foundationalism (see Wolterstorff, *Reason within the Bounds of Religion*, 63–84).

302. Thiel, *Nonfoundationalism*, 50.

303. Barth, *Church Dogmatics*, II/1, 5.

and is connected with a salvific experience of God's grace and mercy.[304] Evangelical scholars drawn to Barth's perspective on theological knowledge are likely to be intent on retaining the highest possible commitment to special revelation and the I-Thou encounter as uniquely—if not exclusively—disclosing the knowledge of God in Jesus Christ, rejecting foundationalist appeals to alleged external sources of verification.[305]

POSTLIBERAL OR POSTMODERN EPISTEMOLOGIES

In *Renewing the Center*, Stanley Grenz describes some major features of postmodern philosophy, particularly relative to epistemology and emphasis on language and meaning. This nonfoundationalist approach includes 1) movement toward belief systems and a communal view of truth; 2) focus on "language games" (i.e., the use of language within particular self-contained systems having unique rules); 3) abandonment of a correspondence theory of truth; 4) meaning and truth not necessarily, directly, or primarily related to an external world of objective facts waiting to be discovered; 5) concentration on contextuality of meaning (i.e., sentences have as many meanings as contexts); 6) utterances deemed true only within the context spoken; 7) language as a social phenomenon; and 8) meaning and truth as internal functions of language.[306]

Clearly the features of postmodern philosophy and epistemology cited here by Grenz sharply contrast with the elements of modern foundationalism examined earlier. Postconservatives pursuing the postmodern or postliberal route are turning primarily to one of two options for theological epistemology: holism or virtue. As we briefly examine both models—with an eye to discern how evangelical theology might be constructed without foundations—it must be kept in mind that these knowledge theories share much in common. One of these common features is appreciation for, as well as differing degrees of dependence on, the philosophy of Ludwig Wittgenstein, and thus we begin with a look at the influence Wittgenstein's philosophy has had upon postmodern epistemology.

---

304. See Erickson, *Christian Theology*, 188–89.

305. D. Z. Phillips, for example, represents a strongly fideistic viewpoint from a philosophical perspective in *Faith after Foundationalism*.

306. Grenz, *Renewing the Center*, 194–95.

The Impact of Wittgenstein

Ludwig Wittgenstein (1889–1951) was influenced by the idea that philosophical problems could be resolved in the arena of *language*. His posthumously published *Philosophical Investigations* effectively overturns the conclusions of his earlier works (e.g., *Tractatus Logico-Philosophicus*) regarding language theory, offering a unique view of the meaning of language as *use*—a move that would have consequences not for only philosophy, but also for many other disciplines, including theology.[307] Thiel provides a cogent description of Wittgenstein's later work:

> Wittgenstein argues that meaning of any sort behaves like a language. . . . While language as elementary expression may be a universally human phenomenon, the grammars of this language or that are formed in the most culture-specific and practical circumstances of social life. Wittgenstein finds this contingent and particular quality of linguistic meaning to be helpful in understanding the workings of the intellect and the will. Just as the meaningfulness of a language is governed by its grammar, so too are the activities of thinking, deciding, and acting defined by the particular frame of reference in which their meaningful practice thrives. . . . [Wittgenstein] referred to meaningful practices in general as "language games." Language-games, like games in general, are not universally purposive but defined by the specific rules which govern their play. Like grammatical constructs, the rules of a language-game are "arbitrary." They are products of the coherent system they regulate rather than the starting points for the play of meaning that engenders them.[308]

Moreover, Wittgenstein clearly rejects the Cartesian idea of intuitive first principles. Thiel continues:

> Wittgenstein insists that there can be no private language that defies the practical and public setting of meaning as use, and so no way in which the inner realm of subjectivity or any of its issue can be privileged as the basis of knowing. . . . There are no first principles on which a context of meaning rests but only the context itself, a network of interrelated and mutually constitutive meanings.[309]

---

307. As we will see, postliberals like George Lindbeck attribute much of the impetus for their theological method to Wittgenstein.

308. Thiel, *Nonfoundationalism*, 10–11.

309. Ibid., 11.

If Wittgenstein is correct, the implications for theological knowledge are considerable; two will be noted here. First, claims to rational and intuitive ideas being ontologically *universal* are simply false. Second, the correspondence theory of truth, intertwined with foundationalist epistemology, must also be abandoned in favor of some other account of truth, as Thiel explains:

> The utterly contextual character of language-games precludes the possibility of fashioning some final purpose or meaning from the ways in which they work. . . . Philosophical investigations of how thinking "means" must also expose the pretensions of universal perspectives, truth claims, and methods that so easily pass for legitimate philosophizing. Like the pragmatists, Wittgenstein considers metaphysical or dogmatic understandings of truth to be exaggerations of the actual and more modest situations in which human beings make and appreciate meaning. He is satisfied to speak of truth as a value shaped by the vast complex of ad hoc circumstances that life offers and which life itself is.[310]

Wittgenstein's perspective on meaning—a network of beliefs that are practically verified—corresponds with the earlier writings of pragmatists such as Peirce, Dewey, and James. Each was seeking ways of arguing for a *contextual* understanding of truth, rather than from an Archimedean point of sanctioned noetic certainty. Wittgenstein is concerned with human recognition of limits of knowledge, whether theological or otherwise. Fergus Kerr illuminates Wittgenstein's thought:

> Compared with a god's way of knowing either mathematical truths or people's mental states, our mere human forms of knowing such matters seem hopelessly inadequate and indirect. We may put on the sacred vestments but we lack the mana to work the magic. We dream of the direct route to the centre of the mystery but we are never allowed to make it. The knowledge that is accessible to the gods is offered to mere human beings only in the materiality of signs. Wittgenstein's wry, self-mocking remarks are intended to provoke us into reflection on the limits of our knowledge, and why we find these limits so chafing and restrictive. Why do we have to, or want to, devalue human ways in comparison with the unmediated knowledge that a god must presumably have? In questioning the validity of this (often hidden) object of comparison, Wittgenstein invites us to remember ourselves as we really are. Once and for all, that is to say, we need to give up comparing

310. Ibid., 11–12.

ourselves with ethereal beings that enjoy unmediated communion with one another.[311]

Following the publication of *Philosophical Investigations*, nonfoundationalist philosophies proliferated, capitalizing on the ideas of Wittgenstein. Thus the Linguistic Turn entailed significant changes for epistemology. Among postmodern/postliberal options, the move for some thinkers was toward an epistemic holism, for others it meant shifting the focus toward a virtue epistemology.

HOLISM

In 1951, philosopher and logician W. V. O. Quine (1908–99) introduced his epistemological holism with a "web of belief" concept, proposing that individual beliefs are modified in order to rationalize retaining the whole of the belief system.[312] Murphy elaborates on Quine's scheme:

> Quine's new model pictures a belief system as a web or net. Beliefs that are most likely to be given up in the face of recalcitrant experience are located at the edges; beliefs less subject to revision are nearer the center. These latter beliefs are less subject to revision not only because they are further from experience, but also because they are interconnected with more elements in the rest of the system. When experience necessitates some change in the system, there are usually many ways to revise, including changing the meanings of some terms, revising theories, or even, Quine hazards, revising logic. The decision among these possibilities will in the end be pragmatic—how best to restore consistency with the least disturbance to the system as a whole.[313]

Quine's theory of knowledge, then, calls into question at least two major foundationalist assumptions: the need for there to be fundamentally indubitable beliefs, and a merely one-way direction of reasoning (i.e.,

311. Kerr, *Theology after Wittgenstein*, 45.

312. Quine would also develop a *naturalistic* epistemology, saying that theory of knowledge should become a branch of psychology. In later writing, Quine evidently revised his view to include epistemology under the field of engineering.

313. Murphy, *Theology in the Age of Scientific Reasoning*, 8. Even if Quine's system obtains, it appears that he fails to address cases of individuals exchanging one belief system for another. For instance, belief resulting in a trusting commitment to Jesus Christ has evidently altered not only more peripheral beliefs of its subject, but in certain cases the most central beliefs, not infrequently accompanied by an apparent lack of concern over "disturbances" to the system. In fact, it is not unreasonable to surmise that some have actually desired such radical interruption to their web of belief.

upward from the foundation). Instead, Quinean holism asserts that there are no sharp distinctions among types of belief, "only degrees of differences in how far a belief is from the experiential boundary." Additionally, there is no preference in the direction of reasoning, there are many kinds of relationships among web beliefs, and facts are theory-laden as well as dependent to some degree on the theoretical knowledge structure.[314]

Quine's epistemic holism has generated a great deal of discussion within theological circles, garnering both detractors and followers. Perhaps the leading representative of the latter group is postliberal theologian George Lindbeck. In *The Nature of Doctrine* Lindbeck proposes that a cultural-linguistic approach to religion and doctrines provides a community-oriented framework within which epistemological questions may be addressed.[315] Influenced by both Quinean holism and Wittgensteinian "language-games," Lindbeck commends the importance of viewing language acquisition within a religious community as part of the knowledge-gaining process. He draws correlations between how learning the language within religious communities parallels what transpires in the larger culture and other subcultures (e.g., business).

Much like John Courtney Murray's argument in *The Problem of God*,[316] Lindbeck views our knowledge of God not so much having to do with ontological considerations, but rather, having to do with God's character and his relationship with us, i.e., "the interaction of his deeds and purposes with those of creatures in ever-changing circumstances."[317]

The evident postliberal skepticism toward both foundations and apologetics is due in part to what Lindbeck views as the "intratextual" nature of religion (e.g., via its practices):

> To the degree that religions are like languages and cultures, they can no more be taught by means of translation than can Chinese or French. . . . Resistance to translation does not wholly exclude apologetics, but this must be of an ad hoc and nonfoundational variety rather than standing at the center of theology. The grammar of religion, like that of language, cannot be explicated or learned by analysis of experience, but only by practice.[318]

314. See Murphy, *Beyond Liberalism and Fundamentalism*, 94.

315. Lindbeck, *Nature of Doctrine*.

316. Murray, *The Problem of God*.

317. Lindbeck, *Nature of Doctrine*, 121.

318. Ibid., 129.

But for many evangelicals—even those in agreement with the cultural-linguistic framework and its *performance* focus—postliberalism's failure to disclose adequately an ontology with respect to the *signified* (i.e., God) leaves vacuous any substantial place for metaphysical or eschatological realism. Hence, some postconservative scholars like Robert Webber have adopted aspects of Lindbeck's model while arguing more robustly for the reality of the propositional or narrative referent of doctrinal claims (e.g., God's presence and promises).[319]

As for Quine's holism, reformists may find challenging its application to theological knowledge, certainly with respect to ontological considerations; nevertheless, certain theses of *epistemic* holism (e.g., "web of belief") seem useful—for instance, the interconnectedness of our beliefs and the change in one area affecting other areas, as well as the whole web.[320]

Consequences for evangelical theology based on a critical appropriation of epistemological holism are potentially far-reaching. It may entail several significant conceptual modifications that traditionalists will find problematic: 1) modern foundationalism must be abandoned, 2) the representational (or referential) theory of language (or meaning) will need to be superseded by an emphasis on language (or meaning) as use, and 3) individualism must be supplanted by a renewed community orientation. Hence, embracing epistemic holism virtually entails adopting a postliberal/postmodern nonfoundationalism.

VIRTUE

Alasdair MacIntyre agrees with the postliberal/postmodern emphasis on interpretive communities. He considers the historical situatedness of the community a given, and therefore, the impossibility of finding a "standard of standards" of rationality for knowledge beyond one's community due to theoretical and conceptual structures inherent within interpretive communities differing from rival standpoints.[321] Still, MacIntyre thinks one ought not despair over not having some Archimedean vantage point that would guarantee objectivity and complete knowledge; rather, one should gladly accept that knowledge within the community has primarily to do with being taught in an *apprenticeship*, under others who are skilled in

---

319. Later we will examine some postconservative adaptations and modifications of postliberal theology, primarily through the approaches of Webber and Vanhoozer.

320. Audi, *Cambridge Dictionary of Philosophy*, 391.

321. MacIntyre, *Three Rival Versions*, 172–73.

learning and living. This entails acquiring knowledge through a proper understanding and practice with reference to *telos*, *prudentia*, virtue, and wisdom, and retaining the interdependent relationship between intellectual and moral virtues.[322]

With this move, MacIntyre wants to connect *post*modern with *pre*-modern epistemological concerns, while viewing the modern era's preoccupation with foundationalism (in his terms, the encyclopedia tradition) as a sort of epistemic parenthesis or aberration.[323]

For MacIntyre, Thomas Aquinas and the Thomistic method[324] best exemplifies the way in which adherents to a community can develop habits and practices that respond properly to the object of faith while also incorporating selectively features of other conceptual schemes into their own, without diluting the central or essential beliefs of their own framework.[325] (Later we will consider postconservative adaptations of virtue epistemology for evangelical theology.)

CONCLUSION

The story of foundationalism is the story of the quest for certainty in the modern era. Since Descartes, this pursuit appears to have repeatedly ended in failed assumptions and faulty conclusions. Reformists, along with many other evangelicals, believe that the modern foundationalist method was bound to fail for a variety of reasons: It failed to recognize its own historicity and contextual-boundness. It proposed an untenable individualism, rather than embracing tradition and community. It stressed the logical and propositional, to the exclusion of more practical human ways of knowing. It proclaimed possession of universal standards of knowledge and truth,

322. See MacIntyre, *Three Rival Versions*.

323. Incommensurability between interpretive schemes leads MacIntyre to suggest an evaluative approach toward each tradition, which must accord with its own standards of rationality, implying the need for each tradition continuing to justify its existence throughout changing historical situations.

324. It should also be noted, however, that as Wolterstorff points out, Thomas is essentially a foundationalist in that he affirms a body of propositions that can (by the light of reason) be known as self-evident (e.g., that God exists), and that faith merely complements reason. One particular nonfoundationalist modification to Thomas would be to include *control beliefs*, replacing the foundationalism apparent within his program. See Wolterstorff, *Reason Within the Bounds of Religion*, 30–31, 67.

325. Nancey Murphy has shown what she sees as potential benefits of MacIntyre's project for evangelical thought (see *Beyond Liberalism and Fundamentalism*, passim, especially 103–9).

rather than considering its own prejudice and provincialism. It frequently bred hubris, rather than appropriate humility. And it imprudently assumed that religion is more related to science than to personal knowledge.

Nonetheless, philosophical frameworks continue to be used by evangelical thinkers in attempting to explicate Christian faith and beliefs. As we have clearly seen, the influential work of nonfoundationalist philosophers and theologians—including of the postmodern/postliberal variety—is effecting change within contemporary theology, philosophy of religion, and philosophical theology. Consequently, Christian nonfoundationalist (and soft foundationalist) thinkers are gaining in number and influence. And from what has been argued to this point, it seems clear that evangelical theologians are being encouraged to abandon foundationalism for alternative epistemological models. Yong's observation summarizes one possible course for evangelical intellectuals to follow:

> Given their . . . robust doctrines of sin and the Fall, evangelicals should be some of the first rather than the last to embrace fallibilism and dispense with epistemological foundationalism. That all knowledge is partial and open to correction should be the hallmarks of an evangelical theology articulated in a posture of humility before others and especially before God. Evangelicals can and should acknowledge the fallibilistic nature of knowledge and the relative or contextual form of all interpretation, without surrendering to a skeptical or nihilistic relativism with regard to truth.[326]

Nevertheless, evangelical philosophers and theologians must exercise appropriate caution when aiming to contextualize the Christian story by way of any philosophical system. Consider Bernard Ramm's sagacious advice and prudent warning:

> If a theologian rests the case for Christianity completely on some philosophy, and that philosophy be discredited, then the whole case for Christianity is undermined. If Hegel's philosophy is completely routed by twentieth-century philosophers, then all those Hegelian theologians of the nineteenth century believed in the truthfulness of Christianity for all the wrong reasons. They smashed their heads against Hume's advice: Don't believe a religion for all the wrong reasons. . . . I think when a theologian is totally committed to Heidegger, or Whitehead, or Wittgenstein, or any great name of the past, he has not heeded Hume! We may believe the right thing for the wrong reason. Therefore, especially in philosophy, proceed

326. Yong, "Demise of Foundationalism and the Retention of Truth," 580.

with caution. As the old maxim goes: whoever married the philosophy of *his* generation, finds himself an orphan in the next.[327]

We have concluded our study of the impetus for the emergence of postconservative theological epistemology, including foundationalism, its theological utilization at Old Princeton, and the several nonfoundationalist alternatives available for evangelical theology. Next, we move from the *emergence* to the *essence* and *development* of postconservative approaches to theological knowledge.

---

327. Ramm, *The Devil, Seven Wormwoods, and God*, 143.

3

The Essence and Development
of Postconservative Theological Epistemology

CLARK PINNOCK'S PIONEERING WORK IN EVANGELICAL THEOLOGY (AS discussed in chapter 2) has been instrumental in the development of postconservative theological methods. His efforts have led many—especially younger—evangelicals to embrace to varying degrees alternative approaches to mainstream evangelical theology. No place has this been more apparent than with the movement's rejection of methods that privilege Enlightenment-based rationalism for theological knowledge—something reformists charge traditionalists with doing regularly. Followers of Pinnock on this issue prefer to envision reason as operating *within* a tradition, a context, a culture, rather than operating as somehow external and neutral to what they see as the concrete situatedness of all theology.

It seems rather clear now from our study of his intellectual journey that many of the mid-to-late evolvements of Pinnock's theological method correlate very closely with Roger Olson's observations about postconservatism, as told in his important 1995 article.[1] Hence, it is not difficult to draw the conclusion that Pinnock's writings contributed rather substantially to Olson's assessment of postconservative evangelical theology. Moreover, a great deal of what is transpiring among younger evangelicals today would appear to be the result of the groundbreaking labors of Pinnock (along with those of Bernard Ramm), especially in connection with *Tracking the Maze.*

For the purposes of this study, our focus in this chapter will be on the essence and continuing development of postconservative theological epistemology. To begin with, we will introduce several important moves underway from primarily younger evangelical and reformist theologians, concentrating on three particular areas—history, theology, and apologet-

---

1. Olson, "Postconservative Evangelicals."

ics.[2] Recent shifts within these three disciplines call for careful consideration.[3] We will explore these developments primarily through the lens of Robert Webber's book, *The Younger Evangelicals*.

Next, we will discuss the so-called Wesleyan Quadrilateral, attending initially to the content of the Bible respecting the knowledge of God. After assessing the biblical data, the remaining components of the Quadrilateral will be explored as a way of getting beyond a limiting *sola scriptura* notion in our goal to ascertain additional ways of viewing the knowledge of God from a biblical basis.

Three Major Areas of Evolvement among Younger and Postconservative Evangelicals: History, Theology, Apologetics[4]

In *The Younger Evangelicals*, Webber documents important and far-reaching moves being made within these fields by "younger evangelicals."[5] Among this group are an increasing number of postconservative scholars seeking to persuade evangelicals to embrace the post-Enlightenment repositioning, characteristic of these younger evangelicals. Hence, the immediate task herein involves using Webber's taxonomy of history, theology, and apologetics as a foil for probing crucial developments within postconservative evangelical thought, with special emphasis on approaches to theological knowledge. (Doubtless the influence of Clark Pinnock will become evident as we move through this study.) We begin by exploring the shifting terrain within history—the move from *a*historical to tradition.

2. I view these three disciplines as highly integrated, and thus the separate treatment of each field below is done primarily for the sake of analysis. For a much more sweeping analysis of change within evangelicalism, see Webber, *The Younger Evangelicals*.

3. Several general trends may be observed within each of these major divisions: moving toward greater unity within diversity, moving away from Old Princetonian Calvinism and Scottish Common Sense Realism, favoring Arminianism and themes on a so-called Wesleyan Quadrilateral model, and embracing the "Great Tradition of Belief" (see Olson, *The Mosaic of Christian Belief*) in looking beyond the Quadrilateral for additional sources of theological knowledge.

4. Especially as it pertains to this section, I am deeply indebted to Robert Webber, as much of the information herein is based on his book *The Younger Evangelicals*.

5. While the modifiers "revisionist" (or "postconservative") and "younger" are not synonymous, the philosophical and theological approaches shared between these evangelical thinkers indicate a great deal of common ground in approaches to theology and epistemology.

History—From Ahistorical to Tradition[6]

In rapid decline within both academic and popular cultures is general acceptance of a universally objective knowledge (i.e., a "God's eye" point of view or *a*historical perspective) available to humankind.[7] In the present societal context, one could say it no longer preaches. Insights from postmodern and premodern sources demonstrate the shaping influence of history and culture upon human thought; this perspective is winning the day at the philosophical (as well as "worldviewish") level, agitating evangelical theology in the process.

Webber agrees that "there is a movement both outside the evangelical culture and within it that takes seriously the need for evangelicals to grow past their preoccupation with a Christianity enmeshed in modern categories of thought."[8] Hence, he is encouraged to see that younger evangelicals are turning, for instance, to a more tradition-informed theology:

> This commitment to recover the past calls into question the ahistorical nature of the traditional evangelical articulation of the faith. It also sets in motion a search for evangelical roots and a desire to connect with the faith communicated in all the paradigms of history (e.g., ancient, medieval, Reformation, and modern).[9]

Revisionist evangelicals like Webber point to the problem besetting their traditionalist counterparts: attempting to defend a theology interlocked with Enlightenment philosophy's encyclopedic view of reason and knowledge.[10] Postconservatives who see a demise of this epistemological framework are calling for incorporating the wider tradition of the church. This shift necessarily entails re-evaluating and implementing insights, wisdom, and exegetical methods practiced by the church fathers and other ancient as well as medieval, Reformation, and modern Christian thinkers.[11]

6. Each of the subtitles (e.g., "From Ahistorical to Tradition") used for the main sections (e.g., "History") are also taken from *The Younger Evangelicals*.

7. With the sometimes exception of "hard" sciences and mathematics.

8. Webber, *Younger Evangelicals*, 79.

9. Ibid.

10. In brief, the encyclopedic view, taken from MacIntyre, *Three Rival Versions*, 23–24, envisions a) universal conception of rationality, b) a rationally neutral and incontestable scientific method, and c) rationality and science as "part of a history of inevitable progress." Postmodern thought has revealed the obvious ethnocentricity of this perspective.

11. For a recent and helpful publication from an evangelical on the subject of incorporating patristic wisdom and insight for evangelical theology, see Hall, *Learning Theology*

Revisionists also note that contemporary evangelicalism—however linked with earlier particular Christian traditions—is deeply influenced by its rootedness in a purportedly modernist, separatist, and largely anti-intellectual fundamentalism: an evangelical tradition that has normally eschewed church history and tradition, at least between the time of the Apostles and the Reformation. There is simply no escaping this reality, they claim, however much one may want to shake off the dust. But as Richard Mouw has convincingly argued, there are several reasons evangelicals should not be too eager to dispense with the "smell of the sawdust" from which they were forged; there remains a great deal to learn and appreciate about this spiritual heritage.[12] This granted, there is exponentially more to glean from a recovery of the whole Christian tradition and its wide variety of practices: for instance, spiritual disciplines. Toward this goal, evangelical revisionists and others are advancing with increasing vigor.[13]

Moreover, it is widely recognized that the modern authorities of science and reason have lost some of their luster and power in the new era—especially among younger generations—since neither have been able to bring to fruition the promise of universal progress and agreement regarding the constitution of knowledge, truth, justice, and the like.[14] As a result, return to the wisdom and practices of traditional societies is accelerating. Revisionists are likewise urging evangelicals to explore the wisdom of ancient and medieval Christian thought and praxis, pointing to the importance of connecting with the "Great Tradition of Belief."[15] Conjoined with this call is acknowledgment of the real and shaping influences of history, community, and context upon theological understanding and construction: no less as it concerns communication of the unchanging gospel of Jesus Christ.

Postconservative strategies for recapturing tradition vary according to the purpose and focus of re-engaging with the past. For instance, some evangelical scholars desire a full-scale reconnection with the ancient Christian tradition. According to some, reforming theology ought not be

---

with the Church Fathers.

12. See Mouw, *Smell of Sawdust.*

13. See, for instance, Oden, *Rebirth of Orthodoxy.*

14. Nevertheless, within the postmodern cultural shift significant exceptions are still to be found: for instance, within the high technology industry.

15. The phrase "Great Tradition of Belief" is taken from Olson, *Mosaic of Christian Belief.*

done in a innovative way, but rather "in an old and familiar way," believing that "what the ancient church *least* wished for a theology was that it would be 'fresh' or 'self-expressive' or an embellishment of purely private inspirations, as if these might stand as some 'decisive improvement' in the apostolic teaching."[16] Hence, this model of reconnecting with the church tradition effectively requires a return to classical Christianity.

Other revisionists are more inclined to call for a return to Christian memory.[17] This move is perhaps seen most clearly with Stanley Grenz and his plea for retrieving the Christian tradition as a significant element in recovering authentic spirituality—an indispensable measure since "this believing community is the true apology for the faith in a postmodern setting."[18] Grenz avers that theology

> becomes an intellectual enterprise by and for the Christian community, in which the community of those whom the God of the Bible has encountered in Jesus Christ seeks to understand, clarify, and determine the community's interpretive framework as informed by the narrative of the action of this God on behalf of all creation as revealed in the Bible.[19]

Hence, Christians ought to be reading the Bible *in community*, approaching the text with the knowledge that "we are participants in the one faith community that spans the ages."[20] Necessarily, this also calls us to reconnect especially with the *modus operandi* of early and classical Christian thinkers and practitioners.

Other (especially younger) evangelicals continue to look elsewhere for connections with the larger mosaic of ancient and medieval Christianity, and for recovery of theological wisdom and spiritual practices of premodern times (e.g., the Celtic tradition). Virtually all tradition-recapturing thinkers are committed to moving away from what they view as an aberrant ahistorical articulation of the Christian faith, manifested in Enlightenment-enchanted evangelicalism. Perhaps the idiom most clearly capturing the return to tradition among revisionist and younger evangeli-

---

16. Oden, *After Modernity*, 22, as cited in Webber, *The Younger Evangelicals*, 76.
17. See Webber, *The Younger Evangelicals*, 77–78.
18. Grenz, "Conversing in Christian Style" cited in Webber, *Younger Evangelicals*, 78.
19. Ibid., 78.
20. Ibid.

cals is "the road to the future runs through the past."[21] Webber aptly summarizes this perspective:

> In this attitude they express their involvement in the cultural transmission of the faith. They want to immerse themselves in the past and form a culture that is connected to the past, a culture that remembers its tradition as it moves into the future.[22]

Theology—From Propositionalism to Narrative

Besides the arena of history, theology is a second major area in which we find shifting terrain. The postmodern flight from reason and science captivity reveals itself in the move from propositional thinking to *narratives* or *stories*. Post-Enlightenment philosophy dismisses the idea that any single narrative is universally valid or globally applicable, yet evangelicals have rightly refused to dismiss the cosmic applicability of the Christian (i.e., gospel) *metanarrative*, viewing it as an all-encompassing story of reality.

Moreover, growing (re)acceptance of the view that virtually *all facts are interpreted facts* has altered the way contemporary culture views value, reality, and truth, especially as it pertains to arenas of science, reason, and religion. Trust in prevailing indigenous narratives is replacing the modern concept of competing rationalities; *reasonableness* is viewed as merely one component among many others internal to the preferred story. Put differently, objective reason no longer holds pride of place in the discussion, having been demoted because of mid-to-late-twentieth-century criticisms, especially by leading thinkers in philosophy, linguistics, and science. And as we have noted previously, epistemological shifts are compelling evangelical revisionists to question the use of modern categories for theology. Webber notes that many evangelicals are continuing to pursue stability, but via ancient and medieval approaches to presenting the Christian story:

> The younger evangelical sees theology as the way to understand the world. It is an understanding based on the biblical narrative. This is the approach to faith that has captured the postmodern mind. Postmoderns have abandoned the modern worldview in which the supremacy of interpretation is given to science. In this context, younger evangelicals are calling on us to see the world primarily through the Christian story. They believe in the God revealed in the great events of creation, incarnation, and re-creation, inter-

21. See ibid., 82.
22. Ibid., 82.

preted first by the prophets and apostles in Scripture, protected in creeds, and handed down to us in the worship of the church. This is the growing vision of the younger evangelical, a vision that stands within the historic confession of faith. Theology is not a science but a reflection of God's community on the narrative of God's involvement in history as found in the story of Israel and Jesus.[23]

This situation is largely a matter of theological method. Thus, for many postconservative scholars, this involves a shift away from rationalistic and empirical approaches to knowledge and truth, to *theology as a worldview based on the scriptural metanarrative*. Naturally, this methodological change leads one to ask whether such a move entails halting speech altogether concerning propositions (for instance, will one no longer be able to affirm that, say, God *is* love?). Adopting such a conclusion would fail to consider the normally *holistic* vision of revisionist theological methodologies. The main point of the narrative approach is affirmation of the gospel itself being a meta-story that speaks authoritatively and universally in the midst of alternative schemes of reality, truth, and value. Certainly, the story encompasses crucial propositions such as "Jesus is Lord." But the Christian story itself is holistic, composed of abundant literary devices— promises, poetry, commands, etc. So, while not less than propositional, the Christian metanarrative is more than *merely* a set of propositions. In sum, it is a *particular* narrative with *universal* applicability.

Apologetics—From Rationalism to Embodiment

In addition to some of the major changes in attitudes toward history and theology that we have noted, we also find shifting terrain in the area of apologetics among postconservatives. Webber notes what he sees as an unfortunate apologetical move made by Christian leaders during the Enlightenment period:

[I]nstead of remaining faithful to an embodied apologetic through the life of the Christian community, [they] turned to a new apologetic that followed the secular empirical method. The raw data of the Christian apologetic was the revelation of God put to the test of reason. The liberals put reason above revelation and proceeded to "demythologize" Scripture to find the truth, which stood behind the myth, namely love. On the other hand, the conservatives placed reason under and in the service of revelation, seeking to

23. Ibid., 92.

"prove" revelation and then to systematize and analyze it to arrive at propositional truth.[24]

Throughout the modern period, the church was urged to embrace the scientific method for theology. Intellectual respectability and the alleged *certain* results of the empirical method were but two of the major persuasive forces beckoning Christian scholars to revise their apologetic for the faith. Many Christian traditions acquiesced to the Enlightenment demands, including several Protestant denominations. This move yielded foundations being built that would provide supposedly incontrovertible evidence for the truth of the Christian faith. Webber summarizes these developments:

> In this way the emphasis on truth as embodied by a people was replaced by truth as objective and observable fact. This became the primary apologetic that shaped fundamentalism and evangelicalism of the twentieth century and is known as foundationalism. This apologetic dominated college and seminary education in evangelical circles throughout the twentieth century. It is now being called into question by the younger evangelicals.[25]

As was shown in detail earlier, modern foundationalism began to crumble under the weight of expanding criticism and counter-evidence midway through the twentieth century. Those who had rested their entire theological method on the most influential epistemology of the modern period were soon to face the music, having failed to heed the warnings of previous eras among certain traditions where Christianity was excessively wedded to prevailing philosophical systems of the day.

Evangelical scholarly responses to the demise of strict foundationalism have run the gamut of possibilities. On the whole, fundamentalist approaches to apologetics continue to work based on the foundationalist model, as the use of reason and evidences remains high atop the defense-of-the-faith strategies; belief in the objectivity and neutrality of facts continues to spawn recycled evidentialist arguments aimed to convince even the harshest of critics of the certainty of Christianity.[26] Other evangelical

24. Ibid., 96.

25. Ibid.

26. It should be pointed out again that this author believes that evidences comprise an important *part* of the whole Christian apologetic; the problem is more a matter of trotting out evidences as the centerpiece (i.e., foundation) of the Christian faith, in effect resting everything on the supposed objectivity and assured results that so-called neutral facts pres-

thinkers have chosen to embrace a modified or modest foundationalism that lacks certain provisos essential to the classical view.[27] Still others have opted for one of several other epistemologies born in the modern era: most often coherentism or pragmatism.

Many revisionist evangelicals are interested in (re)claiming a more dynamic theory of knowledge, and thus have moved in the direction of epistemological holism. This holistic method entails a *post*foundationalist (or *post*modern) method, which "asserts that Christianity can stand on its own; it needs no rational defense."[28] Hence, such an approach is free to recover premodern insights relative to ideas of knowledge and truth, and to (re)impart interpretive responsibility to the domain of the Christian community.

Shifting from modern to postmodern apologetics—rationalism to embodiment—has opened a new "scripture first" hermeneutic[29] for post-conservative evangelical theology: a position advocated by postliberals like George Lindbeck via an "intertextual" vision of the Christian faith.[30] Beginning with the biblical worldview entails as the starting point *belief* that God has revealed and entrusted the church with the meta-story of all stories. Believers are primarily called to an apologetic of *embodiment* rather than reason. In the postmodern age, "the power of embodied experience to communicate the reality of the gospel" surpasses the power of rational arguments for truth void of personal or communal embodiment.[31]

Replacing the modern authority of reason with the authority of the church is due to recognition that the scriptures *belong* to the church—the guardian and interpreter of the divine-human written word of God:

> The goal of postmodern apologetics is to recover the role of the church as the interpreter and the embodiment of truth. Thus faith is not born outside the church but within the church as individuals see themselves and their world through the eyes of God's earthed community. . . . [T]he community embodies the Christian narrative, the unchurched "step into" the narrative, the narrative grasps

ent to every "honest" inquirer.

27. For instance, the access requirement.

28. See the important discussion on postfoundationalism in Webber, *Younger Evangelicals*, 99–105.

29. Ibid., 100.

30. See Lindbeck, *Nature of Doctrine*.

31. See Webber, *Younger Evangelicals*, 97.

them even as they grasp it, and eventually the individual embodies the reality of the church's story as he chooses to live his life from the standpoint of the community of faith.[32]

Particularly important to epistemology centered in Christian community is appreciation for the early church affirmations and creeds demonstrate rootedness of the faith not in certain, detached, individualistic attempts at foolproof reasoning and argumentation, but in a shared heritage and embodied experience with "the ecumenical faith of the church throughout its history."[33] By acknowledging the authority and value of the early church fathers in demonstrating the apologetical way forward for the Christian faith in the postmodern context, a growing number of evangelicals are embracing a "classical Christianity" model, advocated by revisionist thinkers like Webber.[34]

Looking beyond evangelicalism, however, entails more than (re)considering past Christian tradition; it also entails looking to alternative Christian traditions (e.g., Eastern Orthodox) in the present context for theological and epistemological perspectives.[35] Focus on the *essentials* or *center* of Christian faith among revisionist evangelicals is enhancing dialogue with scholars of other Christian traditions, including Roman Catholicism and Eastern Orthodoxy.[36] Perhaps recognition that all Christians are *people of the gospel metanarrative*—in contrast to any alternative meta-story—will continue to provide opportunities for fruitful discussion and growth among evangelical academics and nonevangelical intellectuals. But going beyond discussion toward finding common ground in apologetics may call for revisioning distinct approaches to theological and epistemological questions.

Hence, greater dialectical and dialogical openness among postconservative evangelicals makes them more poised than traditionalists to consider sources of theological knowledge not generally associated with contemporary evangelicalism—virtue, for instance. Whether widening the conversation to include diverse Christian traditions proves beneficial to the future

32. Webber, *Younger Evangelicals*, 104.

33. Ibid., 101.

34. See Webber, *Ancient-Future Faith*.

35. See Pinnock, *Flame of Love*, for an example of gleaning from Eastern Orthodox thought for evangelical theology.

36. For a recent book on evangelical and Roman Catholic dialogue, see Colson and Neuhaus, *Your Word is Truth*.

of evangelical thought may depend upon (among other things) revisionist views of essential versus *adiaphora* theological convictions.

In addition to the major shifts in attitudes that we have seen taking place within history, theology, and apologetics—primarily among postconservatives and younger evangelicals—several more moves are underway that deserve brief mention, and that intersect with the three disciplines previously discussed. In considering these additional shifts, we may want to ask whether there is a discernible common thread respecting these associated moves. Are these changes likely to further alter the face of evangelical thought? And what traditionalist responses or reactions to these primarily postconservative repositionings ought to be anticipated?

Additional Evolvements Related to Postconservative Theological Epistemology

Moving Toward Accepting Diversity within Unity

A central feature associated with recent postconservative shifts is the appeal for evangelicals to move beyond appreciating *unity* on essential doctrine to showing a similar appreciation for *diversity* of options within evangelical theology. Some reformist scholars are committed to delineating the *live options* for evangelicals, rather than dogmatically clinging to what they see as evangelical *adiaphora*.[37]

For an increasing number of evangelical thinkers, this less segregated approach to Christian faith stems from commitments to preserving the unity while allowing the diversity. Thus, two key methodological moves are requisite.[38] First, envisioning as a vital task for theology, comprehension and communication of distinctions between evangelical core/essential convictions and secondary/peripheral beliefs. Second, treating the gamut of evangelical options on a given topic with fairness and sensitivity; hence, an irenic approach respecting extant choices. It may be that the second move is the most difficult, calling for patience and wisdom void of gratuitous

---

37. The number of books of this tenor is increasing. Two more recent works intended to present competing (yet theologically acceptable) positions available to Christians are Boyd and Eddy, *Across the Spectrum*, and Olson, *Mosaic of Christian Belief.* Boyd and Eddy focus almost exclusively on evangelical rather than non-evangelical Christian or non-Christian perspectives, whereas Olson seeks to incorporate a wider Christian tradition approach to various doctrinal and theological positions.

38. See Olson, *Mosaic of Christian Belief,* 43–44.

suspicion or judgment. Yet, this appeal seems certain to gain momentum, as demand for returning to the "center" grows louder.

Moving Away from Old Princeton Calvinism and Scottish Common Sense Realism

The theological trajectory of postconservative scholars is key to the cry for a more "generous orthodoxy."[39] The majority of these thinkers do *not* adhere to a Calvinist theological tradition: more precisely, a certain *form* of Calvinism. Among the designations given this form are "strict Calvinism," "paleo-Calvinism," "classical theology," or "conventional theology."[40] As we saw in an earlier chapter, the theological method of Old Princeton exemplifies this model, personified vis-à-vis Princeton's famous trio of theologians—Charles Hodge, B. B. Warfield, and J. Gresham Machen. These men represent the theological aura and approach of nineteenth- and early-twentieth-century Princeton Seminary. A critical rejection of Old Princeton's underlying Scottish Common Sense Philosophy and its scientific approach to the Bible perhaps unifies postconservative scholars even more than the traditions to which they belong.   *Carl Henry*

Reassessing Authority and Authoritative Sources for Theological Knowledge

As we have mentioned, both theological and philosophical questions are being raised with increasing frequency relative to authority and authoritative sources, having particular relevance to claims of theological knowledge. Is there a sole foundational authority or authoritative source for the knowledge of God? If so, then how would the truth of such claims be adjudicated? And if not, does this spell the end for strong evangelical claims concerning the knowledge of God? How does the postmodern condition, including its epistemological skepticism, figure into the question of authority for evangelical theology?

Some evangelical scholars continue to envision the Bible *alone* as authoritative for all theology and theological knowledge.[41] Ironically, as-

---

39. See, for instance, *Renewing the Center*, 326–51, where Grenz calls upon evangelicals to fulfill what Hans Frei envisioned as a "generous orthodoxy."

40. For instance, Pinnock speaks of these designations in *Most Moved Mover*, passim.

41. For instance, Carl F. H. Henry appears to claim that the sole foundation of theology rests on the presupposition of the Bible uniquely revealing the truth of God—and in

suming this posture does *not* lead to a unified view among such thinkers regarding what is entailed by affirming a strict *sola scriptura*. To some, this results in focus on *doctrine alone*—especially as found in the scriptures and systematized in particular creeds or confessions—as the totality of the knowledge of God available to humankind; anything beyond the doctrinal dimension is viewed as problematic, dangerous, or even heretical. Others seem to hold that the mere *act* of reading the Bible is what provides authoritative knowledge of God, rather akin to scripture serving as a magical charm.[42] It seems, then, that in such cases fear of "enthusiasm" or loss of absolute certainty—frequently displayed by means of defensiveness—drives this vision. As might be expected, this "scripture only" model is hotly debated among evangelical scholars. As will be shown later, postconservative scholars are calling for reassessment of traditionalist evangelical views about authority for Christian belief.

Viewing Knowledge as Personal, Subjective, and Collective

Modern epistemological notions[43] of theology have made it difficult for many conservative evangelicals to imagine additional sources of theological knowledge beyond scripture, or at most, scripture and reason. Yet, it is also the case that evangelicalism becomes impoverished whenever it fails to embrace the thickness and richness of theological knowledge understood biblically, personally, and communally.[44] Reformists point out that knowledge includes a personal (i.e., subjective) dimension, embedded in communities and traditions. As we have seen, a near consensus declares

---

propositional form (see Grenz and Franke, *Beyond Foundationalism*, 14).

42. Many members of the fundamentalist community of faith to which I belonged in the 1980s and early 90s regularly practiced Bible reading with the idea that the mere reading of passages—regardless of whether one actually grasped any meaning there—provided the central way to know God. This claim ought not be taken as insinuating that reading scripture cannot or does not provide any knowledge of God. Certainly, it can and does. The point I am making, however, is that it was not unusual for members of my particular fundamentalist faith community to forego actual *study* of the biblical text in favor of esoteric approaches to the Bible that claimed to "bless" the reader and reveal "the will or knowledge of God," simply as a result of reading words on the page without respect to either what the words communicated or the context of the passage.

43. E.g., the idea that knowledge is virtually always a matter of scientific findings or facts.

44. For instance, using a thoroughgoing modern epistemological scheme is bound to yield systemic difficulties when attending to the book of Proverbs due to the book's frequent linking of *wisdom* with the knowledge of God.

fallacious the idea of neutrality of "facts," no less as it involves the alleged objectivity of the interpretation of those facts.

As we have noted, acknowledgment is growing as to the powerful role played by *cultural* and *historical factors* in shaping worldviews, including epistemic beliefs and practices. Recognition of this insight within the *academe* and popular culture has prompted a de facto return to *opinio*.[45] Hence, the notion of postmodernity being a recapturing in some respects of premodern views of knowledge—however critically—is essentially correct.[46]

Embracing the Great Tradition of Belief in Looking Beyond the Quadrilateral

Dialogue between Roman Catholics and evangelicals over the authority and priority of sources for theology has now crossed the seeming theological Rubicon—with increased frequency in recent years. Furthermore, this discussion appears cast in a hopeful and irenic dialectical approach.[47] We must reiterate that there are important moves being made by both traditionalists and reformists that involve looking beyond evangelicalism in order to find a more consensual understanding of theology and theological knowledge in the new millennium; Roman Catholic and Eastern Orthodox thought, for example, are being gleaned with greater frequency within contemporary evangelicalism—part of a move toward giving due consideration to the "Great Tradition."

Distinguishing between Knowledge of God and Salvific Knowledge of God

Postconservatives appear to be uncomfortable with theological epistemologies that inevitably link *all* that is associated with the knowledge of God directly and/or exclusively to salvific concerns.[48] This attitude may stem

---

45. For explanations of *scientia* and *opinio*, see the section, "The Rise of Cartesian Foundationalism and the Fall of *Opinio*," beginning on page 71.

46. One such instance is post-Enlightenment reinstating—across disciplines—of the elemental role of *wisdom* (or *virtue*), inspiring receptivity to non-modern ways of conceiving theological knowledge.

47. One such commendable example of this growing Evangelical-Catholic dialogue is Colson and Neuhaus, *Your Word Is Truth*. Also see Rausch, *Catholics and Evangelicals*.

48. Later, I will seek to demonstrate that attempts to *inexorably* connect knowledge of God with salvific concerns are unjustified and fail to comport with the biblical witness.

in part from an understanding that scripture itself affirms a multiplicity of authoritative theological knowledge sources: for instance, doing justice and mercy, which does not necessarily equate with *salvific* knowledge of God. Therefore, the practice of justice and mercy—and these terms require definition—qualifies, at least to some extent, as knowledge of God, notwithstanding apparent vagueness compared to, say, God's self-revelation in Jesus Christ. It would also seem that *virtue* is yet another source of theological knowledge, reflecting a sharing in divine knowledge (e.g., God's character) since virtuous living accords with evangelical views of God's will for human beings.[49] Consequently, reformists are interested in more nuanced accounts of theological knowledge: versions that draw what they view as necessary salvific distinctions.

Favoring Arminianism and Themes on a Wesleyan Quadrilateral Model

The shift toward broadening evangelical ways of understanding theological knowledge comes on the coattails of an increased emphasis on primary Christian beliefs as opposed to denominational distinctives, especially within Arminian, Wesleyan, and Pentecostal traditions. Postconservative scholars reject a virtually singular focus on the *sola* of scripture, preferring to embrace the *prima* of scripture alongside additional (albeit subordinate) sources of theology.[50] This perspective is often explicated in terms of the so-called Wesleyan Quadrilateral: scripture, tradition, reason, and expe-

49. Conversely, *foolish* living fails to reflect the knowledge of God or relating to the Lord in an acceptable manner; choosing to perennially live "as a fool" would appear to deny the very relationship one might claim to have with God.

50. While appreciating the *prima* scripture motif, in the concluding chapter of this study I intend to encourage evangelical thought to move beyond the fourfold limitation of most current revisionist epistemologies, which are generally based on a Quadrilateral model or slight modification thereof. Further broadening sources of theological knowledge entails several shifts, including a) critically incorporating a more robust vision of the scriptural witness to expression of the human knowledge of God, and b) assimilating contributions to theological knowledge—thus far inadequately hewn by evangelicalism—from amidst the larger and historical Great Tradition of Belief. Thus, I envision what may be thought of as several additional sources or norms for theological knowledge, all which are adequately visible within the biblical narrative and well attested within the annals of the Christian tradition. These norms or sources of theological knowledge ought not be viewed as being in competition, but rather as complementary parts to the whole witness of the knowledge of God. Hence, a holistic understanding is envisioned with reference to the variegated ways by which the triune God of creation and redemption is (or may be) known.

rience.[51] Some thinkers modify the number and/or level of authority of these sources, while others point to alternative norms for theology,[52] not seldom to the consternation of their critics.[53]

Summary

This brief overview of major shifts in postconservative approaches to theological knowledge—especially in relation to history, theology, and apologetics—demonstrates that significant changes are taking place within contemporary intellectual evangelicalism. Some of these changes are *responses* to the status quo within mainstream evangelical intellectual thought. The integration of evangelical theology with scientism—even in light of the latter's waning authority—has (re)awakened an increasing number of evangelical scholars. The crumbling of modern foundationalism within practically all disciplines has revealed much evangelical theology tethered to a cracked base, forcing structural reassessments of the whole enterprise. If this assessment is essentially accurate, then ought mainstream evangelical theology continue its philosophical commitments to Enlightenment claims of indubitable knowledge and truth? Should some alternative to reason, science, and evidence be asked to shore up the failing groundwork laid for much nineteenth and twentieth-century evangelical theology? Is there some other sure footing on which to base Christian faith? Are radical postmodern philosophers correct in claiming all knowledge as a matter of will to power, and truth as human invention?

Postconservatives are searching for—as well as proposing—answers to these and other epistemological questions facing evangelical theology. We have already examined some of their historically, theologically, and apologetically oriented moves, giving special attention to the ramifications for evangelical theological epistemology. Nevertheless, it remains to be seen whether a postconservative approach to theological knowledge will yield superior results for twenty-first-century evangelical thought. Hence, we turn now to consider the potential benefits of utilizing the so-called Wesleyan Quadrilateral for evangelical theological method.

---

51. We take up this topic in greater detail in a later section.

52. For instance, Grenz proposes *culture* as a source for theology alongside the *kerygma* and the church's theological heritage in *Theology for the Community of God*, 25–26.

53. See the particular cautions expressed by Erickson in *Evangelical Left*, 56–57.

Utilizing the Quadrilateral
for Postconservative Theological Epistemology

Introduction

Although many academics have moved away from epistemological considerations to linguistics, praxis, and postmodernism, considerations of theological knowledge remain of great interest to evangelical scholars. Part of this appeal is due to the very nature of evangelical theology: proclamation of a Christian perspective on the knowledge of God. Nevertheless, the somewhat standard traditionalist emphasis on theological knowledge as derived primarily—even solely—from the scriptures, has come under increasing criticism from postconservative theologians and philosophers more in agreement with so-called Wesleyan Quadrilateralism[54] than with *sola scriptura*.[55] So, while no true consensus exists among evangelical intellectuals as to the authoritative sources and norms for theology, many reformists are looking to the Quadrilateral—or slight modifications thereof—for theological epistemology. Hence, we need to understand something of this model before examining uses of each of the "quads" by postconservatives and others.

The Wesleyan Quadrilateral, or Wesley and the Quadrilateral

Contrary to a popular myth that attributes the emergence of the Quadrilateral directly to John Wesley, the nascence of this *theological frame of reference* is evident very early in church history, partially anticipated in the writings of the church fathers, while its modern and more systematic development is found in early Anglican theology—particularly in the work of Richard Hooker.[56] Methodist author W. Stephen Gunter argues that modern Methodism has "formalized" this framework, turning it into a formula.[57] Gunter succinctly explains as well as suggests how to use the paradigm:

54. Following our survey of the biblical data, we will consider the other three parts of this model—tradition, reason, and experience. From this point forward, we will generally use only the term "Quadrilateral" to stand for the so-called Wesleyan Quadrilateral.

55. I.e., *Sola scriptura* used in the sense of scripture *alone* rather than scripture *foremost*.

56. Indebtedness for this section on the Quadrilateral is primarily to W. Stephen Gunter et al., *Wesley and the Quadrilateral*.

57. Gunter, "The Quadrilateral and the 'Middle Way'," 38.

Perhaps we unintentionally capture and sterilize this dynamic when we "quadrilaterilize" it into the formula Scripture, tradition, reason, and experience, especially if this "box" is perceived to be an equilateral. To avoid this dilemma of our own [modern Methodist?] making, perhaps we should reconsider the contours of our parameters and return to a dynamic more appropriate to the Anglican framers and to the Anglican who gave rise to Methodism.[58]

In order to carry out this suggesting, Gunter encourages the following way of viewing this dynamic:

> We begin with the rule of Scripture, for it is primary. Tradition (the early centuries being privileged) instructs the church, especially regarding the doctrinal interpretation of the Bible. Reason, individually but especially collectively, elucidates God's way of being active in the creative order. And experience, especially as religion *experienced* in celebration and worship, brings to life in the heart and mind of the believer the saving work of God in Christ. We of the Methodist persuasion are direct heirs through John Wesley to this way of theologizing.[59]

And it was, of course, John Wesley's writings that popularized (originally for Methodists) what has become known as the *Wesleyan Quadrilateral*, giving us good reason to consider Wesley's own explanation and use of this theological framework[60]—keeping in mind the important point that Wesley presumably "never focused at any one time on four sources, much less used the word 'quadrilateral'."[61]

According to Professor Scott J. Jones, there is little doubt that for Wesley, the Quadrilateral was

> a single locus of authority with four unequal parts. Scripture is primary, and always interpreted in the light of the other three. . . . all four terms are mutually interdependent. Reason correctly employed testifies to the authority of Scripture, and Scripture must always make sense. Not all Christian tradition is authorita-

---

58. Ibid.

59. Ibid.

60. Of course, we do not intend this statement to be an anachronism; Wesley did not refer to this four-fold pattern of authority as "the Quadrilateral," but rather the name was apparently coined in 1970 within a United Methodist report (see Gunter and others, *Wesley and the Quadrilateral*, 10).

61. Miles, "The Instrumental Role of Reason," 77.

tive—only the parts where Christians were faithful to Scripture. Only those experiences where the goals of Scripture are actualized count in the theological arguments. Thus, it is thoroughly non-Wesleyan to play off any part of the Quadrilateral against the other parts, and particularly so if one part is used to nullify the authority of Scripture.[62]

Moreover, for Wesley the scriptures are both the *source* and *norm* of authority for Christians: the source in the sense of where we find the fundamental teaching of Christian doctrine, and the norm in the sense of serving as our final arbiter in disputes about proper teaching or conduct—whether Christian or not.[63] In fact, Jones goes on to say:

When it comes to authority for Christians, Wesley frequently claims that the Bible alone has that authority. Other sources of authority for the Christian community must be seen as essentially related to the one, central authority which is Scripture. It is Scripture alone that is the rule of our faith.[64]

Tradition is the second part of the Quadrilateral, and for Wesley, it plays a significant—albeit subordinate—role to scripture.[65] He appealed to different streams of Christian tradition for a variety of reasons, including polemical, apologetical, and cultural. Wesley seemed to view the primitive church "as being the purest when it was nearest its apostolic roots, and as degenerating from that time, with a particular precipitous decline in morals coming in the age of Constantine," yet in at least some ways "pure Christianity" continued—for instance, via the works of Eastern church writers Chrysostom, Basil, Ephrem Syrus, and Macarius.[66]

Perhaps more importantly, Wesley "found tradition to be a resource for the renewal or revitalization of the church. . . . [He] called on the resources of ancient Christianity and of the early Anglican church as offering an idealized vision for the renewal of the church in his particular social and cultural context."[67]

62. Jones, "Rule of Scripture," 42.

63. See ibid., 47.

64. Ibid., 48.

65. One author believes that the way in which Wesley understood tradition may best be viewed as two separate types of tradition: (1) Christian antiquity, and (2) the early Church of England. See Campbell, "Interpretive Role of Tradition," 65.

66. See ibid., 69.

67. Ibid., 74.

As to the Quadrilateral's third part, scholar Rebekah L. Miles summarizes Wesley's understanding of the essence and function of reason:

> [F]or him, reason could not serve as an independent source of knowledge. For Wesley, reason was limited not only by sin, but also by its own nature and role. Reason does not generate knowledge on its own, but only processes data and knowledge that originate in experience. It is *a tool, not a source.*[68]

Although reason is a tool and not a source for knowledge, as Wesley saw it, reason and faith are clearly compatible, and the latter without the former is unthinkable. Christians, for instance, must be reason*able*, and this from the use of reason applied toward the other three features of the Quadrilateral—scripture, tradition, and experience.[69] But it appears that Wesley most frequently conjoined religion and reason as inseparable "authorities for Christianity."[70] Unlike many of his modernity-driven contemporaries, however, Wesley did not displace the authority of the Bible with the authority of reason; rather reason *supports* the inspired and authoritative teaching of scripture. Miles's bold claim regarding Wesley and his dedication to reason deserves serious attention:

> We see Wesley's commitment to reason . . . not only in response to charges of enthusiasm, but also in his life and character. He wrote and lived by reason. If Wesley's words flowed from Holy Scripture, the structure of his arguments evolved from Aristotelian logic. If Scripture formed the heart and soul of his theology, logic provided its shape and method. His style and personality were driven by rationality. Wesley was logic on horseback, reason enfleshed.[71]

Nonetheless, Wesley rejected reason as an independent, innate source of knowledge. Hence, natural knowledge of God is derived not as Descartes saw it, but through "the data of creation" as reason interacts "with external data from experience."[72] Still, reason gives only a rudimentary knowledge of God via creation, and that only because of the "moral sense or conscience"—a supernatural gift of God, not a natural endow-

---

68. Miles, "Instrumental Role of Reason," 77. Emphasis mine.

69. The philosophical context for Wesley was primarily British empiricism, which clearly affected his view of reason as "a tool" (see ibid., 78).

70. See ibid., 80.

71. Ibid., 83.

72. Ibid., 86.

ment.[73] Even here, we cannot get to a direct or personal relationship with God. Paradoxically, it is our ignorance that should lead to humility, to faith in God, which actually leads to greater knowledge of God as our senses open to trust in God. In summing up Wesley's view of reason, we can see that reason has both its limits and its benefits for Christian theology and living. Miles' puts it this way:

> Without the revelation of Scripture and without faith, it [reason] cannot produce the things most essential to Christian life. . . . It is subject to error and can never, this side of eternity, reach full knowledge of the spiritual realm. Yet, for all these limits, reason is still necessary, not only to survive and to fulfill our basic obligations, but also to read Scripture, to preach the faith, to teach doctrine, and to live a righteous life.[74]

Turning to the fourth and final elements of the Quadrilateral leads us to Wesley's view of experience. Randy Maddox has observed at least six different conceptions of the term that Wesley would have been aware of,[75] and several of these Wesley seemed to use in his writings.[76] But he was most interested in discussing experience in the sense he conceived as "direct inward awareness"—in reaction to Enlightenment empiricism "typically allowing knowledge of God only on the basis of rational inference from experience" since "God does not appear directly to the senses."[77] Maddox spell outs what he envisions as Wesley's predicament and solution to the problem:

> Wesley feared that such secondary inference could not provide sufficient confidence in God's love to empower our Christian lives. This led him to postulate that God created us with a set of "spiritual senses" in addition to our physical senses, so that we can be directly affected by spiritual realities like God's loving embrace. This proposal involved more than adding another set of senses to the Enlightenment model. Wesley was actually rejecting the appropriateness of the Enlightenment conception of experience, with its focus on objective observation, for explaining experience's empow-

73. Ibid., 96–97.

74. Ibid., 99.

75. See Maddox, "The Enriching Role of Experience," 136.

76. Ibid., 136.

77. Ibid., 118.

ering affect upon Christian life. His alternative was the conception of experience as direct inward awareness.[78]

To this awareness of the work of the Spirit by "direct affect," Wesley adds—in response to "enthusiasts" and others claiming to be led by the Spirit—the need to "test the spirits," including individual interpretations of scripture, dialoging with Christians (past and present) who had much experience in, and wisdom to share from, their spiritual pilgrimage.[79]

On the range of doctrinal issues, Wesley appealed to experience as both "a source and criterion for doctrinal discernment."[80] However, experience never played a *solitary* role, but rather served as part of the ongoing dialogical process between the sources. And on more peripheral issues—i.e., *adiaphora*—Wesley "assumed that scriptural and traditional warrant played roles in discerning where specific theological proposals fit within this spectrum, but his distinctive emphasis was on experiential evaluation of how the proposal either helped nurture or undercut holiness of Christian life!"[81]

Our survey of Wesley and the Quadrilateral may be summarized by making at least four important general observations as to Wesley's approach that *prima facie* correspond in meaningful ways to the methods and goals of various postconservative thinkers: first, a commitment to the primacy of scripture; second, the value of tradition as a source of renewal or revitalization for the church; third, reason as a tool helping to understand scripture, doctrine, Christian living, etc.; fourth, the value of experience as a matter of Christian living and spiritual pilgrimage, especially in conference with others. All of these are crucial to the health and future of evangelical theology, and no doubt to its theological epistemology. Moreover, as with Wesley, scripture is the starting point.

Scripture: The Biblical Record on Theological Knowledge

Introduction

Practically all postconservatives who advocate utilizing the Quadrilateral maintain that the Bible is *ultimately* authoritative, i.e., the "norming

---

78. Ibid.
79. Ibid., 118–19.
80. Ibid., 122.
81. Ibid., 123.

norm."[82] Their approach recognizes the scriptural evidence for various ways of understanding and experiencing the knowledge of God, together with the salvific work of God via the church and in the world in the contemporary context.

Reformist scholars, though, seem increasingly willing to embrace an *expanded* view of "the word of God," reflective of a Barthian three-fold equation: Christ as word, scripture as word, and the word proclaimed. Some postconservatives (following Ramm, for instance) accept a *distasis* between the words of the Bible and the actual word of God,[83] therefore being less willing than traditionalists to focus attention on defending inerrancy positions.[84] Robert Webber, for instance, prefers to see the written word as part of the entire authoritative apostolic tradition, which includes the "Rule of Faith," the liturgy, etc.[85]

These philosophical and methodological disagreements among evangelical thinkers call for re-examination of evangelicalism's norming norm *itself* with respect to what the biblical data reveals about knowledge of God. Several relevant questions will need to be addressed in the process. Is theological knowledge *intrinsic* to canonical scripture or arrived at *through an instrumental use* of the written word? Is there considerable diversity or significant harmony between Old and New Testament presentations of the knowledge of God? How do postconservative theologians and philosophers fare with respect to continuity with the biblical record on theological knowledge? These and other crucial considerations will be the focus of this section concerned with discovering and evaluating biblical assertions about theological knowledge, as well as exploring plausible consequences for evangelical scholarship and practice.

It is hoped that reassessment of the biblical record's account of theological knowledge will provide a sense of the multiplicity of meanings having to do with knowledge of God as disclosed in scripture, as well as a modest framework for discussing and evaluating an evangelical

82. See Grenz and Franke, *Beyond Foundationalism*, ch. 3.

83. The *distasis* concept is viewed by some postconservatives as inescapable because of the adaptation of the word to the linguistic and cultural context in which it was given. See, for instance, Grenz, *Renewing the Center*, 111.

84. Some reformists, however, are *philosophically* committed to belief in inerrant *autographs*, but since the original writings no longer exist, they refrain from attempts to *prove* inerrancy, preferring to focus on the *functional/instrumental* authority of scripture.

85. See Webber, *Ancient-Future Faith*.

understanding of theological knowledge, so that we can gain insight into the correspondence between particular postconservative ideas and biblical presentments of the knowledge of God.

Focus, Presuppositions, and Method

This section will focus on the biblical witness regarding theological knowledge, i.e., biblical conceptions of the knowledge of God as evidenced within the diverse genres and historical-cultural setting within the Bible.[86] We will seek to observe commonly accepted hermeneutical and exegetical principles while also making use of extra-biblical categories.[87]

Some of the *a prioris* at work here include accepting scripture as the written word of God: *functionally, derivatively, and intermediarily;*[88] envisioning the Bible as containing more than (but not less than) propositional truth; viewing human reason as ultimately incapable of achieving or discovering *certainty* with regard to knowledge or truth prior to the eschaton, and thus the need to settle for *practical* certainty; trusting God's light to shine forth through the prism of scripture, as the Holy Spirit interacts with the inscripturated word;[89] and believing that God is faithful in blessing and ministering to and through those diligently engaged in faith-seeking-understanding endeavors.

In addition, we also expect that God can be—and is—known in *various* ways, and thus suggest a multidimensional approach to the knowledge of God. Furthermore, we recognize a *salvifically*-oriented dimension to theological knowledge, considered as uniquely *Christian* (or *evangelical*) in nature. Therefore, the assumption we make is that not *all* theological

---

86. In a later section, we will briefly consider whether postconservative theological epistemology comports with the biblical witness to the knowledge of God. Analysis will be limited to the approach of a select few evangelical theologians, generally considered postconservative: Stanley Grenz, Robert Webber, and Kevin Vanhoozer. Obviously, minor evaluation of their particular perspectives will not wholly explain or represent all of the epistemologies available to postconservatives (see the earlier section on alternative epistemologies), but I hope to present a general outlook of the postconservative approach to knowledge of God and how it corresponds to the record of scripture.

87. We will also consider particular Hebrew and Greek terms, phrases, and concepts pertaining to theological knowledge. English translations from the biblical texts will be from the NRSV, unless otherwise noted or when citing authors who may be using alternative translations.

88. See Grenz, *Revisioning Evangelical Theology*, 133.

89. This point reflects Donald Bloesch's perspective as quoted in Dorrien, *Remaking of Evangelical Theology*, 189–90.

knowledge is salvific in nature, but when characterized by some measure of a knowingly- and mutually-*relational* component within the divine-human engagement (i.e., an I-Thou dimension).

When questions concerning the knowledge of God are posed from a Christian theological perspective, certain key thinkers may come to mind: Augustine, Aquinas, Theresa of Avila, Calvin, Wesley, and more recently, Rähner, Bultmann, Barth, Alston, Plantinga, Pannenberg, and John Frame. Additionally, it is no secret that evangelicals have long held the Bible to be central to faith and practice—no less so regarding the knowledge of God.[90] This is as it should be for those who take the scriptures—solely or primarily—as indispensable for theological knowledge. As David Bebbington and others have asserted, *biblicism* is one of several essential components of evangelicalism,[91] and no other source for theology occupies as central a place in considering the knowledge of God.

Even while evangelical intellectuals of different traditions continue to debate the question of *sola* as it pertains to theological knowledge, consensus persists as to the *primacy* and *priority* of the written word above all other sources of theology. Consequently, study concerned with evangelical sources of theological knowledge ought to consult scripture *first*: a move both faithful to the tradition, and more importantly, central to the theological task of consistently illuminating and contextualizing supreme insights of written revelation—in this case, the ultimate question of the knowledge of God. In contouring an evangelical theological epistemology, faithfulness to scripture must be the foremost consideration.

As we begin this study, it should be noted that this will be merely an overview of the data rather than a comprehensive account, with our focus

90. This also includes certain Pentecostal or "Apostolic" denominations that strongly emphasize *experiencing* God. While other sources of theological knowledge may take (or appear to take) *practical* prominence, a Protestant "seed-flower" principle remains foremost. In essence, this idea entails that scripture (seed) is the measure whereby experience or doctrine (flower) must be tested or approved, in order to ensure that the flower is truly representative of the seed. Evangelical thinkers have generally been critical of Roman Catholicism with respect to the flower (dogma) failing to appreciably correspond to the seed (e.g., as with the dogma respecting the assumption of Mary). It should be noted, however, that Protestants and evangelicals are not immune from growing rather extravagant flowers of their own (e.g., the Westminster Confession), if not complete mutations (e.g., the "health and wealth" gospel or prosperity-oriented theologies). The seed-flower analogy is borrowed from Murray, *Problem of God.*

91. See Bebbington, *Evangelicalism in Modern Britain*, and Vanhoozer, "Voice and the Actor."

on theological knowledge divided into Old and New Testament categories
(i.e., Hebrew and Greek).

THEOLOGICAL KNOWLEDGE IN THE OLD TESTAMENT

The Hebrew idea of the knowledge of God occurs in various Old Testament
historical books, prophetic writings (especially Hosea and Ezekiel), and
wisdom literature (prominently in Proverbs). Interestingly, what is lacking throughout is the notion of speculative contemplation, the type of
knowledge so frequently encountered in classical and later Greek thought.
Rather, ancient Hebrew conceptions of the knowledge of God have more
to do with *acknowledgement, faith, obedience, behavior, and moral responsibility*: all as effects of God's self-revelation, especially vis-à-vis divine acts
among the people of God. Theological knowledge is central to the creation
story itself. God *knows* both Adam and Eve, and is *known* by them. The
pre-fallen Garden state is a sharing of fellowship—a relational interplay
between God and creatures made in the *imago dei*, and among human
beings. The most significant aspect of the Fall, as portrayed in Genesis 3,
is the brokenness of harmonious fellowship, seen as a disobedient response
to the divine command to not eat from the tree of the knowledge of good
and evil (Gen 2:9, 17). The question of knowledge continues to play a
significant role throughout the biblical account.

The two most frequently used terms in the Hebrew Bible with reference to knowledge are *yāda* (יָדַע) and *da'at* (דַעַת). Over a thousand oc-
currences of the root *yd'* are found in the Old Testament, more than eight
hundred in the *qal* tense.[92] A wide variety of uses for these terms exists
(which space and focus preclude discussing at substantial length).[93] Since
there is a multiplicity of connotations respecting the notion of human
knowledge of God and God's knowability, the way selected to proceed is to
consider particular *families of meaning* made apparent from Old Testament
(and later, New Testament) textual analysis. Generalizations are risky, and

92. Hubbard, "Knowledge of God in Hosea," 32.

93. The central concern of this chapter is the more specific concept of knowledge *of
God*. For an expanded discussion on the question of "knowledge" in the Bible and Ancient
Near Eastern usage (in general, or concerning theological knowledge), see Botterweck,
in *Theological Dictionary of the Old Testament*; Bultmann, in *Theological Dictionary of the
New Testament*; Fretheim, in *New International Dictionary of Old Testament Theology &
Exegesis*; Henry, "Know, Knowledge," in *The International Standard Bible Encyclopedia*;
Zimmermann, "Knowledge of God," in *Bauer Encyclopedia of Biblical Theology*; and van
Imschoot, "Knowledge of God," in *Encyclopedic Dictionary of the Bible*.

this is certainly the case with the question of the knowledge of God according to the Old Testament. The impossibility of a generalized meaning reveals the breadth and depth of concepts of theological knowledge in the Hebrew Bible. Thus, what follows is an attempt to grasp the kaleidoscope of meanings with reference to human knowledge of God.

In the widest sense, four major (and sometimes overlapping) categories or families of meaning may be detected: God's self-revelation, the divine-human relationship or fellowship, human obedience to God and proper moral conduct, and God's unique salvific work toward Israel.[94] These categories provide a theological window to the various ways in which the Old Testament reveals that God can be known.

First, knowledge of God in the Old Testament is based on the self-revelation of God. God's greatness and otherness are everywhere declared in the Old Testament. With nearly the same regularity, the ability of human beings to know this supreme One is clearly proclaimed. How can this be explained? Only as a divinely initiated state of affairs. As Pannenberg notes, the knowledge of God is the starting point in religion because the reality of God is presupposed in the very worship of God. However, he argues, a true knowledge of God must *originate* with God's own self-disclosure:

> [H]uman knowledge of God can be a true knowledge that corresponds to the divine reality only if it originates in the deity itself. God can be known only if he gives himself to be known. The loftiness of the divine reality makes it inaccessible to us unless it makes itself known. . . . [T]he knowledge of God is self-evidently possible only as a knowledge that God himself discloses. If the knowledge of God be understood in such a way that in our own strength we can wrest from deity the secret of its nature, deity is lacking from the very outset. This kind of knowledge would not be knowledge of God, for it would contradict the concept of God. Hence the knowledge of God is possible only by revelation.[95]

Within the Old Testament, the self-revelation of God apparently occurs in a general way to some (e.g., Cain [Gen 4:6], Noah and his sons [6:13]), and in a special way to others via unique promises (e.g., Abraham and his successors) or by way of self-revelation as YHWH (e.g., to Moses). Regardless the content of the divine revelation, E. D. Schmitz asserts that

94. As we proceed with our study, further potential demarcations within these broad categories will become evident.

95. Pannenberg, *Systematic Theology*, 1:189.

"knowledge of God is always linked with God's acts of self-revelation. This is illustrated in the formula, 'And you (or they) shall know that I am Yahweh' . . . it is always linked with the proclamation of some specific act by Yahweh . . ."[96]

This *self-revealing* is fundamental to human knowledge of God—or at least a more clearly determined knowledge of God—being apprehended by human beings.[97] The questions respecting theological knowledge can be asked only because of the reality of divine revelation.[98]

Old Testament knowledge of God is envisioned as being constitutive of the *imago dei* (Gen 5:1f), making theological knowledge possible for human beings at a level unavailable to other created life on earth. Exactly what the image or likeness of God is has been variously understood by Christian scholars.[99] For instance, Carl Henry declares "the knowledge of God that continually penetrates the human mind and conscience even in sinful rebellion . . . is attributed biblically to the universal revelation of God and to mankind's divine creation in the image of God."[100]

Old Testament theological knowledge seems to lack any association with purely *theoretical* knowledge; rather, the interest centers on "practical recognition of God's dominion and man's consequent obligations. To know God, therefore, is to acknowledge with reverence and obedience His supreme power."[101] The Creator-creature distinction, and the ramifications of such, is evident throughout all Old Testament genres, and entails human expression of homage and obedience due the Sovereign Lord (e.g., 1 Sam 2:12; Jer 2:8; Ps 9:11).[102]

96. Schmitz, "Knowledge, Experience, Ignorance," 395.

97. If Pannenberg is correct, a type of general revelation that effects a prethematic knowledge of God "precedes the event of revelation" (*Systematic Theology*, 1:233). More will be forthcoming on this topic.

98. Of course, this does not entail that all divine revelation ought to be considered equal in content or manifestation.

99. See some of the positions outlined in W. Mundle and others, "Image," in *New International Dictionary of New Testament Theology*, 284–93; and in von Rad, "Divine Likeness in the OT," in *Theological Dictionary of the New Testament*, 390–92.

100. Henry, "Know, Knowledge," 49. I would expand on Henry's reference to "mind" and "conscience" to say that the individual *in the entirety of her being* is a recipient of God's universal revelation.

101. van Imschoot, "Knowledge of God," 1290.

102. In the LXX (for instance, Isa 26:11), γινώσκειν is used to speak of "the shattering knowledge of the power of God's wrath" (Bultmann, *TDNT*, 699).

God's sovereignty includes choosing the particular method of creation and redemption, as well as the means associated with self-revelation and communication to humankind. The biblical *drama of redemption* demonstrates the powerful, sovereign plan of a highly exalted yet graciously giving God. Thus, a human knowledge of God, according to Timothy Phillips, "entails acknowledging him as Lord in obedience and praise. As a result, human knowledge of God is decisively shaped by the fall and God's salvation."[103]

If the various shades of meaning of "knowledge of God" in the Old Testament were in fact held together by a central theme, it would appear to be *relationship*.[104] This second major Old Testament theme pertaining to theological knowledge is deeply intertwined in the fabric of the historical books, the writings, and the wisdom literature. The biblical drama of redemption has as its common thread, relationships: God and human beings, humans together, and God and humans with non-human life. Nothing compares to relationships in God's economy, in part because they touch every aspect of being, including the intra-Trinitarian relationship itself. Certainly there is much more connected to the question of the knowledge of God, but this primary nexus is decisive regarding the meaning and purpose of theological knowledge; the breath of life, as it were, is infused into every relevant feature encompassing theological knowledge.[105]

The relational dynamic of the knowledge of God is expressed in a myriad of ways: in the deliverance of Israel from the Egyptians (Exod 6:6–8) and God's dwelling among them (Exod 29:46); God's miraculous keeping of Israel, and meeting of their needs (Deut 29:6); vis-à-vis God's authority over the nations (1 Kings 20:28); by God's openness to being found when sought and served (1 Chron 28:9); in God's exaltation among the nations and in the midst of trials and violence (Ps 46:10); and through the practice of worship and praise (Ps 100:1–3). In addition, Yahweh is known through the deliverance and protection of those who know the divine name and choose to cleave to this relational God (Ps 91:14).

---

103. Phillips, "Knowledge of God," 458.

104. At first blush, this might seem obvious; knowledge of someone generally implies a relationship with that person. Nevertheless, this is not *necessarily* entailed from knowledge, depending on how it is defined and to what extent that person is known (not to mention whether the knower is also known by the one known).

105. Keeping this centering aspect in mind throughout this study should provide the critical connectivity necessary in forming a coherent theological knowledge model.

Hosea provides an illustration of the knowledge of God being "a personal relationship growing out of a living encounter with God."[106] This relationship between the people of God and the Lord involves "communication with God," and "respect, love, and trust shown toward God."[107] Likewise, the wisdom literature assumes that knowing Yahweh leads to full trust from the heart (e.g., Prov 3:5a).

As John Courtney Murray has argued, a *functional-relational*—rather than *ontological*—emphasis pervades the Old Testament with respect to the knowledge of God; knowing God centers on encountering Yahweh with unbounded trust in concrete situations, not in disengaged abstract reflection.[108] Schmitz adds to this insight in noting that

> while the Gks. were concerned with a detached knowledge and a speculative interest in the metaphysical nature of things, the OT regards knowledge as something which continually arises from personal encounter. . . . knowledge of God is related to the revelation of God in the historic past and the promised future, in the earthly sphere where God's creatures have their being.[109]

This privileged personal encounter, however, occurs not without a proper understanding of the ontological distinction between Creator and creatures, and the necessity of abiding by the relational rules determined by the Lord of the covenant.

The importance of *covenant relationship* is unmistakable appertaining to God and the people of God in the Old Testament; as to the knowledge of God, certain characteristics can be seen within the divine-human covenant. Phillips elaborates on this point:

> The biblical terms associated with knowing God, like trusting, acknowledging, and believing in God as Lord . . . have a covenantal context. As a result, knowledge of God is not simply propositions about God, but encountering and embracing God

---

106. Botterweck, *TDOT*, 478.

107. See Botterweck, *TDOT*, 477. Hosea uses both "Yahweh" and "Elohim" designations for the name of God. "To know God is to be in a right relationship with him, with characteristics of love, trust, respect, and open communication. . . . Negatively, not to know Yahweh is to be unfaithful, guilty of harlotry . . ." (Fretheim, *NIDOTT*, 412–13).

108. See Murray, *Problem of God*, 9–28.

109. Schmitz, "Knowledge, Experience, Ignorance," 396.

as Lord . . . so that God becomes the center of our desires, affections, and knowledge.[110]

John Frame agrees that "knowing God is knowing Him as Lord, knowing His name *Yahweh*."[111] Similarly, Rudolph Bultmann claims that "to know Him or His name is to confess or acknowledge Him, to give Him honour and to obey His will."[112] Not being utterly forsaken is promised to those who give due recognition to Yahweh as Lord; however, a lack of knowledge of God carries no such affirmations, but instead culminates in serious, negative repercussions.[113] It is essential to remember the importance of what Murray terms the *onomastic* problem among the Old Testament people of God. As Murray explains:

> In the case of God, the Hebrew impulse was not to know his existence or essence; these were alien concepts. It was to know his Name, which was an operative entity in its own right. Knowledge of God's Name was empowering; one could address him as God, call on him, enter into community with him, make valid claims upon him. Similarly, for the people to have the name of God "put" upon them was to come into God's possession and under his protection: "Thou art in our midst, Yahweh; and we bear thy Name. Abandon us not" (Jeremiah 14:9).[114]

Does the covenantal relationship really engender or require this total centering of God into one's life or the life of the faith community? Apparently so, in that the gracious lovingkindness of God should form a desire for encounter and embrace, while God's wisdom and authority ought to compel such a response.

The *human heart* plays a key role in the possibility of theological knowledge. As Murray points out with reference to the Hebrew perspective, "Knowledge is not simply an affair of intelligence; it is an affair of the heart, in the biblical sense of the heart as the center and source of the whole inner life in its full complex of thought, desire, and moral deci-

---

110. Phillips, "Knowledge of God," 459. See 1 Chron 28:9; Isa 43:10; Hos 6:3; Ps 25:4; 119:104.

111. Frame, *Doctrine of the Knowledge of God*, 40. See Exod 14:18; 33:1—34:9; 1 Kings 8:43; 1 Chron 28:6–9; Ps 83:18; 91:14; Prov 9:10; Isa 43:3; 52:6; Jer 9:23; 16:21; 33:2; Amos 5:8.

112. Bultmann, *TDNT*, 698. See Ps 9:10.

113. See, for instance, 1 Sam 2:12; Isa 1:3; and Jer 2:8.

114. Murray, *Problem of God*, 7.

sion."[115] As a term that most captures the center of humanness, the heart is viewed as decisive in knowing God. All who are found to be upright in heart know him (Ps 36:11).[116]

This "heart recognition" is, within the prophetic utterances, a *corporate* one: the people seeing, knowing, taking to heart, and understanding together that the "hand of Yahweh has done this"[117] (Isa. 43:10, 41:23). In fact, in Jeremiah, God's purpose in self-revelation is that they might know him in fellowship with their *undivided* (i.e., whole) heart.[118] In the messianic age, Yahweh is the One who makes knowledge of God possible in the hearts of human beings in order that they may acknowledge, live dependently upon, and be full of faith toward, God. This new heart is for the community of God's people—who have been forgiven of their sins—and is intended to lead to "intimate communion with God," as they return to Yahweh "with their whole heart"[119] (Jer 31:31–34).

On an individual basis, the heart must be discerning and properly attuned if knowledge of God is to be gained (Prov 18:15; Exod 7:23; 9:21).[120] This stipulates that there be no division between the thought and action of the heart, for possessing knowledge of God, according to Hos 4:6 and Jer 31, means that there is "no schism between the intellectual and the practical; the two are united in the integrity of the heart, which in Scripture is the organ of knowledge."[121] Within the wisdom literature (as we have seen), knowing Yahweh should (or will) lead to full trust from the heart (Prov 3:5a). Thus, throughout the Old Testament, the uprightness of the human heart, viewed corporately or individually, appears to always lead to a positive experience of the knowledge of God, whereas a divided or evil heart results in negative—often devastating—consequences.[122]

Uniquely related to the ongoing conflict with paganism that enveloped Israel, ideas regarding the knowledge of God "take on a special

---

115. Ibid., 21.

116. 36:10 in the Hebrew text.

117. Botterweck, *TDOT*, 476.

118. Ibid., 477.

119. Ibid.

120. Fretheim, *NIDOTT*, 412.

121. Denney, "Knowledge," 9.

122. "Negatively, not to know Yahweh is to be unfaithful, guilty of harlotry. . . ." (Fretheim, *NIDOTT*, 412–13). Moreover, according to Isa 5:13, lack of knowledge leads to exile.

significance and come to mean the recognition of the existence of the one sole God and the nothingness of the pagan gods. . . ."[123] Pannenberg sees this move from a belief in the plurality of gods to "the concept of the one God as the origin of the one world" against the historical background of the people of God, asserting that "pioneering in this regard was the development of Israel's faith from monolatry, the worship of only one God, to monotheism, the conviction that only this one God exists."[124] In any case, the people of Yahweh could justifiably claim having knowledge of God as they experienced the reality of the presence and power of the one and only true God in contrast to the neighboring false pagan gods.

Knowledge of God also implies *knowledge of self as related to God*, whether in acknowledging sins and transgressions, gratitude for God's beneficence, or obligations to God because of his graciousness and love.[125] Acknowledging and living in accordance with Creator-creature distinctions, as well as conclusions drawn from these and other crucial premises (for instance, the reality and effects of sin and the need for redemption), anticipates human beings—in varying degrees—partaking of the knowledge of God. Such a response necessitates, among other actions, confession of sins, thankfulness to God for all things, and commitment to following the revealed will of God.

A third category of theological knowledge in the Old Testament is *obedience and right conduct*. Schmitz observes that "in the wisdom literature, fear of Yahweh and knowledge of God are interchangeable terms."[126] Those who know him fear him (Prov 3:7). In the Prophets (i.e., Isaiah and Jeremiah), the knowledge of God is virtually identical to the "fear of God," and involves doing rightly and justly (Isa 11:2; Jer 22:16). The fear of the Lord can be viewed as an experiential, reverential response to God's greatness.

Closely intertwined with the fear of God is the active departure from wickedness that corresponds to knowledge of God. Those who know God turn away from evil (Prov 3:7), demonstrating their fear of the Lord. The story of Lot and the Ninevites dramatically illustrates this turning away from evil in view of fearing God or the judgment of God, and in this par-

---

123. van Imschoot, "Knowledge of God," 1291. See, for instance, Isa 40:21; 44:8f This theme is carried over into the New Testament (e.g., Rom. 1:18ff).

124. Pannenberg, *Systematic Theology*, 1:71–72.

125. See Piper, "Knowledge," 43.

126. Schmitz, "Knowledge, Experience, Ignorance," 396.

ticular case, also demonstrates the potential influence such a God-fearing response may have upon God's announced plans. In Jon 3:6–10 we read:

> When the news reached the king of Nineveh, he rose from his throne, removed his robe, covered himself with sackcloth, and sat in ashes. Then he had a proclamation made in Nineveh: "By the decree of the king and his nobles: No human being or animal, no herd or flock, shall taste anything. They shall not feed, nor shall they drink water. Human beings and animals shall be covered with sackcloth, and they shall cry mightily to God. *All shall turn from their evil ways and from the violence that is in their hands. Who knows? God may relent and change his mind; he may turn from his fierce anger, so that we do not perish."* When God saw what they did, *how they turned from their evil ways, God changed his mind about the calamity that he had said he would bring upon them; and he did not do it* [emphasis mine].

Since Old Testament knowledge of God necessitates obedience to the Lord, Jeremiah makes clear that practicing justice and charity are equivalent to knowing God.[127] Hence, the essential concreteness of theological knowledge, evidenced in God-like concern and behavior toward the truly needy, is set in radical contrast to the practice of activities intended for dishonest and selfish gain.[128] "To know the Lord goes beyond a reaching out for Him with one's mind. For example, it involves embracing God's concern for the poor and needy."[129] As Jeremiah's prophetic, rhetorical question addressed to Jehoiakim in 22:16 reveals, knowledge of God is effectively integrated with upright moral action (in the context, as particularly expressed toward certain groups of people[130]):

> He judged the cause of the poor and needy;

127. The themes of justice and liberation, especially as it concerns the oppressed poor, have been prominent in many twentieth-century liberation theologies. Some of the key Latin American figures include Leonardo Boff, José Míguez Bonino, and Gustavo Gutiérrez. See the important and cogent discussion in Conn, "Liberation Theology," 387–91. See also the valuable contribution (and useful bibliography) provided by Escobar, "Liberation Theology," 330–35.

128. Schmitz purports that "in the rhetorical question of Jer 22:15f, knowledge of God is clearly interpreted as doing justice and righteousness, particularly to the poor and needy" ("Knowledge, Experience, Ignorance," 396).

129. Henry, "Know, Knowledge," 48.

130. Doubtlessly, this godly behavior expresses the very heart of God, and thus demonstrates one's sensitivity to and involvement in the will or work of God in the concreteness of struggle and suffering within the human experience.

> then it was well.
> Is not this to know me?
> says the LORD.

A fourth major theological knowledge category in the Old Testament is that of the particular *salvific work concerning Israel*. In the historical books, Israel comes to know God via "a continual process of salvation, assistance, and deeds of mercy."[131] And as Carl Henry notes, "God was the supreme reality to believers in the OT era . . . [O]ccasionally the Almighty was pleased to reveal Himself by signs and wonders in order that those who did not belong to the covenant people might become cognizant of His power (Ex. 7:17)."[132] In fact, signs and deeds of God were experienced by the Israelites so that they might "know Yahweh is God" alone, as seen in the contest between Yahweh and Baal on Mount Carmel.[133] God's deliverance of the Israelites from Egypt was surely intended to lead to knowledge of Yahweh's being present with them in power (Exod 7:5):

> Thus, through his mighty works, God becomes transparent to his people. He is known to be present in faithful goodness—what the Hebrew untranslatably calls *hesed*—as the Power who alone can save and who graciously wills to save. . . . In all his works, of judgment as of rescue, Yahweh becomes transparent, known to his people, who name him from their experience of his works.[134]

The prophets Isaiah and Jeremiah connect knowledge of God with judgment and salvation oracles. Divine judgment results because of creaturely acts of rebellion, apostasy, faithlessness, adultery, iniquity, and deceit. God's active salvific work results among the people who are seeking to know the Lord, refraining from evil, doing justly and showing mercy (especially to the poor), and remaining faithful to Yahweh.[135]

Closely aligned with *God's signs* and *deeds* and *saving acts* toward Israel is an aspect of knowledge of God involving Israel's *acknowledgement* (or recognition), surpassing a mere *cognition*. This type of knowledge calls for reciprocity, i.e., since Yahweh is Israel's God and "God with us," the

---

131. Zimmermann, "Knowledge of God," 474.

132. Henry, "Know, Knowledge," 48.

133. Botterweck, *TDOT*, 473. See Deut 4:34f.; 1 Kings 18:37.

134. Murray, *Problem of God*, 15.

135. See, for instance, regarding judgment oracles Jer 2:8; 4:22; Hos 4:1; 5:4; 8:2, and for salvation oracles Jer 31:34; Hos 2:22(20); Isa 11:2, 9; 33:6; Dan 11:32; Mal 2:7.

people ought to be "the people of Yahweh" and "walking on with Yahweh." Murray states that

> it has to do not only with propositions and the admission of their truth but also with freedom, decision, and choice. Moreover, the biblical knowledge of God, like the biblical existence of God, is historical-existential. To know God is to recognize that he is here, in the situation of the moment; it is to recognize his action in the situation whether it be a deed of rescue or of wrath, and it is to respond to his action by a turning to the Lord, a "going with" him.[136]

Certainly, this reciprocal relationship is both a matter of divine initiative *and* human decision—to "go with Yahweh" necessitates a resolve to acknowledge "God's presence among us."

For the Old Testament people of God, the history of Israel itself—the tradition—"brings man to the knowledge of God, of his will and of his plans" and links to the fulfillment of prophetic oracles, "a sign by which the supernatural mission of the prophets could be known."[137] According to Bultmann, the Old Testament focus on tradition and the Torah are so strong that they are "the only source and theme of knowledge and instruction" for the rabbis. He argues that

> if in the OT the thought of obedience is regulative in the equation of the knowledge of God and the fear of God, and if this obedience is rooted in knowledge, then the idea of the knowledge which is the presupposition of obedience is dominant for the Rabbis.[138]

Thus, tradition and the Torah are authoritative for knowledge of God and God's will, mandating human obedience to the revealed knowledge of God's will.

Summary of the Old Testament Concept of the Knowledge of God

Considering the Old Testament witness leads one to conclude that knowledge of God, while ultimately dependent upon God's self-revelation, engages human beings in a variety of ways—and for a variety of reasons. And while the God of the Old Testament surely desires to be known, this

---

136. Murray, *Problem of God*, 22–23.

137. Zimmermann, "Knowledge of God," 474.

138. Bultmann, *TDNT*, 701.

same Creator and Redeemer is the determiner of the extent, methods, and requirements for human knowledge of the true deity:

> Knowing God leads naturally into, and cannot be separated from, a more specific content of the knowledge of God as well as the practice of piety, from profession of faith (Deut 4:39; Ps 89:2; 135:5) to confession of sin (Ps 32:5; Jer 14:20) to an assurance that 'God is for me' (Ps 56:9[10] . . . to knowledge of Torah (119:79; Jer 8:7) to a concern for the poor (Prov. 29:7; Mic 3:1).[139]

THEOLOGICAL KNOWLEDGE IN THE NEW TESTAMENT

Importantly, rather than displaying a radical contrast to Old Testament concepts of theological knowledge, the New Testament reveals *substantial unity* with the Old—yet with more clearly delineated and explicit reference to God's self-revelation in visible form, i.e., in Jesus the Christ. It may seem obvious that knowledge of God according to the New Testament writers would be viewed as intimately connected with knowledge of Christ Jesus. This is certainly true, yet not *exclusively* so. In other words, theological knowledge continues to be a multifaceted reality, while most explicitly focusing on the self-revelation of God in the Incarnation. The primary New Testament terms associated with knowledge of God, γινώσκω and οἶδα—along with associated yet less familiar terms— not infrequently offer some surprising insights for the careful observer.[140]

As was the case in the Old Testament, the New Testament emphasizes the self-revelation of God as a primary vehicle of theological knowledge. Creation, rather than being a stagnant reality that merely happens to point to its ultimate Designer, is, as Marianne Meye Thompson puts it, "manifesting God's continued providence and sovereignty over the created order," and "pointing to God not because the world was once created but because God is sovereign over it."[141] The world is moving toward eschatological restoration and teleological fulfillment. The Epistle to the Romans proclaims the message of creation declaring that God is known through it. Pannenberg states that Paul

---

139. Fretheim, *NIDOTT*, 413. The same level of commitment is found among first-century disciples of Jesus (i.e., "followers of the Way") respecting the authority of the earliest Christian tradition and the New Testament writings concerning knowledge of God.

140. See, for instance, the use of these terms in 2 Timothy.

141. Thompson, *God of the Gospel of John*, 137.

speaks expressly of a divinely disclosed knowledge of God's deity from the creation of the world (Rom. 1:20), i.e., long before the historical revelation of God in Jesus Christ. As G. Bornkhamm rightly stresses, this knowledge is not just a human possibility that we must first actualize by our own efforts. It is a divinely based fact which we cannot escape and which proves our guilt when we turn to idolatry.[142]

Ultimately, it would appear that the New Testament view of knowledge of God via creation includes, positively, hope for those who—at the very least—acknowledge the Creator, and negatively, judgment for those rejecting God's presence and work in creation. The creation is taken for granted as the exclusive work of the One and only true Creator, presenting creatures with unequivocal knowledge of God's deity and power. *Human response* to the God of creation holds a seminal place in the question of divine judgment and salvation.

The idea of human beings having an inborn (or infused) knowledge of God "has been common to the theology of the Christian West from the time of Tertullian."[143] Interpretations combining Rom 1:19–20 and 2:15 provide Luther, Melancthon, Calvin, and many other theologians with evidence of a *sensus divinitatis*—a universally internal sense leading to some level of knowledge of God through experiences of the world.[144] Whether or not such a "sense of the divine" is inherent within (or infused into) human nature, Rom 2:15 claims that some human, conscience-level intuition or awareness of God exists.[145] Pannenberg, for instance, prefers

142. Pannenberg, *Systematic Theology*, 1:75. It should briefly be noted here that material differences exist over the question of creation relative to knowledge of God between the majority Protestant view and Vatican I and II Roman Catholic positions. In general, the majority Protestant view maintains that the works of creation are a divine self-declaration; the Vatican I perspective viewed the ability (or capacity) of human reason as the central issue; and the official position of Roman Catholicism following Vatican II incorporates "natural knowledge of God in the framework of salvation history according to the divine decree of revelation" (Pannenberg, *Systematic Theology*, 1:76), opening much wider the door of salvific efficacy via human response to creation. Yet another position (held by Karl Barth, for instance) argues for the absence of such natural knowledge of God, i.e., not that creation was *not* a self-revealing of God, but that this revelation was not a "natural" quality *inherent within* creation.

143. Pannenberg, *Systematic Theology*, 1:108.

144. For a discussion of the "sense of divinity" as understood by Luther, Melancthon, and others, see Pannenberg, *Systematic Theology*, 1:107–13. For Calvin, see *Institutes*, I.3.1, 43.

145. A major philosophical and theological argument here is whether this knowledge

to see this in the earliest stages of one's life as being "set before a transcendent mystery in the sense that the silent infinity of reality that is beyond our control constantly presents itself to us as a mystery," and "only later, in light of an acquired, explicit awareness of God, can we say that what we have here is a nonthematic knowledge of God."[146] Nearly all Christians would seem to agree that there is some capacity or aspect within humans whereby God is known, even if prethematically. If one wants to be known, and has the power to make oneself known *to everyone*, then at least a rudimentary level of knowledge of oneself (or capacity for such knowledge) as a part of all human beings would surely be expected.

One of the clearest connections between Old and New Testament understandings of theological knowledge involves the *acts of God* in self-revelation. In the Old Testament, "knowledge of God arises uniquely from the revealing acts of God and the testimony to them."[147] This theme continues in the New Testament, with primary concentration on the Person of Jesus Christ as *the* revelation of God—more explicitly, the *image* or *impression* of God (2 Cor 4:4). This divine self-disclosure in the person of Christ is clearly articulated in Heb 1:1–3a:

> Long ago God spoke to our ancestors in many and various ways by the prophets, but in these last days he has spoken to us by a Son, whom he appointed heir of all things, through whom he also created the worlds. He is the reflection of God's glory and the exact imprint of God's very being, and he sustains all things by his powerful word.

The pericope of 1 Cor 2:1–16 places emphasis concerning the knowledge of God's mystery, culminating in Christ and his saving work, on God's Spirit rather than on anything within natural human nature.[148] The revelation of God's mystery—the making known of God's wisdom—is to be gratefully acknowledged as a *gift* from God to the ones who have been given this special revelation of knowledge in "demonstration of the Spirit and power." Those who know, or are known by, God and Christ also know the Holy Spirit, and can count on the Spirit's continued presence: specifically, teaching and reminding with respect to Jesus' communication

---

of God is *innate* (as Luther believes) or *acquired* (as Masäus holds).

146. Pannenberg, *Systematic Theology*, 1:114–15.

147. Schmitz, "Knowledge, Experience, Ignorance," 396.

148. As employed here, "natural" is intended to indicate an unregenerate or fallen condition.

to them (John 14:16–26; 16:7–15). Moreover, 1 John 3:24 emphasizes the Spirit's unique role in supplying obedient believers the knowledge of God's presence remaining in them.

Therefore, a proper recognition of God results from recognizing this knowledge as a gift from God, not merely something natural. The basis for this theological knowledge is revelation: "I give thanks to my God always for you because of the grace of God that has been given you in Christ Jesus, for in every way you have been enriched in him, in speech and knowledge of every kind . . ." (1 Cor 1:4–5). This knowledge, as a spiritual gift, is evident in 1 Cor 12:8,[149] while the Pauline prayer of Eph 1:17–19 speaks not only of the gift, but of the associated response and desired outcomes of the proper manifestation of this knowledge:

> I pray that the God of our Lord Jesus Christ, the Father of glory, may give you a spirit of wisdom and revelation as you come to know him, so that, with the eyes of your heart enlightened, you may know what is the hope to which he has called you, what are the riches of his glorious inheritance among the saints, and what is the immeasurable greatness of his power for us who believe, according to the working of his great power.

The Epistle of James asks readers to consider the biblical text concerning Abraham's faith and deeds and its fulfillment (Gen 15:6) as evidence for Abraham's personal knowledge of God—even his being known as "the friend of God" (James 2:20–24). The Pentateuch is referenced for its authority in communicating how human beings may be said to have true knowledge of God, and how *trust* and active *obedience* demonstrates a living relationship, i.e., friendship, with God. Paul also references the same text that James indicates, focusing on the important of faith in contrast with works of the law for obtaining justification before God. In each instance, the written revelation of God is seen as authoritative for determining issues relevant to knowledge of God.

John Calvin eloquently summarizes the importance of scripture in clarifying theological knowledge:

> Just as old or bleary-eyed men and those with weak vision, if you thrust before them a most beautiful volume, even if they recognize it to be some sort of writing, yet can scarcely construe two words, but with the aid of spectacles will begin to read distinctly;

149. "To one is given through the Spirit the utterance of wisdom, and to another the utterance of knowledge according to the same Spirit . . ."

so Scripture, gathering up the otherwise confused knowledge of God in our minds, having dispersed our dullness, clearly shows us the true God. This, therefore, is a special gift, where God, to instruct the church, not merely uses mute teachers but also opens his own most hallowed lips.[150]

Somewhat surprising, however, is the unanticipated lack of reference to the written word *in and of itself* being a means of attaining theological knowledge.[151] A looking *through* or *beyond* the page, rather than *at* the page itself, appears to be the focus of scripture pertaining to knowledge of God.[152]

While the Old Testament people of God had had revealed to them the name Yahweh for the name of God, in the New Testament period God's name is revealed in plurality: God, Jesus Christ, and Spirit. Thus, the ancient Hebrew quest to know God's name (epitomized in Moses' onomastic question) is now answered, "*We* shall be there as who we are

---

150. Calvin, *Institutes*, I.6.1 (Battles, 70).

151. This finding seems rather astonishing, given my formative influences within evangelical—especially fundamentalist—communities of faith, and the unending appeals made by preachers and teachers that "knowing the Bible means to know the Lord." It may be that such intentions were meant to call attention to the various ways in which the scriptures reveal how God is known. However, the primary emphasis seemed to fall on seeking the Lord *within the Bible itself* rather than through its instrumentality or functionality, as if by the very act of reading something in the Bible, one was to be certain to know God better, regardless the content, or understanding of the original context, setting, or audience. In stark contrast to this method, it seems rather obvious that the focus of written revelation is to *point to the ways in which God is revealed*, and the means by which humankind knows—or may come to know—God.

152. Even hymnology is not unfettered from the trend within "Bible-centered" communities to focus on the Bible's *ontological* status at the expense of its *instrumental* or *functional* purposes. One rather clear indications of tampering with the original meaning or intention of the text was discovered during the process of reviewing this section of my work with my mentor, Richard Mouw. It was found that the *Trinity Hymnal* (1961) used by the Orthodox Presbyterian Church contained an altered first verse of the hymn, *Break Thou the Bread of Life* (#256), originally written by Mary A. Lathbury (vss. 1–2) and Alexander Groves (vss. 3–4) in 1877. The focus of the verse is on seeking the Lord. Interestingly, the textual revision changes "beyond *the sacred page* I seek Thee, *Lord*" to "throughout *the sacred page* I seek thee, *Lord*." This conscious move would appear to reflect the Orthodox Presbyterian Church's agenda of placing primacy on the *ontology* of scripture, while ignoring the *mediatorial function* of the inscripturated word. It should also be noted that in the fourth verse of the original, Groves had already declared that "in Thy Book revealed *I see the Lord*" (emphases mine).

shall we be there."[153] Murray captures this developing revelation with regard to the onomastic question:

> As Father he is more intimately known, and he is more than ever truly named by all the many names that had long been used but are now laden with new meaning because they are read by men from the new works of God in our midst, more wonderful than ever—the Son's ransoming deed of love, and the Spirit's ceaseless energizing in the Church. Thus stated in triadic terms, the New Testament problematic of the presence of God exhibits a substance that transcends the Old Testament substance.[154]

Hence, the triadic formulas found throughout the New Testament indicate that God is known among believers as a *community of Being*: each member of the divine community named, and as a result, accessible to those who know the Name.

Moreover, the New Testament transposes knowledge of Yahweh with knowledge of Christ. The Old Testament phrase, "Know that I am Yahweh" (especially prevalent in Ezekiel), is juxtaposed with Christ in the New Testament. One of the so-called "seven 'I am' statements" in the Gospel of John most clearly captures this transpositioning: "So Jesus said, 'When you have lifted up the Son of Man, then you will realize that I am he, [ἐγώ εἰμί] and that I do nothing on my own, but I speak these things as the Father instructed me'"[155] (John 8:28). Numerous other New Testament passages repeat this move, i.e., attributing to Jesus Christ the attributes or character of Yahweh (e.g., Rom 11:36; Rev 22:13). Consequently, to know Jesus is to know Yahweh God. The onomastic concern for access to God and knowing God's character is answered in the person of Jesus Christ—"Jesus said to him, 'Have I been with you all this time, Philip, and you still do not know me? Whoever has seen me has seen the Father. How can you say, "Show us the Father"?'" (John 14:9).

Although one might suspect that John's use of the *logos* carries with it Hellenistic overtones, in reality, as Piper observes, the concept is more closely akin to the Hebrew *dābār* [דָּבָר]. "Far from being the basis of a rational world, it interprets the universe as a divine communication destined to lead people to personal fellowship with God (1 John 1:1–3)."[156]

153. Murray, *Problem of God*, 28.
154. Ibid.
155. See also Rev. 2:23.
156. See Piper, "Knowledge," 45.

John's writings are the clearest in expressing the idea that the Logos, who has always been with God (John 1:1), has come to humanity (1:14), and has made the Father known (14:7–9).[157]

In conjunction with the *Logos* made flesh, *Wisdom* is also enfleshed in Jesus Christ. According to Johannine scholar, Marianne Meye Thompson, the implications of this for theological knowledge are considerable: "The whole tenor of John's depiction of Jesus as incarnate Wisdom is to stress the manifestation of God's presence which, though hidden, nevertheless remains accessible to those who have eyes to see and ears to hear."[158] Even more profoundly,

> because Wisdom is not only *from* God but is also *of* God, to speak of Jesus as the embodied Wisdom of God is to speak of the embodiment of God's own presence. To know God through Jesus is not merely to know things about or from God but is rather to know God.[159]

The crucial relationship between the Father and Jesus is therefore to be *seen* and *heard* in terms of not only representation of the former by the latter, but as Jesus being the *Revealer of God*, demonstrating in his person and work a total unity with God—even embodiment of God's character and attributes.

The New Testament offers many polemical and apologetical arguments against other kinds of knowledge (e.g., religious) that claim to enlighten one to a true knowledge of God in contrast with the self-revelation of God in the person of Jesus Christ. Consequently, knowledge of God in the *explicitly salvific* sense is knowledge of Jesus, the Christ of God. As O. A. Piper illustrates, the Pauline corpus gives center stage to this far-reaching theological claim:

> The Christian knowledge transcends all other knowledge, including that of the OT, by the fact that in Jesus Christ for the first time in the history of mankind the glory of God has been manifested in a human life (II Cor. 4:6). Hence, there can be no true knowledge of God except in his manifestation in Christ (e.g., Gal. 4:9; Col. 2:2–3). . . . Paul focuses his attention upon the moral and spiritual character of Jesus. In him the goal of God's "mystery"—i.e, of his saving purpose—becomes visible (1 Cor. 2:7; Eph. 1:2–4; Col.

157. Ibid.
158. Thompson, *God of the Gospel of John*, 134.
159. Ibid., 135.

1:9; 3:23–24), and thus he determines our moral obligations (Eph. 5:5; Col. 3:16). . . . knowledge of Christ is the realization of his saving significance (1 Cor. 2:12–13; Phil. 1:9–10; Philem. 6).[160]

For Paul, the knowledge of Christ is determinative for fullness of life and salvation; indeed, absolutely nothing rivals this knowledge in significance:

> Yet whatever gains I had, these I have come to regard as loss because of Christ. More than that, I regard everything as loss because of the surpassing value of knowing Christ Jesus my Lord. For his sake I have suffered the loss of all things, and I regard them as rubbish, in order that I may gain Christ and be found in him, not having a righteousness of my own that comes from the law, but one that comes through faith in Christ, the righteousness from God based on faith. I want to know Christ [lit., him] and the power of his resurrection and the sharing of his sufferings by becoming like him in his death . . . (Phil 3:7–10).

Matthew and Luke, in the so-called "Johannine logion in the synoptics," record Jesus as saying, "All things have been handed over to me by my Father; and no one knows the Son except the Father, and no one knows the Father except the Son and anyone to whom the Son chooses to reveal him" (Matt 11:27; Luke 10:22). This dynamic relationship of incomprehensible depth between the Father and the Son is now opened for those to whom the Son grants to know the Father. As Pannenberg states, "By his revelation in the Son the essence of the otherwise incomprehensible God is disclosed. It is disclosed in such a way that the hidden God himself is manifest. The God who is not revealed is now revealed."[161]

The phrase "and no one knows the Son except the Father" cannot imply *utter* unknowability of the Son by human beings, in view of the whole purview of the New Testament and its focus on knowing the Son. What is intended therefore? Perhaps depth, quality, clarity, or other terms may be utilized to speak of the *level* or *plane* of relationship that may be in mind.[162] The context apparently suggests a knowledge incorporating both ontological and relational features, in that Jesus is depicted pronouncing

160. Piper, "Knowledge," 45.

161. Pannenberg, *Systematic Theology*, 1:340.

162. Certainly, a unique kind of knowledge is intended, whether it refers to intimacy or specificity of persons, since God (not necessarily as Father) is known to some degree in various ways, as we have seen (e.g., in creation).

an impending future judgment for those rejecting him, i.e., not repenting and not choosing to welcome and receive the Son, even though he had performed great deeds among them. Therefore, they show their ignorance as regards Jesus: about where his power is from—the Father rather than the devil—and even unawareness of who the Father is. Perhaps then, this passage is not to be viewed as an exclusive claim regarding the only way to know God *at all*, but rather a claim suggesting that one can experientially know the Father *in ways not otherwise possible* by receiving Jesus as being of and from the Father.[163]

Moreover, possessing a religious knowledge "after the flesh" concerning the earthly ministry of Jesus is insufficient for apprehending "the manifestation of God in the earthly life of the man Jesus"[164] and his exaltation as Lord and Christ (Acts 2:23; 5:31; Phil 2:9). In both the humanity and divinity of Jesus—pre- and post-resurrection—the knowledge of God is publicized.

Much of what has been claimed regarding our first major New Testament category bearing on theological knowledge—the self-revelation of God—connotes something crucial, extending beyond the divine self-disclosure itself; the very purpose of such personal revelation is that those to whom the knowledge of God becomes manifest may attain a proper and personal salvific relationship by means of trusting in God and Christ. As Piper explains,

---

163. It seems likely only a rather nuanced account will penetrate to the core of the issue and help to break the exclusivist/inclusivist divide often associated with these texts: there is something crucially definitive, yet not utterly exclusivist, about knowledge of the Father through the Son. The depth and power of the Father-Son relationship can never be fully comprehended, but certain aspects and ramifications of the divine "dance" are declared within the New Testament. As van Imschoot states, "Mutual knowledge supposes equality of nature; both the Son and the Father are on the same plane, so high above man that no man of himself can come to a knowledge of Their nature; only the Son, who alone knows the Father, can make Him known to others. . . . [The] mutual knowledge of the Good Shepherd and His sheep is not a speculative, but a practical knowledge, which includes love (cfr.1 Jn 2,3ff; Jn 14,21). It is indeed compared to the mutual knowledge of the Father and the Son, but the comparison is not perfect. For in man this knowledge is not possible without faith (Jn 6,69; 10,38; 16,30; 17,7f; 1 Jn 4,16), while the Son knows the Father by His own personal knowledge (Jn 7,29; 8,55; 17,25). In fact, He alone knows the invisible God (1,18; 6,46; 1 Jn 4:12) and He alone can make Him known to men (Jn 1,18; 14,6–9), because He is God and is in the bosom of the Father (1,18; cfr. 10,38; 14,11; 17,21), because He is with the Father (10,30; 17,22)" (van Imschoot, "Knowledge of God," 1291–92).

164. Piper, "Knowledge," 46.

Those only who are willing to believe that in his actions Jesus is doing the will of the Father, receive the light which enables them to discern the Son of God in his hiddenness. In Jesus, one sees eventually God (John 14:17). Thus knowledge, which has reached this level, is not a mere acceptance of God's revelation, but rather an ontic relationship with God has been established therein.[165]

Thus, trusting the *kerygma* is essentially trusting that knowledge of God has been made manifest *by God* in the Person of Jesus, providing us with our second general New Testament category for knowledge of God. Such privileged theological knowledge is grounded in hearing and receiving the *kerygma*:

Though all men are capable of knowing God, the knowledge of Christ is given to those only in whom the Holy Spirit operates (e.g., I Cor. 2:12–13; Eph. 3:4–5; Phil. 3:8). . . . True spiritual knowledge originates in the hearing of the message in which God's revelation in Christ is proclaimed (Rom. 10:17; I Cor. 8:1; Col. 1:6; I Thess. 4:9). Faithful acceptance of the "word of Christ" (Rom 10:17; Eph 1:13) or the "gospel" (e.g., Rom 1:15; 10:16; 1 Cor 1:17; 2 Cor 4:3; Eph 3:6; Col 1:5) leads to spiritual experience, both of its reality and of its implications (Rom 15:14; 1 Cor 1:5; 2 Cor 8:9; Gal 2:9; Eph 1:18).[166]

Hearing and receiving the gospel carries with it the privilege of intimate spiritual relationship, as well as particular responsibilities accompanying this knowledge.

Linked to hearing and receiving the *kerygma* is the idea of *conversion* to the Christian faith. This is emphasized in 1 Thess 1:9–10, where the radical change of allegiance made by the new converts to the faith is highlighted:

For the people of those regions [lit., they] report about us what kind of welcome we had among you, and how you turned to God from idols, to serve a living and true God, and to wait for his Son from heaven, whom he raised from the dead—Jesus, who rescues us from the wrath that is coming.

Focus on conversion is especially evident in the later epistles.[167] Evidently, a body of truth exists that is to be known about God and Christ,

165. Ibid., 45.

166. Ibid., 46.

167. For instance, in 1 Tim 2:3–7 (situated between appeals to pray and proper com-

demonstrating a theological move toward *gaining saving knowledge*: belief in the *facts about* the saving will and work of God in Christ. People are to be converted to the Christian faith in virtue of realizing this knowledge.

Thus, certain essential features of the *kerygma* were apparently solidifying in response to growing crises within the church, with adherence to "the truth" (e.g., the sacrificial work of Christ Jesus) viewed as indispensable for salvific knowledge of God. Still, this later New Testament emphasis on the *saving* proviso associated with having "knowledge of the truth,"[168] did not negate personal knowledge of God, i.e., relationship *with* God.[169]

The personal nature of the divine-human relationship is an Old Testament concept pertaining to knowledge of God (as discussed earlier). But with the development of the New Testament canon, this notion is extended toward—and modified in its focus upon—Jesus the Christ. In the Gospel of John, for instance, this personal knowledge of God and Christ is wedded, leading the knower to ζωῆς, life (John 17:3). In addition, a Pauline presupposition is that Christ Jesus is the possessor of all wisdom and knowledge, and who, as the mystery of God, is the One to be known *personally* (Col 2:2–3), above all else that may be known in this way (1 Cor 2:2[170]). Such experiential knowledge includes knowing Christ in a way that includes "the power of his resurrection and the sharing of his

---

munal and societal behavior) the author writes, "This is right and is acceptable in the sight of God our Savior, who desires everyone to be saved and to come to the knowledge of the truth. For there is one God; there is also one mediator between God and humankind, Christ Jesus, himself human [Gk., ἄνφρωπος] who gave himself a ransom for all—this was attested at the right time. For this I was appointed a herald and an apostle (I am telling the truth, I am not lying), a teacher of the Gentiles in faith and truth."

168. See also Heb 10:26; Titus 1:1; 2 Tim 2:25.

169. For instance, the personal intimacy of the divine-human relationship is vividly captured in 1 Tim 1:12–17: "I am grateful to Christ Jesus our Lord, who has strengthened me, because he judged me faithful and appointed me to his service, even though I was formerly a blasphemer, a persecutor, and a man of violence. But I received mercy because I had acted ignorantly in unbelief, and the grace of our Lord overflowed for me with the faith and love that are in Christ Jesus. The saying is sure and worthy of full acceptance, that Christ Jesus came into the world to save sinners—of whom I am the foremost. But for that very reason I received mercy, so that in me, as the foremost, Jesus Christ might display the utmost patience, making me an example to those who would come to believe in him for eternal life. To the King of the ages, immortal, invisible, the only God, be honor and glory forever and ever. Amen."

170. "For I decided to know nothing among you except Jesus Christ, and him crucified."

sufferings . . ." (Phil 3:10). As a result, "to know him means to enter into the personal relationship which he himself makes possible."[171]

Clearly, emphasis on knowing Christ is the centerpiece of New Testament theological knowledge.[172] In fact, the proclamation—and associated Christian experience—of Jesus as Lord and Light is said "to give the light of the knowledge of the glory of God in the face of Jesus Christ" (2 Cor 4:6b).

An indissoluble amalgamation between love (primarily ἀγάπη) and knowledge of God permeates the Johannine corpus. Given that coming to *know* God and Jesus Christ is eternal life (John 17:3), knowledge is supreme. But as Bultmann emphasizes, this knowledge is essentially *love*:

> [M]aterially this [knowledge] is understood to be ἀγάπη. God is ἀγάπη, so that the man who is related to Him is related as one who loves (1 Jn 4:8, 16). To be determined by love is thus a criterion of the knowledge of God (1 Jn 4:7f.; cf. 4:20f.), as also of belonging to Jesus (Jn 13:35). . . . Since the knowledge of Jesus or of God expresses itself accordingly in ἀγαπᾶν, observing the commandments (which have in ἀγάπη their content) might also be called a criterion of γινώσκειν (1 Jn 2:3–5; cf. 3:6). Yet γινώσκειν, as determination by God or Jesus, is ἀγάπη not merely in ἀγαπᾶν as loving action but also in awareness of being loved.[173]

The concept of *passive* knowledge (i.e., being known by God) is for Paul, grounded in God's election and foreknowledge—God having known and predestined us before time (Eph 1:4–6). Thus, the emphasis is on God's precipitating theological knowledge by way of divine love, rather than active human effort seeking knowledge of God.

The New Testament link between knowledge and faith is intensely—and intentionally—close, especially the relationship of faith in Christ to *saving* or *true* knowledge. As Piper states, "Particularly in the Fourth

---

171. Schmitz, "Knowledge, Experience, Ignorance," 396.

172. For instance, the author of Colossians exclaims, "I want their hearts to be encouraged and united in love, so that they may have all the riches of assured understanding and have the knowledge of God's mystery, that is, Christ himself, in whom are hidden all the treasures of wisdom and knowledge" (Col. 2:2–3). Although the passage is somewhat uncertain, the NRSV probably best captures the meaning, that Christ is the knowledge of God's mystery, carrying with it the idea that this knowledge is not open to everyone, but to those to whom Christ has been made known.

173. Bultmann, *TDNT*, 711.

Gospel knowledge of God and faith are practically synonymous."[174] This type of knowledge (γινώσκειν, but never γνῶσις) leads to "eternal life" (John 17:3) and is often used synonymously with πιστεύιν, since "to believe or to have knowledge of God through faith, means to unite oneself to God or to Christ, the source of eternal life (Jn 5,21.26; 11,25; 14,6) or to receive within oneself God or Christ as the object of faith (6,35.37.45; 1 Jn 2,23)."[175] The intertwining and juxtapositioning of faith and knowledge is also evident in Pauline thought. For instance, Eph 3:16–19 records a multifaceted faith/knowledge prayer:

> I pray that, according to the riches of his glory, he may grant that you may be strengthened in your inner being with power through his Spirit, and that Christ may dwell in your hearts through faith, as you are being rooted and grounded in love. I pray that you may have the power to comprehend, with all the saints, what is the breadth and length and height and depth, and to know the love of Christ that surpasses knowledge, so that you may be filled with all the fullness of God.

In describing Christian knowledge of God it remains debatable whether Paul uses Gnostic terminology, adopting a Gnostic approach while selectively modifying its content. What seems beyond dispute is Paul's arguments in favor of a genuine and *uniquely Christian* knowledge of God—grounded in God's divine act of salvation, most clearly revealed in the person and work of Christ and available for all who walk according to the spirit and in love. It is authentic knowledge, not according to excellence of speech or human wisdom, but in harmony with the δύναμις and σοφία of God, which God has revealed to believers in Christ by the Holy Spirit (1 Cor 3:1; 8:1ff.).

John Frame sees unique Christian knowledge linked with the question of lordship and covenant:[176]

> In summary, "knowledge of God" essentially refers to a person's friendship (or enmity) with God. That friendship presupposes knowledge in other senses—knowledge of facts about God, knowl-

---

174. Piper, "Knowledge," 44. Schmitz expands on this point, noting that "the striking equation of faith and knowledge in the relationship of man to God is also part of the polemic against gnosticism which at the very least depreciated faith in contrast to knowledge" ("Knowledge, Experience, Ignorance," 404).

175. van Imschoot, "Knowledge of God," 1292.

176. See Frame, *Doctrine of the Knowledge of God*, 18–61.

edge of skills in righteous living, and so forth. It therefore involves a covenental response of the whole person of God in all areas of life, either in obedience or in disobedience. It involves, most focally, a knowledge of God's lordship—of His control, His authority, and His present reality.[177]

Frame appears to be making the case that Rom 1:18ff. signifies that *all* know God—and not merely *about* God—but that the unbeliever *rejects* or *refuses* to obey God's authority. Frame discards the notion that unbelievers do not know or know about God *at all*, and thus have to be informed or enlightened. Rather, it is a matter of the heart, and of course, being *regenerated* in order to change one's rebellious nature against God (or enmity with God).[178]

A third major category of New Testament knowledge of God involves *practical obedience and edification.* Several New Testament passages connect knowing or doing the will of God with possessing knowledge of God—or the truth of God (John 7:17, Acts 22:14). The Pauline "calling formula" (e.g., 2 Cor 1:1) implies that Paul is obediently acknowledging God's will, thus reflecting his personal knowledge of God. "According to John, knowledge does not lead to a gradual merger of the knower's mind with that of God, but rather to a harmony of their wills in which God remains distinctly the authority to be recognized."[179] In contrast to the people who do not know God (the Father) and refuse to listen to the good news of our Lord Jesus Christ (2 Thess 1:8), the people who know God are those who "'go with' him," and "realize their religious and moral relation to him by a life of faith and obedience." As Murray asserts, "the people of

177. Ibid., 48.

178. While Frame is right about the fact that rebellion and rejection characterize the human condition toward God, his contention seems to simply ignore a parallel reality: that there are religious adherents who know only their own traditional means of worshiping God and their faith community's moral code. Certainly, the vast majority of these worshipers are far from thinking that they are actually *rejecting* God, although it can unequivocally be admitted that they are not worshipping God *as most fully revealed in Tri-unity, or in Christ.* Does this entail, then, that there is an absolute rejection by God of *all* of the countless millions who worship God "without knowledge of Christ?" While this question is not the primary focus of this paper and cannot be adequately addressed herein, in short it seems that there may be significant issues that Frame needs to address that have received the attention of several other prominent contemporary evangelical thinkers (see, for instance, Grenz, *Renewing the Center*; Pinnock, *Wideness in God's Mercy*; Placher, *Unapologetic Theology*; Stackhouse, *No Other Gods before Me?*).

179. Piper, "Knowledge," 45.

God are constituted a people precisely by their knowledge of him, by their faithful, active recognition of his presence among them."[180] Knowledge of God's will, decree, or law carried with it much more than theoretical assent, but rather "the recognition that it applies to the person individually and demands his obedience."[181] The indication from 2 Cor 10:5 is that obedience to Christ and knowledge of God directly correspond.

"Love for God takes the shape in new obedience to the Lord Jesus Christ and freedom from the lordship of sin . . . in fellowship with Christ's sufferings, and in strenuous service in the resurrection power of Christ . . ."[182] What is more, John's use of γινώσκω appears to have a "double application: knowing the love of God shown in the sending of the Son (Jn 17:18; 1 Jn. 3:16), and the obedience of love based on it which is also described as obedience to the message proclaimed (1 Jn 4:6)."[183]

Doubtlessly, the privilege of theological knowledge anticipates moral responsibility. As Zimmermann observes, "Since knowledge is an expression of a loving union with God, it must have its practical effect on the moral life of the Christian. . . . Keeping his commandments is precisely the means whereby one is certain that one knows him (1 John 2:3), for Christ is for the Christian the type of moral conduct (1 John 2:6)."[184] Just as Jesus demonstrates his own love for the Father "by obedience to God's commands (Jn 14:31), so he who knows demonstrates his knowledge by keeping God's commands (1 Jn 2:3ff.) . . ."[185]

Peter wishes multiplied grace and peace (2 Pet 1:2) upon those who, through knowledge of God (or Christ), have received the same precious faith, and have therefore been divinely granted "all things pertaining to life and godliness" (1:3). The illocutionary point of the larger pericope (1:1–15) appears to be the *encouragement* of believers. The author reiterates that they possess knowledge of God and the power of God to strengthen them to live virtuously:

> or this reason, you must make every effort to support your faith
> with goodness, and goodness with knowledge, and knowledge

---

180. Murray, *Problem of God*, 80.

181. Schmitz, "Knowledge, Experience, Ignorance," 399.

182. Ibid., 403.

183. Ibid., 404.

184. Zimmermann, "Knowledge of God," 477.

185. Schmitz, "Knowledge, Experience, Ignorance," 404.

with self-control, and self-control with endurance, and endurance with godliness, and godliness with mutual affection, and mutual affection with love . . . in the knowledge of our Lord Jesus Christ (1:5–7, 8c).

The believers' efforts act as confirmation of their calling and election (1:10b). Still, this particularly faith-engaged level of the knowledge of God anticipates a corresponding practical "virtuousity"—and that not of human origin, since the δύναμις of God provides the ability.

Surely, the connection between knowledge and virtue is grounded in God and Christ. And since (as we have seen) God desired to be known, granting of spiritual knowledge has a crucial purpose: that human beings may be formed into the likeness of Christ (Gal 4:19; Col. 3:10; Rom 8:28–29), implying attentiveness to the moral dimension of our lives. Consequently, the public practice of biblical ethics is never far from the subject of the knowledge of God—in fact, the intertwining is indissoluble. Whenever theoretical knowledge is in view, some sense of practical activity is connected with it.[186]

Pauline and Johannine writings agree that the knowledge of God *necessarily constitutes* love for God and love for others (1 Cor 8:2f.; John 14:20f.; 1 John 3:4), leading to "building up" the faith community rather than "puffing up" oneself by means of intellectual knowledge (1 Cor 8:1ff.). Paul attacks self-centered knowledge, using the edification of the church as the basis for his argument; true knowledge of God results in loving concern with "the salvation of others in the fellowship of Jesus Christ, including the weak (1 Cor. 8:9) who do not possess this knowledge (1 Cor. 8:7), and surely also the outsiders and unbelievers (1 Cor. 14:23)."[187] Thus, this practical expression of love among Christians and toward all people serves to indicate the presence of the knowledge of God among the people of God. Where this love is absent, so is any assurance of true theological knowledge.

Our final category of New Testament theological knowledge is *Christian doctrine and tradition.* The Pastorals picture Christian knowledge of God in terms of knowledge of "the truth," referring to the message of the gospel (e.g., 1 Tim 2:3–7; 3:16—4:3; 2 Tim 2:25—3:15). Regarding receptivity of this truth, Murray ascertains that it involves "both affirma-

---

186. For instance, see Rom 15:14–15, along with the broader context.

187. Schmitz, "Knowledge, Experience, Ignorance," 402.

tion and choice, a knowledge and an acknowledgment, at once an assent and a consent, an affair of both mind and heart."[188] Conversely, "to oppose the gospel is to resist the truth."[189] (2 Tim 3:8). The use of γνῶσις and ἐπίγνωσις are employed technically and polemically in order to equate the former with the "gnostic heresy (cf. 1 Tim 6:20)" and the latter with reference to "Christian knowledge (1 Tim. 2:4; 2 Tim. 2:25; 2:7; Tit. 1:1),"[190] which Schmitz points out has

> quite clearly an intellectual, semi-dogmatic stress. The knowledge of God's truth is of equal important with experiential profession of the Lord, and finally pushes it into the background. Hence, conversion to the Christian faith can be described almost technically as coming to a knowledge (*epígnōsis*) of the truth (1 Tim. 2:4; 2 Tim. 3:7; cf. Heb. 10:26; 1 Tim. 5:3; 2 Tim. 2:25; Tit. 1:1; 2 Pet. 2:21).[191]

For the truth of the gospel of God to remain clearly identifiable, it must remain free from being associated with what various New Testament epistles view as merely human commands and regulations, profane myths and tales, the promotion of speculations, unsound doctrine, teachings of demons, wicked people and imposters, and smooth talkers and flatterers (Rom 16:17–18; Col 2:20; 1 Tim 1:3–4; 4:1, 7; 2 Tim 3:13; Titus 2:1).

One particular New Testament test respecting the knowledge of God involves

> the collective character of spiritual knowledge. It had entered into history through the witness and proclamation of the apostles, who were the ones to see the heavenly glory of the risen Lord (1 Cor. 15:5–9) and who were commissioned to propagate the gospel. . . . The nucleus of spiritual knowledge is formed by the tradition (*paradosis*) of the church (Rom. 6:17; 1 Cor. 11:2, 23; 15:1, 3; Gal. 1:9, 12; Phil. 4:9; 1 Thess. 2:13; 4:1; 2 Thess. 2:15; 3:6).[192]

Paul speaks in rather poetic terms—with polemical intent—of being "vessels of God" through which a "fragrance that comes from knowing him" spreads everywhere, serving as a testimony of the truthfulness of the

188. Murray, *Problem of God*, 29.

189. Denney, "Knowledge," 10.

190. Schmitz, "Knowledge, Experience, Ignorance," 405.

191. Ibid.

192. Piper, "Knowledge," 46.

apostolic witness concerning Christian claims to theological knowledge (2 Cor 2:14).

Second Peter uses ἐπίγνωσις in a rather technical manner, associating it with God's call.[193] "Knowledge is here of the orthodox tradition, of the catholic doctrinal teaching (2 Peter 1:2, 3, 8; 2:20) which, as in the Pastorals, must become effective in a corresponding manner of life."[194]

In later New Testament writings, growing clarity of expectation as to Christian faith is emerging; issues corresponding to knowledge of God are answered more in accordance with the developing body of doctrine—especially concerning the death and resurrection of Christ—and the ongoing Christian tradition. Out of the doctrinal crisis, possibly pertaining to both Judaizers and pre-Gnostics, 2 Tim 2:24–25 makes clear the importance of knowing the truth (e.g., concerning the gospel, cf. 2:8–15) and the corresponding manner of life expected of those who serve and lead the young church: "And the Lord's servant must not be quarrelsome but kindly to everyone, an apt teacher, patient, correcting opponents with gentleness. God may perhaps grant that they will repent and come to know the truth."

In Titus 1:1ff, knowledge of the truth connects with godliness and hope of everlasting/abundant life, and the promise of God regarding the manifesting of the word through proclamation of the gospel. Here again is evident emphasis upon theological knowledge as it concerns preaching and teaching of doctrine, combined with corresponding ethical behavior. Still, it must be admitted that numerous factors inhibit a more thoroughgoing knowledge of God this side of the eschaton, entailing that our theological knowledge—while sufficient—is but partial and somewhat obscured. As Piper asserts, "Paul points out that even the richest spiritual knowledge remains fragmentary here on earth (e.g., Rom 11:34; 1 Cor 13:12–13), both because of the limited range of our experience and because the Spirit of Christ has to operate upon an earthly mind."[195] Pannenberg points to Duns Scotus's insistence that our knowledge of God and God's self-knowledge must be distinguished.[196]

---

193. Schmitz, "Knowledge, Experience, Ignorance," 405.
194. Ibid.
195. Piper, "Knowledge," 46.
196. As cited in Pannenberg, *Systematic Theology*, 1:73, n.26.

Summary of the New Testament Concept of the Knowledge of God

Old Testament perspectives on theological knowledge are repeated throughout the New Testament, especially as it concerns the divine-human relationship, and consequent proper moral conduct. The Christological focus of the New Testament presents the salvific orientation of the knowledge of God as unequivocally grounded in dependence upon God's initiation and self-disclosure in the person and work of the Lord Jesus Christ. Accessing this privileged theological knowledge is linked with a human faith/trust response in acceptance of the *kerygma*, obedient living characterized by proper moral conduct, love, and edification of others, and growing in the knowledge of the truth via the apostolic tradition and teachings.

CONCLUSION

As we have demonstrated, knowledge of God as understood in the New Testament substantially reflects Old Testament concepts, while expanding to incorporate the centrality of Jesus. Both Testaments represent theological knowledge as based on divine self-revelation—a gift of the Spirit. Divine disclosure occurs in a variety of ways, and is intended to draw human beings to respond to the sovereignty and power of God.

Scripture is unified in affirming the primacy of human relationship-fellowship with the true and living God. Whether in the Old or New Testament—in the Name of Yahweh or in the Name of Jesus—the personal and communal nature of human relations with God is a central biblical theme. In addition, both Testaments anticipate the exercise of wisdom and obedience resulting from privileged theological knowledge—even equating such right behavior as an aspect of knowing God.

Tradition, in both the history of Israel and in the ancient church context, is viewed by scripture as integral to knowledge of God via demonstrations of divine speaking and acting among the people of God. This results in not only various expressions within oral tradition, but also more concretely, in the Holy Spirit, inspired written form of God's word among these particular faith communities.

The New Testament places great emphasis on the salvific aspect of theological knowledge, and makes clear that a Person is the centerpiece of the knowledge of God—Jesus the Christ, the divine Logos and Wisdom made flesh—the image of the invisible God. To know Jesus is to know

God, for Jesus is the One who knows God the Father in a unique way, and makes the knowledge of God particularly accessible through him.

Having concluded this look at the biblical data and what it reveals about the knowledge of God, it will now be important to (re)turn to consideration of the larger framework for theological method in which scripture holds the primary place among most reformists—the Quadrilateral—to see what actual and further potential benefits are accessible for evangelical reflection and practice.

Tradition, Reason, Experience, and More: Toward a Socially-Oriented Epistemology

Our focus now shifts to consideration of tradition, a second source for theology within the Quadrilateral model. Part of tradition's significance is in its ability to reveal the significant sociological and historical elements that shape a great deal of our philosophizing and theologizing—including the ways we view reason and experience in different times and settings. Observing theology *through* traditions brings to light the so-called sociology of knowledge, a guiding perspective of postmodern understandings of knowledge and truth.

In addition to the resurgence of tradition within certain evangelical theological methods, both reason and experience are being pictured somewhat differently than during the modernist-fundamentalist controversy and other periods within modernity. Some evangelical intellectuals are becoming (re)acquainted with John Wesley's own approach to the third and fourth components of the Quadrilateral, while others are seemingly more interested in looking at each through postmodern filters. In any case, attention is growing among post-Enlightenment types interested in reconceiving the ways in which experience and reason have often been characterized and used (wrongly, they would say) within conventional evangelical thought.

Overall, though, twentieth- and twenty-first-century evangelical intellectuals have been slow to acknowledge—slower to employ—the ideas and findings of more socially-oriented approaches to theological knowledge. This hesitance notwithstanding, there is a growing trend among reformists to incorporate such epistemological outlooks into their theological method. In our next segment, we will consider certain ways in which this is being done.

Clearly, many postconservative scholars contend for the need for evangelical theology to move beyond the supposed misguided foundationalist assumptions reflected in individualism and lofty claims of neutrality and objectivity. Thus, the forthcoming analysis will consider what we have been introducing to this point as an alternative, socially-oriented framework for theological epistemology. Beginning with a short introduction on the apparent widespread (re)turn to *opinio*, our focus moves thereafter to an examination of several postconservative theological epistemologies that are interested in incorporating to some degree a sociology of knowledge component. This nonfoundationalist assumption—the social embeddedness of all knowledge—will doubtlessly involve looking at tradition, reason, and experience, and therefore stands to contribute to a more holistic vision for evangelical approaches to the knowledge of God.

OPINIO: TO RESTORE OR NOT TO RESTORE

Acknowledging that socio-cultural factors significantly contribute to shaping human knowing is an essential step forward in constructing a new vision for evangelical theological epistemology. Obviously, traditional and communal contexts deeply influence our outlook on all of life. Thus, the divergent responses among evangelical philosophers and theologians are to be expected in light of the postmodern sociology of knowledge move.[197] Many traditionalist theologians continue to equate evangelicalism and evangelical theology with the affirmation of particular propositional statements of the Christian faith, believing that a theological or epistemological shift in any other direction is tantamount to rejecting or reducing the *content* of Christianity.[198] A key question on which this argument pivots concerns what is actually said to be *changing* within evangelical theology. Is it the essential *doctrinal* content of the historic Christian faith (e.g., Christological or soteriological), or is it rather the *emphasis* on different aspects of Christianity (e.g., focusing on praxis and community)? This

197. More accurately, this move involves the *restoration* or *recovery* of *opinio* of the pre-Cartesian period, rather than a novel discovery. Still, articulation concerning such has been substantially different from original understandings in several key ways. For instance, viewing the sociology of knowledge as *detrimental* to religious faith, rather than *supportive* of the value of interpretive religious communities, is a more or less radically *post*modern development. This can be witnessed most clearly with postmodern philosophers who deny the existence of any external Signified or referent (e.g., Nietzsche, Foucault, and Rorty).

198. This is not infrequently the charge made with reference to David Wells's methodology (see his *No Place for Truth* and *God in the Wasteland*).

problem seems to be central to the argument of whether one, as an evangelical, ought to affirm the changes being proposed by particular—mainly postconservative—theologians.

No Place for Truth?

Millard Erickson, in evaluating historian and theologian David Wells and his book *No Place for Truth*, notes Wells's full-scale rejection—and in some respects unawareness—of postmodern contributions to philosophy and theology. Rather, Wells is deeply concerned with what he views as the disappearing of theology among evangelicals, claiming that theology is being broken into areas of specialization and that the articles of Christian belief are no longer central to evangelicalism. In other words, the *theological* definition of the faith is vanishing.[199] As Wells sees it, the goal of *happiness* has become primary for evangelicals, leading to various capitulations to the consumer-oriented and religiously-pluralistic cultural context. Consequently for Wells, the solution to this problem for evangelical Christians (as summarized by Erickson) is "to return to a concern for truth as objective knowledge of reality. Specifically, it is a matter of recapturing the understanding of persons, not as selves, but as human beings who stand before a holy God."[200] Importantly, Wells recognizes the sociological factors in belief, and he has grasped important insights into cultural change, as well as the need to see the inseparable relationship between faith and practice. Still, there are several blind spots making his approach—at least for reformists—suspect.

As Erickson points out, Wells appears to be unaware of the relativizing effect of *his own* sociology of knowledge on the approach that he recommends. This would seem to be the result of his *historically-conditioned* perspective! Wells also fails to deal with important philosophical matters adequately, such as epistemic questions raised by both modern and postmodern philosophers and the predicament of foundationalism. He also appears to be interpreting scripture through his own objectivist presuppositions, claiming *absolute* understanding. And finally, as Erickson notes, Wells actually seems to embrace one aspect of postmodernism with

199. See the full discussion on Wells's views in Erickson, *Postmodernizing the Faith*, 23–41.

200. Erickson, *Postmodernizing the Faith*, 38.

his community approach to truth, yet lacks a practical solution for his call to return to objective truth.[201]

This example perhaps reflects the difficulties involved in attempting to incorporate a community- or tradition-based epistemology into an otherwise strongly individualistic paradigm. It should be readily admitted that the task of integrating is never easy, and in the case of evangelical thought, is likely to be rather slow going, on a rough track, for many who have long-ridden the rails of modernism and Enlightenment epistemology. On a more positive note, some scholars are taking a different route via the trail of postmodern epistemology, while sidestepping several potential theological difficulties along the way. This primarily postconservative move requires careful deliberation.

Some Evangelical Theology Appropriations of Postmodern Epistemology: Returning to Tradition and Opinio

As we introduced earlier, an increasing number of mostly younger evangelical thinkers are readily acknowledging that commitments to historical, cultural, and communal contexts deeply condition human knowledge—including knowledge of God. Facilitating change in the theological agenda, the work of these scholars is becoming increasingly instrumental in guiding the larger evangelical intellectual community toward the vision of a promising (or renewed) evangelical epistemology.

Theologian Stanley Grenz, for instance, strongly criticizes what he sees as an unwarranted reliance on Cartesian epistemology among evangelical theologians. Nonetheless, he also warns against reacting too radically against such an approach:

> [W]e dare not entirely lose the emphasis on the importance of the individual human person indicative of modernity. Indeed, we must always keep in view the biblical themes of God's concern for each person, the responsibility of every human before God, and the individual oriention that lies within the salvation message.[202]

Grenz states that, furthermore, "the twentieth-century examples of totalitarianism are stark reminders that we must continually stand against the tyranny of the collective in all its various forms."[203]

---

201. Ibid., 39–40.
202. Grenz, *Primer on Postmodernism*, 167–68.
203. Ibid., 168.

In discussing this (re)new(ed) role for tradition within evangelical thought, it will be helpful to consider the work of three postconservative scholars—Stanley Grenz, Kevin Vanhoozer, and Robert Webber—whose approaches to theological knowledge recognize and incorporate the formative nature of tradition and community.[204] Taken together, it seems plausible that their views represent a significant number of postconservative intellectuals, and therefore ought to provide a preliminarily glimpse into the shared perspective of the movement in relation to the knowledge of God.[205] It is only hoped that their views are fairly and accurately represented herein. We begin with Stanley Grenz.

STANLEY GRENZ

Echoing the perspective of a growing group of postconservative thinkers, Grenz seeks to move evangelical theology in a *communitarian* direction.[206] He affirms that "we must shake ourselves loose from the radical individualism that has come to characterize the modern mind-set. We must affirm with postmodern thinkers that knowledge—including knowledge of God—is not merely objective, not simply discovered by the neutral knowing self."[207] Descartes' method, according to Grenz, has resulting in several unfortunate outcomes for evangelical theology, especially related to the virtual setting aside of the value of tradition, often looked at askance by evangelicals. He thinks that there were many problems created for Christian theology by Cartesianism, with traditionalists continuing to carry forward a number of Descartes' epistemological inaccuracies.[208] Instead, evangelicals ought to move away from many Cartesian assumptions, and as Grenz views it, toward more postmodern—and biblical—ones. For instance, he

204. The three representative scholars were chosen based on their scholarship, accessible writing, wide influence within evangelicalism, commitment to the gospel, and evident passion for their ideas.

The recent passing of both Grenz and Webber is a tremendous loss for the whole Christian community on earth; both celebration for their work and lament for their absence continues to be expressed within evangelical scholarship, especially among postconservatives.

205. For an overview of several major trends among younger evangelicals, see the section above entitled, "Three Major Areas of Evolvement among Younger and Postconservative Evangelicals: History, Theology, Apologetics," beginning on page 129.

206. Grenz, *Primer on Postmodernism*, 168.

207. Ibid.

208. See Grenz's discussion on Descartes, foundationalism, and the resulting liberal-fundamentalist dichotomy, as well as his proposal for a way forward for evangelical theological method in *Renewing the Center*, passim.

suggests de-emphasizing the modern stress on individualism to support the communitarian view of "the individual-within-community":[209]

> Communitarians point out the unavoidable role of the community or social network in the life of the human person. For example, they affirm that the community is essential in the process of knowing. Individuals come to knowledge only by way of a cognitive framework mediated by the community in which they participate. Similarly, the community of participation is crucial to identity formation. A sense of personal identity develops through the telling of a personal narrative, which is always embedded in the story of the communities in which we participate. The community mediates to its members a transcendent story that includes traditions of virtue, common good, and ultimate meaning.[210]

Grenz then exhorts his readers to take seriously the contemporary communitarian findings, because "they are echoing the great biblical theme that the goal of God's program is the establishment of community in the highest sense." Not only is this God's goal for a future community of faith, but also reflects God's own person since "God is the social Trinity —Father, Son, and Spirit."[211]

Call for a communitarian emphasis is balanced by declaring that it is "personal encounter with God in Christ that shapes and molds us" and is "both facilitated by and expressed in categories that are propositional in nature," but which should not focus attention on propositions *per se*, but rather on leading others into relationship with God in Christ.[212] Conduct, virtue, and "wisdom for living so that we might please God with our lives" demands a "post-noeticentric" articulation of the gospel.[213] Even theological knowledge must focus on the purpose of fostering "wisdom (or spirituality) in the knower" and moving beyond merely intellectual endeavors to matters of the heart and "transformation of character."[214]

This methodology may provide the evangelical scholarly community with a two-pronged contribution: first, a necessary corrective to overstressed *cognitive* or *propositional* knowledge that effectively minimizes

---

209. Grenz, *Primer on Postmodernism*, 168.

210. Ibid.

211. Ibid.

212. Ibid., 170–71.

213. Ibid., 172–74.

214. Ibid., 172–73.

emotive and volitional aspects in favor of a more holistic emphasis that acknowledges the embeddedness of reason and experience within tradition and community; second, a reminder of the biblical concern for Christian virtue and practice.

A *balanced* approach to epistemology, Grenz insists, is vital—one that respects both the significance of every individual made in the *imago dei* and the particular social contexts to which individuals collectively belong.[215] This holistic approach would thus serve to protect from a radical individualism that is "untouched" by historical and contextual factors, while simultaneously retaining the singular importance and undiminished value of each person.[216]

215. For instance, these contexts may include (beginning with the larger) belonging to the twenty-first-century Christian church; then to evangelicalism; then to a particular denominational or nondenominational body; then to the local church of the larger denomination or nondenomination; then to additional smaller communities within one's local church (e.g., a recovery group). All such "networks" would thus necessarily be composed within the larger culture and contextual setting (e.g., the United States, then California, Southern California, Pasadena, etc.).

216. Problems associated with depersonalization of the individual in favor of focusing on a tangential theological stance were clearly brought home to me immediately following the terrorist attacks upon the World Trade Center and the Pentagon. One particular fundamentalist community to which I remain in somewhat indirect social contact (and from which a theological "divorce" over numerous issues has ensued over the past decade, e.g., eschatological views), displayed via certain of its pastors, leaders, and congregants how inexcusable an individually- and communally-impersonal response to such a crisis can be. Rather than demonstrating material concern for those devastated by the tragedies of 9/11, the book of Revelation was marshaled to provide analysis on the horrifying events—events said to point to the next step in the "End Times" scenario coming to pass *in our lifetime.* Far from a compassionate, *personal* response by the community of believers attending this particular local congregation (estimated to have 35,000 attendees—there is no membership), the setting was used to pronounce an *impersonal* judgment upon the entire Islamic religion and all its Muslim adherents, and as an opportunity to "witness" concerning this "truth" to "non-believers" who are asking *why* the evil acts had been committed. The fact that thousands of innocent victims had been murdered, and their families devastated, scarcely entered into the pulpit or interpersonal conversations—at least initially. The focus instead was directed toward where this cataclysmic event (or its correlatives) might be found in the book of Revelation, or what next phase in the move toward the Great Tribulation period might entail. One wonders whether this response was indicative of the personal irresponsibility and corporate anti-intellectualism preached and practiced among the faithful there, beginning with the pastors and teachers, or whether it has more to do with a modernist attempt to bring together a completely comprehendible picture of the state of affairs from an Archimedean vantage point in reaction to the apparent chaos of the situation. Maybe a bifurcation here is unnecessary, and a Hegelian synthesis of the two theories might best explain the rather neurotic religious culture evident to few participants within the community, yet apparent to many external eyewitnesses.

Perhaps most daring and directly important for our study, Grenz calls for fellow evangelicals to include *culture* as a source for theology.[217] Theological method is to employ "an interactive process that is both correlative and contextual," in which theology emerges from "an ongoing conversation" that involves gospel and culture.[218] Grenz also takes seriously the work of the Spirit in culture:

> Because the life-giving Creator Spirit is present wherever life flourishes, the Spirit's voice can conceivably resound through many media, including the media of human culture. Because Spirit-induced human flourishing evokes cultural expression, we can anticipate in such expressions traces of the Creator Spirit's presence.[219]

Still, there is the primacy of the text to be upheld since "hearing the Spirit in the text provides the only sure canon for hearing the Spirit in culture, because the Spirit's speaking everywhere and anywhere is always in concert with this primary speaking through the text."[220]

Finally in this model, the church is to be understood as a culture itself, using its own language, symbols, and other expressions arising from its being united in its "fundamental commitment to the God revealed in Christ."[221] Theology's task is to critically reflect on and evaluate the community's practices, but in so doing, says Grenz,

> we must avoid a foundationalist approach that starts with some complete whole as a given reality which theologians in turn simply explicate or on which they erect the theological knowledge edifice. Rather, the constructive task of theology emerges out of the process of give and take, as participants in the community converse over their shared cultural meanings as connected to the symbols they hold in common as Christians.[222]

KEVIN VANHOOZER

In his contributing chapter for *Evangelical Futures*, Kevin Vanhoozer presents his highly nuanced proviso for a critical adaptation of certain

---

217. Grenz and Franke, *Beyond Foundationalism*, 130–66.

218. Ibid., 158.

219. Ibid., 162.

220. Ibid., 162–63.

221. Ibid., 164.

222. Ibid., 165–66.

postmodern epistemological insights by evangelicals.[223] In short, he argues that the *authority* for theological knowledge is—based on a dramatic model—the divine communication act of the gospel. Yet, the interpretive communities of various Christian traditions are significant *participants* in the structuring and interpretation of that divine drama. Explaining his goal of providing a "hermeneutical theology," he speaks of his aim as being

> to propose what an evangelical theology with a postfoundationalist Scripture principle, and with one ear cocked to the postmodern condition, should look like. . . . The hallmarks of such a theology include performative understanding and creative fidelity. Evangelical theology is a matter of "joyful faith seeking creative understanding" of the Word and Act of God.[224]

Vanhoozer's approach invokes a *canonical-linguistic* model, a method that makes much use of speech-act theory. He claims that this differs significantly from a cultural-linguistic schema like that used by George Lindbeck, which, Vanhoozer asserts, holds central not the canon of scripture but the interpretive community. To make the distinction clearer still, Vanhoozer notes that his "postpropositionist theology" is "better described as postconservative rather than postliberal," since his view focuses

> on the communicative practices of the canon, rather than those of the interpreting community, as the primary locus of the meaning and truth of Christian faith. While meaning may well be a matter of use rather than reference, the authoritative uses of terms such as *God, grace,* and *salvation* are those of the biblical authors, not its readers.[225]

Vanhoozer also points to the centrality of *wisdom* in the knowing process—wisdom being "the ability (which includes knowing but is not limited to knowing) to say or do the right thing in a specific situation."[226] The term Vanhoozer settles on is *phronesis*, an Aristotelian term for moral reasoning in life situations: practical reason or prudence. Noting that the scriptures display a theological *phronesis* embedded in various forms and genres (e.g., epistle, law, narrative), Vanhoozer's thesis is that "theological wisdom and understanding are formed through an apprenticeship to the

223. See Vanhoozer, "Voice and the Actor."
224. Vanhoozer, "Voice and the Actor," 69.
225. Ibid., 77.
226. Ibid., 81–82. See also Wood, *Epistemology.*

biblical texts," and that the "practices that should inform and transform evangelical theology are therefore those of what we might call the 'society of biblical literature.'"[227]

Attempting to strike a balance between a rejection of the "lonely itinerary" of the individual Christian as normative, and a denial of ultimate authority to the interpretive community, Vanhoozer proposes a three-stranded epistemology: loosely conversant with the categories of creation, fall, and redemption. These "cords" consist of 1) right cognitive function—reliabilism, 2) right spiritual relations—the virtues, and 3) sanctification and scholarship—relative to "fallibilism and other fruits."[228] So one may ask, What is the relevance of social epistemology in this model? Vanhoozer explains that

> the understanding performance that constitutes good theology must be corporate in nature. The church is to be a "hermeneutic" of the gospel. The diversity of churches is therefore to be seen in terms of different interpretive traditions. The variety of ecclesial traditions represent so many "masterpiece theatres." And behind every theatrical tradition there is usually a "great performance"— the theology of an Augustine or a Luther or a Calvin. There is value in learning how to participate in the drama of redemption through participating in these venerable companies, so long as one remembers that the ultimate aim is creative fidelity not to an interpreter or to an interpretive tradition but to the divine drama and its script.[229]

Thus, within a particular community, according to Vanhoozer, the task of the theologian involves instructing the community

> in what constitutes a fitting understanding of the faith and to monitor the integrity of its subsequent performance. In so doing, the theologian formulates the wisdom implicit in the community's practices and reforms the community's practice in light of the wisdom implicit in the canonical practices of its authoritative script. In brief, the theologian is to articulate and reflect back to the community what the community really is in Christ. If and when the reality of Jesus Christ contradicts the current beliefs and practice of

227. Vanhoozer, "Voice and the Actor," 82.

228. Vanhoozer, "Voice and the Actor," 87–88.

229. Ibid., 105.

the community, then the theologian must play the fool, the "fool for Christ."[230]

Vanhoozer's canonical-linguistic theology thus advocates a dramatic approach to the knowledge of God, with primary concentration on God's self-revelation in acting and speaking in the Bible—a theological drama.[231] His model reflects clear appreciation for God's revelation to, and covenant with, humankind as recorded in scripture, reaching "its fullest expression in Jesus Christ."[232] The combination of "God's speaking to the readers in and through the biblical text, and the readers' subsequent responses"[233] captures both the divine and human sides of the problem of theological knowledge; while God has self-revealed and the word of God has been addressing humanity, human participants in the drama of redemption (and reading) must response properly—i.e., in terms of relationship and obedient. "Communication action" is central to Vanhoozer's biblical revelation model as it concerns God's self-disclosure: "God does things in speaking and *thereby* reveals himself."[234]

Vanhoozer's model incorporates the idea of *phronesis* or practical reason (i.e., wisdom) with reference to comprehending the biblical communication through different genres, and the necessary "apprenticeship to biblical texts" in order to make correct theological evaluations.[235] Apparently, his emphasis is similar to that of the New Testament concern for obedient living and moral conduct in response to hearing and accepting the *kerygma*—especially as it relates to the realization of knowledge (theological and otherwise) for purposes of wisdom and edification.

230. Ibid. Affirming the importance and value of Christian community and tradition, one still gets the idea that for Vanhoozer the focus remains on the individual theologian, rather than the company of theologians within a tradition (or even across various traditions) working together. This is in no way to infer a reduction in the value of one's giftedness and service to a particular interpretive community of faith: only to point out what looks to be a continued emphasis on the sufficiency of working *solo* (albeit with God's wisdom and grace). It seems that many evangelical thinkers (myself included) have far to go in terms of something akin to, say, Bernard Lonergan's plea for an integrative method that incorporates a variety of theologians, philosophers, and other leaders working together to provide a more corporate theological atmosphere and outcome (see Lonergan, *Method in Theology*).

231. Vanhoozer, "Voice and the Actor," 63–64.

232. Ibid., 64.

233. Ibid., 65.

234. Ibid., 70.

235. Ibid., 84.

Moreover, Vanhoozer is sensitive to, and in parallel with, the clarity of scripture respecting the *personal* dimension of salvific knowledge of God:

> God calls individuals; it is as individuals that we are united to Christ. We do not enter the church of Jesus Christ by being born into it so much as by answering a personal call. "Communion with God in Christ comes first, communion with others second." Let's not forget the lesson that Kierkegaard sought to convey to his age, namely, that persons cannot hide behind or surrender their individual responsibility to the collective, even if that collective is the Christian community.[236]

Individual responsibility, according to Vanhoozer, also touches biblical interpretation of the knowledge of God, being "a matter of right cognitive contact *and* of right covenantal relation, and not of mere information only," which corresponds to the biblical concept of theological knowledge as personal, covenantal relationship with God as Lord.[237]

Combining theology and drama (pace Hans Urs von Balthasar's *Theodrama*), Vanhoozer's model is both imaginative and biblically based, and may serve as a useful paradigm for evangelical scholars concerned with remaining faithful to the biblical record on knowledge of God, while engaging postmodern emphases on linguistics, play, symbol, participation, and mystery. In Vanhoozer's own words,

> The nature of doctrine is . . . directional: Doctrine is instruction ("direction") concerning one's fitting participation in the drama of redemption. Theology, like the Scriptures themselves, aims to communicate "the wisdom that leads to salvation" (2 Tim. 3:15 NASB). And salvation itself may helpfully be viewed as the process of being incorporated into the divine life of the Triune God. The dramatic action includes both a "going out" (incarnation) and a "coming back" (resurrection). The ultimate aim of doctrine, then, is not simply to "picture" the divine drama but to incorporate more players into it.[238]

ROBERT WEBBER

While Grenz and Vanhoozer include the crucial importance of the social for epistemology, Robert Webber *centers* on it. Webber, a former funda-

---

236. Ibid., 86. Internal quotation is of Dalzell, "Lack of Social Drama," 462.
237. Vanhoozer, "Voice and the Actor," 87.
238. Ibid., 93.

mentalist and son-in-law of Harold Lindsell, embraces what he terms a
"classical Christianity" approach, intending to bring sociology of knowledge to epistemic center stage with his theological method. Webber's move
results in part from his awareness and acceptance of significant postmodern
developments. He refers to the "communication revolution" birthed after
1950, which paralleled developments in science and philosophy, noting
the significant changes in vocabulary with respect to knowledge and the
contemporary emphasis on *partaking*:

> In the modern world communication occurred primarily through
> conceptual knowledge. Words that dominated the ways of know-
> ing were "reading"; "writing"; "intelligence"; "analysis"; "clarity";
> "explanation"; "logic"; and "linear sequence." The new postmod-
> ern shape of community has shifted to a more symbolic form. It is
> knowledge gained through participation in community. The new
> words are "the primacy of experience"; "knowledge through im-
> mersed participation"; the "impact of the visual" such as atmo-
> sphere, environment, and space; the rediscovery of "imagination,"
> "intuition," and a sensitivity to "spiritual realities". . . . The shift of
> postmodern communications to the power of symbolic communi-
> cation is a call to return to the classical period when the church was
> an embodied experience of God expressed in life-changing rituals
> of immersed participation.[239]

Moving outside conventional conservative evangelical reflection,
Webber collapses the structural linkage between Christianity and modernism, boldly treading into a postmodern vision of knowledge and
faith. Yet, according to Webber, this move has nothing to do with "rein-
venting" Christianity. Rather, it is an attempt to "restore and then adapt
classical Christianity to the postmodern cultural situation."[240] He avers
the *premodern* church period as *the most productive,* having been "shaped
by mystery, holism, interpreted facts, community, and a combination of
verbal and symbolic forms of communication."[241] This is what Webber
optimistically envisions for the future of evangelicalism and its approach
to theological knowledge.

Apostolic epistemology and *the rule of faith* are central elements of
Robert Webber's tradition-oriented classical Christianity approach to evan-

---

239. Webber, *Ancient-Future Faith*, 24.
240. Ibid.
241. Ibid.

gelical theology.[242] His postmodern vision of knowledge and faith heavily draws upon the practices of the ancient (i.e., apostolic) Christian community, and its emphasis on the center of Christian faith—"Jesus Christ, God incarnate for our salvation."[243] Webber believes that for theological epistemology, contemporary sociology of knowledge methods best reflect the biblical vision of both human noetic limitations and the authoritative rule of faith entrusted to protégés of the Way.

The role of scripture regarding knowledge of God is one of authority, in part due to the New Testament writings serving as a central element of apostolic epistemology that includes "oral tradition, reflected in the liturgy and the rule of faith, and the written tradition, in which the liturgy and the rule are embedded."[244] Thus, for Webber, epistemological authority is composed of "the intertwining of the grand tapestry of faith rooted in Christ and the authority of apostolic interpretation."[245] His *nonfoundationalist, holistic, web of belief model* attempts to obviate an ahistorical, non-participatory, and reason-oriented individualistic approach to theological knowledge. It aims at the narrative history of the church, its "community rules," and its center, Jesus Christ.

Webber's theological method would seem to deserve appreciation, if for no other reason, because of his rootedness in the totality of apostolic practices within the nascent church, including its committing to recording the word of God, culminating in the authoritative New Testament scriptures. He views the New Testament as *part of* the broader "process of the development of authority within the developing tradition of the church" which the Holy Spirit "oversaw."[246] For example, Webber believes that "the Scriptures were written for the church and were to be read in worship. They contain the authoritative accounts of Christ together with the apostolic interpretation of Christ. Thus Scripture is tradition; that is, it hands over Jesus Christ."[247] This is a rather unusual move for an evangelical; but then again, Webber seeks to broaden evangelical theology beyond certain "boundaries" with his classical Christianity paradigm.

242. See Webber, *Ancient-Future Faith*.

243. Ibid., 185. Of course, Webber does not exhaustively embrace the postmodern rejection of metanarratives; he strongly affirms the universality of the gospel narrative.

244. Ibid.,186.

245. Ibid.

246. Ibid., 182.

247. Ibid., 181–82.

Webber's theological epistemology also endeavors to capture the *spirit* of the apostolic period, i.e., the work of the Holy Spirit within the Christian community as a testimony to the truth of the self-revelation of God in Christ. Similarly to Grenz, he discerns the Bible's emphasis on Christian *praxis*, especially the New Testament concern for following the apostolic tradition and being obedient disciples of the Way. Assuming that his emphasis on the communal aspects of participating in the life of faith and the knowledge of God also retains the *individual* dimension so manifest in scripture, it seems that Webber's approach attempts to strike a balance in its effort to communicate the good news of truth in Jesus Christ. In addition, his work stresses *immersed participation* in the community of faith, as well as *embodied reality* as the way forward for experiencing Christian truth, while presumably preserving propositional truth regarding theological knowledge.

Webber's tradition-oriented model also has a distinct *authority* for theological knowledge: the "tradition handed down to the apostles." This is composed of the apostolic social community of the early church, and the faith—including theological knowledge—passed down "through oral preaching and teaching, through the written gospel accounts and letters, and through the appointment of their successors, the bishops."[248] Webber notes that the rule of faith emerged in cities across the Roman Empire and was regarded as "a summary of the salient features of the Christian faith; a framework of the essential truths confessed by those who stood in the tradition of apostolic teachings."[249] He then connects the idea of the rule of faith with "holding out promise of a framework of faith in a postmodern world. It is a rule that functions for us in what Lindbeck refers to as those 'communally authoritative rules of discourse, attitude, and action.'"[250]

After describing Lindbeck's identification of the ancient *regula fidei* as "intratextuality," Webber declares that the Christian faith cannot be known experientially or proven evidentially "outside itself through the scientific method." His fideistic approach centers on the issues of trust, belief, and willingness to "step inside its story apart from any dependence on historical, scientific, or rational persuasion."[251] Modernist

---

248. Ibid., 176.
249. Ibid.
250. Ibid., 184.
251. Ibid., 185.

evangelical theologians will likely disavow this move as purely presuppositionalist, anti-evidentialist apologetics or Kierkegaardian fideism. Yet, such assessments would miss the point. Rather than seeking a reason-centered epistemology that will lead one to pure propositionalism and nonparticipatory observation and judgments, Webber views his method as centered in the narrative history of the church and the community's "rules" for theological knowledge:

> The rule of faith is the rule, the perimeter within which the community talks about its belief system. What stands at the very center of Christian faith is Jesus Christ, God incarnate for our salvation. This conviction regulates all discussions of faith and functions as the primary rule of the Christian community. For this rule derives not from human invention, but from the inspiration of the Holy Spirit given to the apostles who have handed these truths down to the church. Because the rule of faith was formed at the same time that the apostolic writings were being collected, it precedes the scriptural canon in time and functions as the key to the interpretation of Scripture. Anyone, for example, who espouses a doctrine that conflicts with the rule of faith, misinterprets Scripture.[252]

Hence, a cultural-linguistic model, with emphasis on learning the language of the community, may effectively serve evangelical theology in providing an epistemological basis for the Christian faith—based on the authoritative rule of faith and the apostolic tradition handed down to the succeeding generations of followers of Jesus Christ, the wisdom of God.[253] Such a model is attractive, especially considering the postmodern cultural emphasis on community, authenticity, and praxis as it pertains to claim of knowledge and truth. An *exclusive* focus on evidences or a modernist use of the scientific method to "prove" the veracity of the gospel of Jesus Christ is simply unable to credibly or convincingly present the Christian faith and its central message in the changing "after modernity" cultural context.[254]

252. Ibid.

253. "Christ the power of God and the wisdom of God" (1 Cor 1:24c).

254. What is not intended in this statement is an outright *rejection* of the *use* of Christian apologetics, and its subset, evidences. The Christian faith *is* an *historical* faith, as well as a *praxis-* and *existentially-*oriented one, meaning that a presentation of the faith to the world is to encompass a holistic approach. Therefore, to disregard the historical life, death, and resurrection of Jesus Christ—as testified to by *historical* individuals and the *historical* community of faith—is to demythologize (*pace* Bultmann) the historical

Finally, Webber believes that the renewed focus on the importance of unity, spirituality, worship, and involvement in the lives of others evident within postmodern culture means, for evangelical theology, a positive return to "apostolic epistemology." The following quote displays an evangelical commitment to a holistic, tradition-oriented (theological) knowledge that, for some evangelicals—especially postconservatives, postmoderns, and postliberals—helps set the agenda for future epistemic paradigms:

> Apostolic epistemology includes the oral tradition, reflected in the liturgy and the rule of faith, and the written tradition, in which the liturgy and the rule are embedded. To separate these sources of authority is a mistake. The liturgy celebrates the apostolic tradition; the Scriptures are the authoritative apostolic writings. There is one truth, Jesus Christ, one source of truthful interpretation, the apostles. The work of the church is to preserve and hand down this apostolic witness. In this sense, Scripture, tradition, and authority are not three distinct subjects, but the intertwining of the grand tapestry of faith rooted in Christ and the authority of apostolic interpretation.[255]

In the end, Webber is suggesting a theological model that encourages evangelicals to understand the knowledge of God as the church being (or becoming once again) the "metaphysical presence" of God on earth, grounded in Jesus Christ and apostolic epistemology. This paradigm holds that theological knowledge is *constituted* in the ecclesia, and actualized as a result of "immersed participation" of its members. Such an embodied truth—based on the living Christ and the authority of apostolic interpretation—deserves recognition as part of a more holistic evangelical theological epistemology.

---

interpretive community for an *ahistorical* modernist view alleging indubitable certainty of late-nineteenth to early-twentieth-century European Existentialist scholarship. This method amounts to what Helmut Thielicke referred to as *a theology of accommodation*. My point is that using evidences in the role of apologetics is not a worthless endeavor, but in a postmodern culture that emphasizing the role of interpretation of facts and shaping contextual influences, evidences ought not take *center stage* in the apologetical process; rather evidences should be employed as *complements* to the broader task of demonstrating the veracity of Christian faith. Moreover, apologetics itself must also be conducted within the larger framework of Christian praxis, theologizing, and philosophizing based on the historical approach of biblical proclamation as truth ("a theology of actualization") *within community*—Christian community. Only then will the church most effectively engage the *external* community.

255. Webber, *Ancient-Future Faith*, 186.

It seems feasible that Webber's theology—like the theologies of Luther, Calvin, and Barth—serves as a *necessary corrective* to the wedding of evangelical theology with dominant philosophies of the age. It ought to be remembered, though, that Webber's own paradigm is subject to the possibility of an unhappy marriage as well: in his case, postmodern philosophies that underestimate—or even seek to eliminate—the role of human reason as an over-reaction to modernity's primary emphasis. [256] Nonetheless, his commitment to weighing personal theological opinions "up against the universal faith of the church," testing them by the "witness of the Holy Spirit in the church" and "universality, antiquity, and consensus" in submission to the "communal authority of the church's teachings" [257] is refreshingly innovative while traditionally grounded.

Conclusion

The crucial insights provided by Grenz, Vanhoozer, and Webber have served to call evangelical scholarship beyond traditional approaches to theological knowledge—even beyond a broader Quadrilateral model—encouraging integration of culture, *phronesis*, and ecclesia as essential sources in a holistic approach to the knowledge of God. Many postconservatives are likely to welcome this development, viewing it as indicative of the need for evangelicalism to reach beyond its own tradition for constructive ideas considering the postmodern context.

Hence, all three of these evangelical reformists are calling for evangelical theology to adopt particular postmodern epistemological insights. Their methods vary—sometimes considerably—yet each grasps the important shaping influence that tradition and community exert in human comprehension and articulation of knowledge and truth. Clear differences exist across the evangelical spectrum as to *how* and *why* this postmodern restoration of *opinio* ought to impact Christian theology. Nonetheless, some shared viewpoints respecting common and crucial elements may be delineated.

First, there is manifest concern for retaining the authority of scripture. The primacy of place is reserved for the church's inspired and uniquely

---

256. To Webber's credit, it should be noted that he is well aware of the *human garb* of cultural categories that influences theological interpretation (see, for instance, *Ancient-Future Faith*, 197–201).

257. Webber, *Ancient-Future Faith*, 194.

written word. However, what is manifestly absent is a *sola scriptura* emphasis; rather, epistemic considerations are viewed more broadly, incorporating additional theological sources for knowledge of God (e.g., tradition, reason, experience) as we see evident with the Quadrilateral framework. While seeking to present the everlasting gospel in ever-changing cultural garb, the reformist intellectuals we discussed appear to have maintained the highest respect for evangelicalism's foremost authoritative source for theological knowledge—the written word of God. Regardless of their distinctive approaches, each embraces the importance of the Bible for theological knowledge, supporting our argument in favor of the need to study the data of scripture to comprehend what it communicates respective of the knowledge of God. These authors exhibit clear correspondence with the biblical writings as it pertains to theological knowledge.

There is little doubt that evangelical theology will retain the scriptures as the primary interpretive source of theological knowledge; albeit in some cases this may entail reading and reasoning about it *in community*, or via the interpretation within the community's tradition. Thus, biblically-centered theological knowledge is perhaps best viewed as *concrete participation* in the interpretive community—one's own, as well as in a *fusion of horizons* with the apostolic community. The necessarily corrective nature of theology—i.e., rescuing scripture and its witness to the knowledge of God from otherwise inseparable marriages to philosophies and worldviews of every era—bodes well for postconservative thinkers. Furthermore, the evidence appears compelling as to postconservative views corresponding to the knowledge of God panorama as revealed in the biblical canon, as well as in Christian tradition and community.

Second, there is passionate concern for evangelical *praxis* as part of their epistemological vision—not just individual, but also corporate praxis. For instance, Vanhoozer focuses on the parochial role of the theologian in helping the community to reflect Christ as they ought, which sends a clear message that evangelical theology must *practice* what it teaches; what it teaches must be bound up with theological and practical *phronesis*. Mere disengaged reflection, as Webber underscores, neglects the postmodern language, science, and communication revolution. Only a renewed focus on the value of unity, spirituality, worship, and involvement in the lives of others will minister to the postmodern culture, and provide the means for evangelical theology to return to its "apostolic epistemology." Obviously, this emphasis on praxis from an evangelical perspective coincides with the *experience* element of the Quadrilateral, at least in some understandings of it, particularly conceptions more closely associated with Wesley's use of the term when referring to the "conferences" and spiritual pilgrimages of Christians.

Next, there is commitment to a more inclusive theology—one that centers on the *essentials* (e.g., "Jesus is Lord") rather than peripheral or denominational matters (e.g., modes of baptism). This turn to a more generous orthodoxy is especially represented by Grenz and Webber, as they recognize the need for Christian unity in the midst of—and in answer to—postmodern cultural fragmentation and chaos. Here we see *reason* being given an important role in the process of determining important theological matters from within the Christian community. Reason, then, is working—not only here, but alongside each of the Quadrilateral sources for theology—to aid in the effort to increase in our knowledge of the faith, including knowledge of God.

Still, the question remains as to whether evangelical scholars must *limit* their sources for theological knowledge to merely those of the Quadrilateral. Are there additional ways of understanding the knowledge of God? Does not scripture itself point to several further possibilities? And what is to be gained—or lost—if evangelical theology presses beyond the Quadrilateral?

Going beyond the usual "boundaries" of evangelical thought to offer a commendable paradigm for theological method and its epistemology is the focus of the next section of our study. Lesslie Newbigin's approach to theological knowledge is that which we will be commending for evangelical theology. Newbigin's work, along with some broader aspects of his life, will be considered at some length with hopes of presenting evangelicals—postconservatives and interested others—a first-rate alternative to traditionalist, and even Quadrilateral-type approaches to the knowledge of God.

4

Lesslie Newbigin's Theological Epistemology

A Commendable Paradigm for Evangelical Theology

Introduction

SEEKING AN IDEAL THEOLOGICAL EPISTEMOLOGY PARADIGM FOR EVAN-
gelical thought would seem to be an impossible assignment, given the
substantially different proposals defended by traditionalists and reformists. Nevertheless, amidst this sometimes-contentious atmosphere, it can
be productive at least to look for a mediating voice, one that is familiar
with the range of evangelical approaches to theology and epistemology,
and is concerned to facilitate authentic unity among the multivocal perspectives: at the least, a voice that is able to generate a more conciliatory
understanding.

While several possible mediating voices within familiar evangelical
academia were considered for this present task, the decision was made
to look somewhat beyond the familial arena. This voice, while unques-
tionably evangelical in doctrine and mission, is perhaps more recognized
among the broader church body than by evangelicals. A careful look
at the career of Lesslie Newbigin (1909–98), as spelled out in Geoffrey
Wainwright's recent biography,[1] reveals a broad ministry: perhaps something more expected from a team of energetic people. Hence, it will be
helpful—especially since he explored many of the same issues being raised
by North American postconservatives—to consider Newbigin's contributions to evangelical theological method and epistemology.

---

1. Wainwright, *Lesslie Newbigin.* I will be making use of Wainwright's text throughout
this chapter, and it should be understood that when citing or quoting Newbigin from
Wainwright, much of the material exists in unpublished works or in personal conversations
between Wainwright and Newbigin.

Before moving ahead with analysis of Newbigin's approach to the knowledge of God, we will first consider the larger landscape of his life, thought, and ministry that provides the critically important context for his theological and missiological developments, leading to more specific epistemological considerations for evangelical theology.[2]

Newbigin's Intellectual and Theological Development

Born in the first decade of the twentieth century, Newbigin entered life well before many modern technologies and conveniences were either invented (e.g., television) or introduced (e.g., plumbing) to his milieu of Northumbria, England. His early spiritual and intellectual formation occurred within the Presbyterian Church of England and through his studies at Cambridge. Before university, he attended boarding school, where he first moved away from the religious roots instilled by his parents to a historical and scientific determinism, then on to a human "progress" and "mastery of life" perspective. However, the combined influences of William James's book *The Will to Believe* and an apologetical work by a friend of the family and Presbyterian minister, managed to keep him from viewing Christianity as merely an irrational fideism.[3]

Studying at Queen's College, Cambridge, Newbigin was initiated into the theological liberalism of his day, educated to believe in broad and pluralistic views concerning God. On this view, the Bible merely contained subjective reflections of people claiming religious experiences universally felt by adherents of all religious traditions. Christ was not viewed as God incarnate or as accomplishing an atonement for sin on the cross. These were mythical stories devised to encourage early members of the Christian sect. He was also taught that there existed no knowable objective acts of

---

2. While an attempt will be made in the following section to provide a brief but panoramic view of the life and work of Lesslie Newbigin, the focus of this work precludes substantial investigation outside theological and epistemological concerns. Moreover, this has already been masterfully accomplished in large measure in Wainwright's *Lesslie Newbigin*. I am deeply indebted to (and grateful for) the accomplishment of Wainwright's superbly-written theological biography on his friend and co-laborer in Christ.

3. Newbigin, *Proper Confidence*, 59–60. Newbigin also notes (positively) the importance of Martin Buber's *I and Thou* in providing him, along with many others of his generation, with "crucial insights that made it possible to come to Christian faith." However, Newbigin also points out (negatively) the unfortunate false separation that the distinction between two kinds of knowing (made by Buber) could lead to, since it is impossible to "isolate a personal relationship from its actual context."

God—for instance, the Resurrection—that could be looked to for faith: instead, one ought to focus on the subjective, experiential, and ethical realms as suitable foundations for faith. However, Newbigin made friendships within the Student Christian Movement (SCM) and soon began his re-examination of the Christian faith.

His claim to being granted an actual vision of the cross gave him hope and energy as he joined evangelistic outreaches and began participating in what he viewed as a worldwide Christian movement that was taking place among devoted, spiritual, and intellectual believers. Those like John R. Mott, widely acknowledged as the father of the modern ecumenical movement, deeply influenced Newbigin toward an *ecumenical* Christian faith. Only a year after the cross vision and after hearing an unexpected call, he began a journey toward ordained ministry. Upon completing his theological studies at Westminster College, Cambridge, in 1936, he was ordained. That summer he was married and with his wife, left for missionary service with the Church of Scotland, in India.[4]

Newbigin experienced a theological crisis during studies at Westminster College in 1933. His study of the Letter to the Romans proved decisive in the transition:

> That was a turning point in my theological journey. I began the study as a typical liberal. I ended with a strong conviction about "the finished work of Christ", about the centrality and objectivity of the atonement accomplished on Calvary. . . . At the end of the exercise I was much more of an *evangelical* than a liberal.[5]

Thus, by the mid-1930s, Newbigin had abandoned his theological liberalism and embraced a theology that was both conservative and evangelical.[6] The influence of Scottish theologian James Denney was pivotal for his new perspective.[7] Nevertheless, the shaping liberalism of his early

4. Newbigin married Helen Henderson, one of the committee members who hired Newbigin as SCM staff secretary (a job he sought in order to pay for his theological training). Helen's own parents had been missionaries (Irish Presbyterians) to India (see Wainwright, *Lesslie Newbigin*, 4).

5. Newbigin, *Unfinished Agenda*, 29. Emphasis mine.

6. "Conservative" defined as adhering to historic doctrines of the Christian faith, such as found in the early Creeds of the church; "evangelical" broadly defined in terms of being both theologically conservative (e.g., with respect to sin, salvation, grace, and faith) and engaged in furthering the message and mission of the *evangel* (and in Newbigin's case, unassociated with separatist fundamentalism).

7. Denney, professor of systematic and pastoral theology at Free Church College

theological education would make him more aware of its powerful influence, which he would encounter for many years, including within the later World Council of Churches (WCC). These experiences gave him particularly incisive comprehension and articulation of liberal theology, and even more importantly, a powerful polemic against its various assertions (e.g., the idea of the inherent goodness of human "progress").[8] Hence, Newbigin's views of theological knowledge would extend considerably beyond the merely subjective sphere of religious experience (as will be shown later) to the objective province of God's self-revelation in Christ.

Under John Oman and Herbert Farmer at Cambridge, Newbigin was becoming increasingly prepared for his role in what would later become the WCC, in large part due to his association with various ecumenical leaders like J. H. Oldham and William Temple, and movements such as Life and Work. After being commissioned and ordained in 1936 to serve as missionaries in India, the Newbigins began serving in a leprosy colony. Abruptly, they had to return to England as a result of an accident that smashed Lesslie's leg, ultimately requiring ten operations. Yet, during this three-year recovery period, he continued to study the Tamil language and serve on the Church of Scotland's foreign missions committee. They returned to South India in 1939. The missionary experience would come to deeply influence all of his theological work.[9]

---

in Glasgow, and his commentary of Romans had the primary influence on Newbigin's theological shift. Critical to understanding Newbigin's thought are the various shaping influences; unlike many evangelicals, Newbigin did not have a deeply fundamentalist intellectual heritage, but rather, as we have seen, liberal and higher critical theological training. Thus, Denney, an evidently moderately-conservative evangelical, was among a "group of evangelicals, who functioned within the more central church bodies, [which] published distinctly conservative theories of the Bible" with a tendency of affirming "both the Bible's general trustworthiness and the appropriate use of criticism" (see Noll, *Between Faith and Criticism*, 79).

8. In a similar manner, from the vantage point of hindsight, my own decade-long experience with subcultural fundamentalism can now be viewed as having certain advantages for my present and future work. For instance, because of immersed participation within the fundamentalist tradition, I have been granted the opportunity to know firsthand both the strengths (e.g., doctrinal orthodoxy relative to the historic Christian faith) and weaknesses (e.g., naïve biblicism) that accompany this essentially American religious tradition—a tradition I continue to interact with, but now (akin to Newbigin and liberalism) from the *outside* looking in.

9. Between 1939 and 1959, Newbigin served as evangelist, ecumenical negotiator, and (beginning in 1947) bishop in the Madurai and Ramnad diocese of the newly united Church of South India, which he helped create.

By mid-1940, Newbigin had finally arrived at his destination in Kanchipuram, India. His work of evangelism was evident from the start—engaging in street preaching and handing out gospels—as was his involvement with interreligious dialogue.[10] He also found himself engaged in various pastoral and administrative duties, and sought to build up the local congregational leadership. In addition, during his time in Kanchipuram, Newbigin was actively involved as a representative of the South India United Church (SIUC) in negotiations that resulted in the uniting of SIUC, Methodists, and Anglicans, as the Church of South India—an important event in the history of ecumenical relations. He was also selected to serve as one of the first bishops in the newly united church in 1947. The stage was now set for the next five decades involving fullness of life and a great deal of profound and influential work.[11]

From 1965 to 1974, Newbigin served as General Secretary of the International Missionary Council (at the time of its integration with the WCC). Upon his "retirement," he settled down in Britain, accepting a position at the Selly Oaks Colleges in Birmingham where he taught for five years. Newbigin's sermons and services as pastor to a racially and religiously diverse local congregation spanned the 1980s. He simultaneously engaged in several other activities: serving as elected moderator of the United Reformed Church in the U.K., heading *The Gospel and Our Culture* movement in Britain, and participating in frequent and diverse speaking engagements. Probably most telling, however, Newbigin's reputation had become, in his biographer's words, that of "a national sage and finally prophet."[12]

Newbigin flirted briefly with ascendant 1960s secular theology until the *shattering experience* of the 1968 WCC assembly in Upsala, Sweden. Here he saw what he regarded as a mockery of the Christian gospel, and an ushering in of *humanization over salvation*. This would later (in 1989) lead

10. For instance, Newbigin was engaged in sharing leadership—with the head of the Hindu monastic community—of a weekly study group devoted to both the gospel of John in Greek and the Svetasvara Upanishad in Sanskrit.

11. Newbigin's engagement in ecumenical activities is another key reason in selecting him as a model for evangelical scholarship; his committed-yet-teachable approach to theological reflection and praxis deserves fair and full consideration. The *ecclesiastical* methodology and efforts employed by Newbigin in accomplishing the birthing of the Church of South India were exemplary; perhaps critical utilization of his *theological* epistemology may serve to enliven greater unity among evangelicals.

12. Wainwright, *Lesslie Newbigin*, vi.

him to designate the notion of a "secular society" as technically a myth and popularly a falsehood, and the idea of "religious neutrality" as illusory. Accordingly, then, "what has come into being is not a secular society but a pagan society, not a society devoid of public images but a society which worships gods which are not God."[13] As a result, a "secular" theology is nonsense; the true question is more akin to which *supernatural* theology—pagan or otherwise—will win the day. This recognition, which led to a reaffirmation of the central role of the church, including its declaration and practice of the knowledge of God, would forever shape Newbigin's later theological, and more specifically, apologetical, view.

Although Newbigin had at times throughout his career of theological and cultural reflection both embraced and criticized the "idea of progress," by the decade of the 1980s his critique of the Enlightenment in the modern West was in full swing. Modernity's exaltation of Cartesian rationalism and its associated quest for indubitable certainty above faith in all matters of knowledge were seen as seriously flawed.[14] While acknowledging the real benefits of the Enlightenment—especially scientific and technological discoveries and advances—he incisively illuminated its significant philosophical problems, which have led to both the decay of Western culture itself, and, in relation to the church, the end of its once-held privileged position in carrying Christianity—whether in liberal or fundamentalist form—to the rest of the world on the back of "civilized" and allegedly universal self-evident truths.

The missionary years in southern India awakened Newbigin to competing systems of thought that directly challenged the prevailing Eurocentric perspective. He came to see that alternative worldviews, rather than being "barbaric," were highly systematic, and pragmatically viable for particular cultures. His own Enlightenment heritage had not prepared him adequately for effectively engaging with these alternative philosophies and theologies, thus leaving him to seek an apologetical methodology that would seriously consider the worldviews found within particular cultural contexts, while maintaining an irenic yet also vigorously evangelical Christian faith. The way forward for Newbigin was both old and new: both a return to the ancient Augustinian *credo ut intellegam*, and an appropriation of the thought of contemporary philosopher Michael

---

13. *Ibid.*, 254, 353.

14. For instance, see Newbigin's strong critique in *The Gospel in a Pluralist Society*, passim.

Polanyi.[15] He found that together these methods provided a legitimate and material response to both the deeply empirical scientific method, and the reason-driven fundamentalism reflecting Gnostic-like tendencies. Thus, Newbigin's later writings repeatedly focus on Christian apologetics in an increasingly hostile-to-Christianity culture, as he attempts to answer the question asked at a conference more than a decade earlier, "Can the West be converted?"[16]

Eventually, Newbigin would apparently coin the term "out-narrate" to describe the task awaiting the church in the midst of a pluralist society: a society interested more in story than propositional statements; a society interested more in praxis than theory; a society interested more in Christ than Christianity; a society inclined more toward holistic than atomistic thinking; and a society involved more in pluralisms than monisms. For Newbigin, Augustine and Polanyi could be effectively utilized to counter Enlightenment assumptions in a post-Christendom, post-modern world.[17]

The sheer number of multifaceted activities Newbigin engaged in for seven decades is reason enough to command the attention of missiologists, biblical scholars and teachers, philosophers, sociologists and psychologists, ecumenists, pastors and bishops, and *evangelical* theologians. As certain as Newbigin is to raise the ire of those who would prefer either a cloistered fundamentalism or a theological pluralism, his engaged, concrete theology addresses issues that are relevant to both traditionalist and reformist evangelical thought. Given that his theological work has been overlooked by many evangelical scholars, it will be important herein to consider both if and how the fruit of Newbigin's labor may be compatible with evangelical theology, and for the purposes of this study, utilized for theological epistemology.

---

15. Polanyi, an epistemologist, actually began his career in the scientific arena, but became a scientist-turned-philosopher whose writings in the areas of knowledge have had an enduring impact across disciplines. See his most well-known book, *Personal Knowledge.* I am indebted to Wainwright for his many insights into Polanyi's methodology and influence.

16. This question arose from a Bangkok missionary conference in 1973 in which Newbigin heard Indonesian general and theologian T. B. Simatupang muttering the query under his breath (see Wainwright, *Lesslie Newbigin*, 192.)

17. Augustine and Polanyi will also have shaping roles regarding Newbigin's theological epistemology, as will be shown later in this chapter.

Because Newbigin successfully eludes attempts at "label-fixing," he is not typically seen as an evangelical—in the North American sense. However, virtually any primary reading of Newbigin, whether of his theology or his praxis, convincingly shows his steadfast commitment to the centrality of the cross and resurrection of Jesus Christ, with emphasis on the atonement's meaning and significance. Thus, the holistic and balanced approach realized in Newbigin's life, thought, and work, could perhaps serve as a model for contemporary evangelical scholars and practitioners.

Selecting a practicing missionary in looking for a proper perspective on evangelical epistemological questions might appear especially odd, since herein we are not only going beyond the boundaries of American evangelicalism, but also looking outside the academic guild altogether. But in this case, it can prove helpful to move beyond the compartmentalization that often characterizes evangelical thought. Newbigin is a thinker *for the church*, someone less concerned about a particular academic title or label than *being* evangelical, *doing* theology well, and *knowing* God. He is someone not confined by standard notions of what it means to be a theologian, evangelical, or epistemologist, but rather someone immersed in holding together the larger holistic mosaic of life. No wonder Newbigin flowed so freely in and out of diverse positions and contexts. His model reflects commitment to a holistic approach vis-à-vis evangelical theological epistemology.

In Newbigin's life and work, *mission* (rather than *missions*) served as his centerpoint, grounded most centrally in Christ, and within a trinitarian framework. For Newbigin, God has given the church a mission of reconciliation, and this is the highest priority. Even theological reflection must be done through the lens of mission, as well as concrete experience. Nevertheless, as he would make clear on more than a few occasions, unless the church has been reconciled *to itself*, the hearing of the call of reconciliation of others to God in Christ will largely go unheeded; the household of God must actively seek reconciliation and reunification.[18] Mission, theology, apologetics, ecclesiology, religious dialogue, worship, teaching and preaching—all are part of the same larger picture: the Creator's desire for his creatures to know and glorify him as universal Lord, experiencing and growing in reconciliation and wholeness by means of the redemptive work of Jesus Christ on our behalf.

18. Newbigin's years in India provide the rich backdrop and framework for what later would become his classic works in ecclesiology and apologetics.

Before examining Newbigin's theological epistemology in detail, a brief consideration of several of his key theological and epistemological developments is in order. Each of these characteristics of Newbigin's thought figures within his holistic conceptualization of the knowledge of God.

Newbigin's Theology and Epistemology

Contextualizing Theology

The contexts in which Newbigin lived, worked, and thought varied significantly. In each setting, his theological reflection was informed by the tangible milieu. This characteristic is not meant to call into question the objective reality of God and the transcendence of the work of Christ. Rather, it highlights Newbigin's insistence that history and culture influence theological and epistemological views. God calls the theologian to a particularity in time, which in turn requires authentic living and thinking *within* one's environment when reflecting upon the knowledge of God.

This thoroughly engaged attitude must be recommended for contemporary evangelical thinkers wishing to retain and respect God-given truths concerning Jesus the Christ and his sacrificial atonement for all, while employing—as much as possible within a framework of fidelity to the Gospel—contemporary thought-forms. In this way, Newbigin has led many others, and remains an important example of the value and priority of doing theology in context.

From Modernity to Postmodernity

Perhaps one of Newbigin's most formative moments came as he stepped back onto British soil—having been away for nearly forty years—to experience repercussions of the cultural shift underway in the West. The considerable philosophical change that had begun years earlier in U.K. universities and other educational institutions was seeping into popular culture and revolutionizing virtually everything. The Enlightenment project had utterly failed to provide the backbone, the values, or the "utopia" expected of it by so many who had placed their faith in its supposedly objective and "foolproof" system. Droves of thinkers, especially younger ones, escaped into despair or deconstruction, embracing both tolerance and multiculturalism—partly because of disillusionment with an exclusive exaltation of the Eurocentric vision of truth and values.

Forms of Enlightenment-entangled Christianity met with similar intolerance. Questioning all claims to truth and authority came to characterize the last several decades of twentieth-century Britain (and for that matter, most if not all of Western Europe). This was a new era with a new philosophy. How would—or even *could*—the gospel be heard again in the new context? This question occupied much of Newbigin's mature years.

Newbigin's engagement with the culture from such diverse positions and ministries made his already incisive observations that much more compelling, even prophetic at times. He spoke and wrote ahead of his time, perceptively grasping cultural changes and their effects, sometimes years before his contemporaries.[19] Because of the compass and quality of his reading, Newbigin kept pace with significant developments in multiple disciplines, once again authenticating his personal devotion to a holistic focus.

Authors influencing Newbigin represent a wide range of fields and disciplines. He frequently makes substantial use of their work.[20] Newbigin's openness and willingness to draw from a wide spectrum of thought, provided by his Reformed philosophical commitment to the proposition that "all truth is God's truth," helped to alleviate potential fundamentalist-like fears of finding other "truths" contradicting the Bible. Hence, Newbigin steadfastly retained a strong confessional stance in line with historic Christian doctrine, while holding that God has not limited truth to merely biblical or theological realms.[21]

Theological Tradition, Method, and Doctrine

Newbigin's theology was not defined by a single theological system, although on most issues, as a Presbyterian, he clearly favored Reformed over Arminian or Anabaptist themes. Nonetheless, Newbigin's ecumenical experiences made him much more open to—and at times accepting of—views not espoused, and sometimes rejected, by his denominational tradition.[22] Newbigin's breadth of experience and depth of reading and

19. The bishop's detection—descriptively and prognostically—of the changing situation was, as some have said, simply uncanny.

20. For instance, the thought of scientist-turned-philosopher Michael Polanyi, which will be discussed shortly.

21. Perhaps, too, the methodology of Christian philosopher Arthur Holmes may have influenced Newbigin's own thinking with respect to considering and articulating God's work amidst the world, e.g., within the Arts. See Holmes, *All Truth is God's Truth*.

22. One such example involved Newbigin's affirmation of the theological validity of cer-

reflection, including from outside his own denominational and confessional boundaries, allowed him to develop alternative ways of viewing God's character and works than those generally reflective of his own theological tradition.[23]

Newbigin's willingness to hold his own and other Christian traditions to the standards of the gospel—and to principled criticism—provides a refreshing as well as exemplary model for evangelicalism: remembering to consistently judge one's own religious tradition in light of the gospel that Christian traditions are called to proclaim and practice. Apologetically, Newbigin (in his later works) would conclude that only the God-honoring praxis of the proclaiming faith community would serve as the ultimate witness to the truth of its given message to the world; Christianity stands or falls not on whether it passes the "acid test of modernity," but whether the local Christian community is properly and attractively a living witness in its particular context. Is it any wonder, then, that Newbigin is deeply concerned with the unity of the whole body of Christ, since division therein destroys its compelling beauty and witness?[24]

Evangelicals can find much to appreciate in Newbigin's outspoken and well-documented commitment to essential, historic Christian doctrines. For example, his approach encompasses a systematic trinitarianism—one that is strongly christocentric while also possessing an exceptionally high level of openness (among Reformed-minded theologians) to the work of the Holy Spirit.[25] Newbigin's display of tolerance for views not naturally associated with his own liturgical tradition is perhaps due to several crucial factors: an ecumenical heritage and spirit focused on a mission of unity and agreement on the core essentials of a shared faith in Jesus Christ, rather than a centering upon soteriological or sanctification issues; the shaping influences of the missionary field, increasing his personal level of tolerance and widening his ministry perspective concerning the triune God;

---

tain charismatic movements. Even as early as 1952 in *Household of God*, Newbigin showed remarkable openness to Pentecostalism, dedicating one chapter to Pentecostals. Moreover, his involvement with Holy Trinity Brompton in the 1990s helped to put Newbigin in greater touch with charismatics.

23. For example, with reference to one's normative spiritual journey and salvation, Newbigin attributed primacy to the Christian community rather than to the individual (as we will see later in this study).

24. Cf., John 17.

25. For instance, Newbigin was even willing to grant the so-called Toronto Blessing as a work of God's Spirit.

an "all truth is God's truth" philosophy, providing him with a willingness to learn and to be corrected, as opposed to accepting a potentially stifling separatism; interpersonal relations and shared ministry experiences with Christians originating from a multiplicity of traditions and being used by God for the sake of the Kingdom; and the testing of theological and philosophical thought and practice by authoritative Christian sources.[26]

Consistent with practically all evangelical traditions, Newbigin focuses on the self-disclosure and atoning work of God in Christ; regardless his context or setting, whether missional, educational, dialogical, etc., he consistently returns to the reconciliatory act of Christ on our behalf as definitive for all human history. Absent from his confessional position, however, is dogmatic epistemological certainty. Hence, Newbigin's theology may seem tentative to some because of his usual pattern of qualifying statements and curbing unwarranted dogmatism. This method often involves employing forms of the phrase, *If this is true* or *If God truly said.* Whether one judges Newbigin's qualification as unfortunately cautious or as properly humble, such an assessment will most probably surface from one's own theological and apologetical tradition—including linkage with modern or postmodern approaches to knowledge and propositions—since Newbigin *unequivocally affirms* that God has truly and definitively acted in Christ.[27]

What follows is a more thorough engagement with Newbigin's approach to theological knowledge, attempting to answer the question of compatibility with contemporary evangelical thought. In recommending Newbigin's method as a model for evangelical scholarship, we will consider several significant complements. We will also analyze one potentially major problematic contrast that will necessitate determining whether the divergence renders this effort unworkable.[28]

---

26. See Newbigin, *Truth and Authority in Modernity*, 25–63.

27. Hence, taking Newbigin's "if" in the sense of "since" (i.e., since God has done this), rather than "whether" God has acted, seems reasonable. His style is modest and judicious, considering Newbigin's rejection of unbecoming modernist arrogance, whether in theological or apologetical form, along with his dismissal of the Enlightenment's enamored quest for certainty. This precludes him from making unwarranted proclamations to absolute knowledge relative to his own Christian—or any other—faith, while not shrinking from a robust belief in and commitment to proclaiming the gospel of Jesus Christ in word and deed. By this example, we glimpse yet another facet of Newbigin's methodology that evangelicals are certain to gain wisdom from, if embraced and applied.

28. Several other less potentially troubling issues will receive brief treatment under the

Systematic Analysis of Newbigin's Theological Epistemology

General Characteristics and Observations

With reference to the following analysis, it is helpful to keep in mind that Lesslie Newbigin's theological epistemology is *integrative* in a way that defies precisely defined boundaries and categories. Nevertheless, dividing his approach to theological knowledge into several major categories may be expedient, if not necessary, for the immediate purposes of reflection and assessment. Thus, we begin with Newbigin's characteristically holistic theological methodology.

HOLISTIC

Newbigin's prominent *whole life approach* counters the standard modernist method of viewing *reason* or *experience* as singularly authoritative sources for knowledge of God. For Newbigin, *interconnectivity* between scripture, tradition, and proclamation is essential. Reason and experience are *part of* the whole Christian faith and life; they are not disconnected, uninvolved sources for theological knowledge. *Our* story must be connected to the *gospel* story, and within that connection—via scripture, the community, experiences within the community, the use of reason and apologetics within the community, and the Holy Spirit's work within the community—people come to know God intimately.

ECCLESIAL

Long before many contemporary evangelical scholars began moving toward a more ecclesial-centered theology (i.e., theology *for* the church) in place of a prevailing academy-oriented focus, Newbigin's theological method had been church-centered for decades. The conviction that God was made explicitly known in Jesus Christ—and to the church—gave Newbigin cause for keeping his theological epistemology closely linked with the body of Christ. His theologizing was largely devoid of the "professionalism" of many of his contemporaries, primarily due to his engagement with the culture and religions in India,[29] along with concrete concerns

---

section, "Some Final Concerns," beginning on page 245.

29. For example, teaching English and scripture to Hindu high school boys, and eventually founding a schoolboys' camp "where Hindu and Christian boys shared in a few days of fellowship and teaching" (Newbigin, *Unfinished Agenda*, 51–52).

issuing from that context. In addition, his work at uniting the Church in South India was a powerful force in keeping his theological reflection church-centered.

PERSONAL

Another critically important consideration shaping Newbigin's view is his identifiable reliance upon Michael Polanyi's *Personal Knowledge*. He is deeply influenced by Polanyi's insights into knowledge within the scientific arena, and its applicability to religious and theological spheres. A main theme of *Personal Knowledge* is that all human knowledge has a *fiduciary character*, regardless of whether the topical arena is theology, psychology, or natural science. For that reason, Newbigin envisions the Incarnation showing *ultimate truth* to be *personal in nature*: made known to humanity only by self-revelation of the Creator.[30]

HISTORICAL-CULTURAL-CONTEXTUAL

Another reason for commending Newbigin to evangelical thinkers concerns his ability to effectively engage in theological reflection and praxis within diverse communities and contexts. For Newbigin, an *a*historical, *a*contextual, *a*cultural theology was truly no theology at all. It purports to be "above and beyond" historical-cultural frameworks—a pretended "God's eye" point of view more akin to what the human mind conceives when utterly dependent upon reason, which is subversively shaping the thinker who is being molded by his context. Is it any wonder that Newbigin—in the strongest of terms—rejects Enlightenment rationalism and the scientific method as paradigmatic for theological knowledge?

The *contextual* emphasis of Newbigin's thought is obvious, showing an awareness of the necessary interplay between theological reflection and praxis within concrete situations. He demonstrates an ability to comprehend—even prophetically—the cultural and historical shifts in philosophy, behavior, technology, ethical and moral standards, and trends in religion. At times he seems to be simultaneously standing in numerous places in the past, present, and future, seeing complexities and connections between a great number of relationships on a mega scale, both within the church and larger cultural contexts.[31] No doubt, this ability calls evangelical thinkers

30. See Wainwright, *Lesslie Newbigin*, 49–50.

31. At a local café in Santa Ana, CA, my brief conversation with a lay friend who had just recently been introduced to one of Newbigin's books (*The Gospel in a Pluralist Society*)

to respect, learn from, and at least to some extent follow, Newbigin's own thought and praxis.

Beyond the Modernist-Fundamentalist Divide

Newbigin's ability to think from "both sides of the aisle" adds to his already strong résumé. For instance, relative to the modernist-fundamentalist debate, he seems to stand equally well on either side of the divide in fairly appraising strengths and weaknesses of both perspectives, and without resorting to the rhetoric familiar in North American discussions. His ability to successfully understand various positions in addition to his own, and to see the problems and potential solutions therein, as Wainwright points out, reflects the ability to "'out-narrate' the stories told by those whose ultimate commitments lie elsewhere—and this for the achievement of the Father's purpose, and so to the glory of the Triune God."[32] This capacity reveals wisdom evangelical thinkers can glean from Newbigin. To begin this process, we must now consider his philosophy respecting sources of theological knowledge.

Theological Knowledge Sources and Norms

Self-Revelation of God

Lesslie Newbigin's earliest theological writings—perhaps reflected most distinctly in a paper written during his studies at Cambridge (1935–36)—demonstrate his nascent theological epistemology. There, Newbigin focuses on faith as being the reception of revelation, and on God's self-revelation as necessary for human knowledge of God. Sensitivity and trustfulness in responding to God's revelation is the way to know God in his self-disclosure. However, as to our knowledge being true, Newbigin is concerned with both "inward understanding and valuing" and "a reality external to our minds." Moreover, because revelation is passed down through historic

---

yielded his comment that Newbigin sounds like a futurist. I noted that the inimitable Alvin Toffler "had nothing on him," at least as to feeling the pulse of national and world level culture. More to the point, Newbigin's perceptabilities reminds me of what a different friend told me years ago about another elder statesman in the faith: "he seems to be able to see how everything connects, and then to be able to actually articulate it with great success!" While much of this depth of perception was arrived at later in Newbigin's life, the seeds and gifts were evident even early on: as far back as his years at Cambridge, as evidenced in several of his papers.

32. Wainwright, *Lesslie Newbigin*, 230.

community, *the church is the location of, and the Bible is an instrument for, reception of the divine self-disclosure.*[33]

wdw.
chpt 1
ending.

Newbigin's belief in the preeminence of divine initiative in the process of human knowledge of God is ontologically based: "If the reality that we seek to explore, and of which we are a part, is the work of a personal Creator, then authority resides in this One who is the Author." This is due to knowledge of a *person* being necessarily connected with that person's willingness to self-disclose—something that the Enlightenment has seen fit to reject as it concerns God's own authority. And "because personal being can be known only insofar as the person chooses to reveal himself or herself, and cannot be known by methods that are appropriate to the investigation of impersonal matters and processes, then authority, in this view, must rest on divine revelation."[34]

This divine authority, according to Newbigin, was powerfully evident in the teaching and healing work of Jesus, as he "embodied final authority," not binding himself to the authority of the Torah, as had the scribes. Thus, ultimate authority rests not with "the way of thinking that came to dominance in the intellectual leadership of Europe . . . that rejected appeals to revelation and tradition as sources of authority," but rather directly with the revelation-based authority of the personally disclosed Creator—most clearly and finally seen in Jesus Christ.[35] Here, Newbigin has opted for a Barthian move: rejecting all allegedly authoritative arbitrators of truth set to judge the confessed authority of God's self-revelation. Responsibility for this perspective also lies with Newbigin's general acceptance of the findings of Thomas Kuhn, Michael Polanyi, and others who have demonstrated the fiduciary character of all knowledge.

Newbigin is convinced that the most significant impact on Western thought in the Middle Ages—and its subsequent influence upon Christian theology—was the translation of the great Islamic commentaries on Aristotle into Latin, which "led to the creation of the universities and the rise of 'the new science.'" For theology, this rediscovery of Aristotelian thought laid the groundwork for Aquinas's restating of "Christian tradition in light of the new intellectual situation."[36] What did this mean

33. Ibid., 34.
34. Newbigin, *Truth and Authority in Modernity*, 1–2.
35. Ibid., 2–3.
36. Ibid., 4.

Rollins – Newbigin. ontic - epist

for human knowledge of God? It entailed a *breach* in the once unified method of theological epistemology: now two distinct approaches would be pursued, primarily depending upon the subject matter being discussed. Certain things about God could be known by means of *reason*—quite apart from revelation, e.g., the existence of God and of the human soul. However, reason was limited, and thus only through revelation and faith could other aspects of the knowledge of God be grasped, e.g., Trinity, Atonement, Incarnation, Resurrection. This "division of labor" concerning human knowledge of God meant that Aristotle would be called on to answer significant theological questions (for instance, concerning the existence of God) previously reserved for the Christian tradition. Thus begins a deep and pervasive kind of intertwining of Christian theology and philosophy previously unknown.[37]

Unfortunately for Christianity, this major methodological shift, in certain theological realms, from faith to reason—from biblical to natural revelation—was unable to hold ground against sweeping changes in cosmology under Galileo, Copernicus, Kepler, and others, eventually leading to a "climate of extreme uncertainty and skepticism,"[38] preparing the way for reception of René Descartes' views. Descartes, as we saw in an earlier chapter, would construct an entirely different foundation for knowledge, the self: beginning from a position of *doubt* rather than faith, and seeking indubitable certainties over against a growing conflict of traditions (*opinio*). Descartes' powerfully influential method effectively *reversed* Augustine's maxim; the course to knowledge would now *begin with doubt* rather than faith, dominating practically all of Western thought for 300 years. However, since the mid-twentieth century, this *scientia*-focused quest has encountered insurmountable problems and is now in the process of effectively self-destructing. The death of modernity (in this sense) is at the doorstep. Newbigin acknowledges the situation:

> The Cartesian program proves to be inherently self-destructive for the simple reason that doubt, if it is to be rational, must rest upon something that is believed to be true. . . . Plainly, both faith and doubt have necessary roles in the enterprise of knowing; but the

37. Whereas with, say, Augustine, Christian thought naturally *utilized* contemporary philosophical categories and themes to effectively contextualize and communicate the gospel and Christian theology *within* that culture and era, with Thomas comes a clear *distinction* between two equally authoritative realms of theological knowledge.

38. Newbigin, *Truth and Authority in Modernity*, 5.

role of doubt, as necessary as it is, is secondary, and that of faith primary. We can know without doubting, but we cannot know without believing. The Cartesian invitation to make doubt the primary tool in the search for knowledge was bound to lead to the triumph of skepticism and eventually of nihilism, as Nietzsche foresaw. The demand for a kind of indubitable certainty that does not depend upon faith has led inexorably to despair about the possibility of knowing anything. We are in the situation that Nietzsche anticipated where rational argument ceases and the only arbiter is power and the will to power. Even science . . . is no longer seen as a pathway to wisdom, to a true understanding of the human situation; rather, it is seen as a means to power.[39]

Noting the obvious fallacy and failure of the scientific method to provide an unassailable objectivity respecting knowledge and truth, Newbigin keys in on the *post*foundationalist approach that views all knowing as intertwined with believing and *a priori* commitments. Thus, one must begin not with Aquinas, but instead with Augustine: not with a strict division between what can be known by faith and revelation on the one hand, and by reason on the other, but rather with *credo ut intelligam*—I believe in order that I may know.[40]

Hence, for theological knowledge, the way out of this conundrum is the way back: back to a *starting point of faith*—committed belief in the divine self-revelation of God. This does not entail, however, a precritical naïveté, but instead a christocentric interpretive model, grounded in a larger trinitarian framework. Newbigin proposes that the starting point be God's personal revelation in the history of Israel, and finally in the person of Jesus Christ: *God spoke and acted.* Thus, no distinction ought to be permitted between revelation and reason as sources of, and criteria for, truth, but rather between the different ways in which reason is employed *in the service of faith and revelation.* Finally, Newbigin concentrates on the *gift* aspect of the self-disclosure of God: "Faith in God's self-revelation is a gift of God, not an achievement of the autonomous reason and conscience."[41]

While Newbigin insists on divine self-revelation as essential to human knowledge of God, he flatly rejects natural theology, viewing it as closer to idolatry than providing partial theological knowledge:

39. Ibid., 7–8.

40. See Newbigin, *Truth and Authority in Modernity*, 3–4.

41. Newbigin, *Truth and Authority in Modernity*, 17.

> [E]ven if we are thinking only of revelation as the communication
> of knowledge about God, we have to reject the claim that this
> knowledge can be given added certitude by the support of natural
> theology. For, if one thing is obvious, it is that the "god" whose
> existence natural theology claims to demonstrate is not the God
> whose character is rendered in the pages of the Bible, not the God
> and Father of our Lord Jesus Christ, not the blessed Trinity. It is
> hard to deny that this "god" is a construct of the human mind and
> that therefore has the essential character of an idol. One has to ask
> whether idolatry is a step on the way to the worship of the true
> God, or a threat to it. If our starting point is the kind of reasoning
> provided by "the Philosopher" [Aristotle] or his many successors, it
> becomes difficult to accept the possibility of a true incarnation and
> almost impossible to regard the blessed Trinity as anything other
> than a piece of mystification. If this is so, must we not say that the
> knowledge of God given through "natural theology" is not merely
> a partial knowledge but is a distored and misleading knowledge?[42]

What seems most transparent with Newbigin here is his underlying
belief in the *non*-neutrality of all knowledge. Thus, the idea that some
objectively neutral body of facts in the universe awaits discovery is an illusion at best, and idolatry at worst. One's underlying worldview, he might
say, on the authority of scripture in relation to the revelation of God,
will determine the starting point—reason or faith and revelation—for
theological knowledge. Newbigin would acknowledge that such divergent
views entail radically different methodological consequences for Christian
thinkers. For those holding to the primacy of faith and revelation, "we
do not possess indubitable knowledge, but we press forward on the path
of faith, looking forward to the day when we will know as now we are
known." For those holding to the priority of reason, "a natural theology
that purports to offer us grounds of assurance more reliable than those
given to us in God's own self-revelation in Jesus Christ is no service to faith
but a subversion of it."[43]

Grace and Faithfulness of God

In opposition to the Enlightenment idea that knowledge, including theological knowledge, must come by way of eternal and ultimate truths, "a
kind of objective knowledge wholly sanitized from contamination by any

---

42. Ibid., 18–19.
43. Ibid., 20.

apoditic statements

'subjective' elements," and the often belabored point by some conservative Christians that "only by asserting the *objective* truth of the gospel" can one affirm its authority, Newbigin claims that such a model effectively "severs the knowledge of God from the grace of God."[44] This is a mistake, since

> the knowledge of God can be only by grace through faith. The attempt to eliminate this deeply personal element in the knowledge of God, out of fear of subjectivism, can lead only to a kind of hard rationalism that is remote from the gospel. Certainly we must insist on the objectivity of what we affirm in preaching the gospel if that means that we are speaking of realities "beyond ourselves" and not just of our own feelings. But God is not an object for our investigation by scientific methods in the style of Descartes. God is the supreme Subject who calls us by grace to put our faith in Him. . . . [C]ertainty rests not in my own competence as the knower, but in the faithfulness of One whom I have learned to know, and the knowing is a matter of believing that looks forward to a day when we shall know in full and without possibility of doubt.[45]

Hence, for those who have become believers in the gospel, it is inappropriate to turn to other "collateral sources of information" in attempting to know the truth: "the truth surely is not that we come to know God by reasoning from our unredeemed experience but that what God has done for us in Christ gives us the eyes through which we can begin to truly understand our experience in the world."[46]

Perhaps the issue is Rollins appropriation of the language of continental philosophy in articulating Newbigin's theologian.

THE GOSPEL METANARRATIVE

Newbigin declares as the *ultimate* standard of faith "the revelation of God in Jesus Christ." Scripture, rather than tradition, is where through the testimony of his first followers, Christ is encountered in his person, words, and works: they bear witness to "God's redeeming act once for all at a point in history." Thus, rather than going to the Bible to discover for the church its earliest forms of the traditions and rules, we instead seek in the scriptures the *object* of faith: Christ and his work, in trinitarian terms.[47]

---

44. Ibid., 78.

45. Ibid., 78–79.

46. Newbigin, *Proper Confidence*, 97. Clearly, Newbigin would, in apologetical terms, be classified as a "presuppositionalist" rather than an "evidentialist."

47. From Newbigin, *Reunion of the Church*, pages not cited, as quoted in Wainwright, *Lesslie Newbigin*, 89.

Newbigin rejects a bifurcated fundamentalist-modernist divide in seeking to understand scripture, preferring to center on the *narrative pre-eminence* of the biblical writings—narrative that "structures human experience and understanding. . . . [I]t is essentially a story that claims to be *the story*. The true story both of the cosmos and of human life within the cosmos." He continues:

> History is to be understood as the patient wrestling of God with a stupid, deluded, and rebellious people—stupid and rebellious precisely because they insist on seeing themselves as the center of the story. The Christian message . . . is that the real point of the story has been disclosed in the events of the cross and resurrection of Jesus.[48]

Newbigin emphasizes *the instrumental use of scripture*—a looking *through* rather than *at* it—that calls us "to *indwell* the story, as we indwell the language we use and the culture of which we are a part."[49] Living *in the story* of the Bible, as well as within our own contextual story, necessitates (as foreign missionaries experience) the setting up of "an internal dialogue as the precondition for true interpersonal dialogue."[50] Even though we are yet unable to capture or comprehend many mysteries concerning God's nature, wisdom, knowledge, and judgments (Rom 11:33), we are nevertheless called to embrace the mystery of grace—divine love and holiness for the unholy and unlovely. Attending to the Bible brings one into the presence of this unique story, and tends to give shape and clarity to what otherwise would remain hidden or nebulous. Indwelling the story in John 15:15, for instance, provides us with

> the clearest indication of Scriptural authority. The truth is not imposed upon us, for indeed truth has not done its work unless and until we have learned to honor and love it from our hearts as truth. But we do not reach truth unless we allow ourselves to be exposed to and drawn by a truth which is beyond our present understanding. . . . *The important thing is not how we formulate a doctrine of biblical authority but how we allow the Bible to function in our daily lives.* We grow into a knowledge of God by allowing the biblical

---

48. Newbigin, *Truth and Authority in Modernity*, 38–39.

49. Ibid., 42.

50. Ibid., 42–43.

story to awaken our imagination and to challenge and stimulate our thinking and acting.[51]

This approach would seem to imply a necessary humility before the scripture as it pertains to theological knowledge, admitting that we are unable to know God *exhaustively*. Instead, we continue to grow in theological knowledge, as well as corresponding reflection and praxis, through deference to the gospel metanarrative. This view of the knowledge of God coincides well with Aquinas's idea of *cognosci* over *comprehende*.[52]

Rejecting the Cartesian-Newtonian pursuit of "timeless realities governed by eternal laws," which aim for "a total knowledge that leaves no room for either faith or doubt," Newbigin seeks to ground his apologetic for theological knowledge in *the* story—proclamation of it and immersion within it:

> If our model of truth is embodied in a story, a story of which we are ourselves a part, then the only available form of knowledge is by faith in the One who is the author of the story. . . . The only knowledge we can possibly have of the purpose, and therefore the meaning of this entire cosmic story of which we are a part, is by faith in the One whose purpose it is and who has, by grace to us who had shut ourselves off from this knowledge, called us to be co-workers with him in the fulfillment of this purpose. It follows that the only way in which we can affirm the truth and therefore the authority of the gospel is by preaching it, by telling the story, and by our corporate living of the story in the life and worship of the church . . . reject[ing] a conception of "objective truth" that seeks it in a series of timeless propositions in the affirmation of which we are not personally involved, for which we do not have to commit our whole lives; it means that we affirm that truth is to be found only in the personal commitment to a

---

51. Newbigin, *Proper Confidence*, 90–91. Emphasis mine. Perhaps it would have been advisable for Newbigin to use the qualifier "merely" between the words "not" and "how" in the statement *the important thing is not how we formulate a doctrine of biblical authority but how we allow the Bible to function in our daily lives*. Otherwise, it appears that Newbigin's instrumental use of the Bible is *merely* pragmatic, which, from indications elsewhere, it is not. It seems most probably that he is interested not in denying the need for a doctrine of biblical authority, but rather emphasizing the need for our submission to its functionality, and thus implied, its authority.

52. See the insightful discussion of these important distinctions Aquinas made in Benson, "End of the Fantastic Dream," 159–60.

life of discipleship with Him who is himself the truth. We have to tell and enact the story.[53]

Clearly then, human participation in the story must be in *real time*—presently living in obedient faith towards the central character to whom the story points definitively: the word of life.

The Word of God Incarnate

Newbigin's christomorphic life and theology is central to his wider trinitarian theological method, and thus has application to the question of his theological epistemology; namely, knowledge of God is most clearly gained through knowledge of the word of God made flesh, Jesus Christ. Such knowledge brings one into (intimate) relationship with God. Nevertheless, Newbigin notes that the context of the Bible *as a whole* is critically important and protects against wrongly detaching Jesus from the story, in effect making him a mythical figure, or interpreting the whole story apart from Jesus who is the authoritative word of God. This important point is worth quoting at length:

> If we do not know the whole story and context of Jesus, then we cannot truly know him and thus cannot truly know God the Father. We need to see this God of Israel both in his wrath and his infinite mercy. We need to learn a holiness that reject all compromise with evil and a generosity that seeks and saves the lost. We need to learn to know God as he is. There is no way by which we come to know a person except by dwelling in his or her story and, in the measure that may be possible, becoming part of it. . . . As we live with the tension between the awesome holiness of God and his limitless kindness and as we bring this tension always to the person of Jesus himself in whom these seeming opposites are held together in a single life and death of judgment and mercy, we are led into a knowledge of God. To be more precise, we are enabled in growing measure to be admitted into that intimacy that Jesus had with his Father . . . [54]

Throughout each stage of Newbigin's developing theological epistemology, *Jesus remains central and definitive*. For Newbigin, all that the scriptures, and for that matter, tradition, have to say concerning the knowledge of God ought to be read and understood through the person and work of

---

53. Newbigin, *Truth and Authority in Modernity*, 80–81.
54. Newbigin, *Proper Confidence*, 88–89.

the incarnate One, who is the clearest and most definitive self-disclosure of God. The *personal* nature of theological knowledge necessitates God making himself known; by becoming flesh in the man Jesus Christ, God has become fully—though not exhaustively—known in a Person. Thus, Jesus makes God known to humanity since, according to the Fourth Evangelist, he is the very word of God incarnated. As Newbigin states concerning the biblical author's message, "only when the reader has come to know Jesus himself will he be able to understand that it is Jesus who is the word, that in him all things were created and in him all things hold together . . . that he himself is the gospel which is preached, and that it is in his name 'that there is life' (John 20:31)."[55] Newbigin finds unequivocal correlation between Jesus and theological knowledge at the end of the Prologue to the Fourth Gospel (verse 18):

> Jesus *is* God's word. There is, therefore, only one way to know God, and that is to attend to his word. All men share the longing to know the ultimate secret of their life. Without this they are in darkness. The 'good news' which John is about to tell is that the light, the only light there is, has come into the world, that the word of God has become flesh in the man Jesus Christ, and that here, therefore, in this life, God has made himself fully known. For the beloved Son, who is the word of God, is God, and only God can make God known.[56]

TRUST AND OBEDIENCE TO GOD

Perhaps the single most important contemporary thinker to influence Newbigin's theological epistemology is Michael Polanyi. Among his most profound insights is that *all* knowledge has a fiduciary character—*trust is inherent to the process of knowing.*[57] To begin with, there is the given, including the data (or facts) and the tradition of knowing, which includes its language and conceptual method. Knowing involves being open, mind and senses, to "the great reality which is around us and sustains us." Thus, "in order to be informed, we have to make acts of trust in the traditions we have inherited and in the evidence of our senses."[58] And as E. J. Carnell

---

55. From Newbigin, *Light Has Come*, page not cited, as quoted in Wainwright, *Lesslie Newbigin*, 310.

56. Ibid., 312.

57. See Polanyi, *Personal Knowledge*, 266–67, 280–86.

58. From Newbigin, *Proper Confidence*, 25, 49, 96, as quoted in Wainwright, *Lesslie*

astutely remarks, "God is not rightly known until one is spiritually moved by a sense of his own moral distance from God."[59]

In connection, then, with knowledge of God, Newbigin claims the Christian faith

> offers the most comprehensive of clues to reality, for it proclaims that the divine Word which creates and sustains all things has been made flesh in Jesus Christ. The primary witness to this act of God, this fact (*factum*), is contained in the Scriptures; and the interpretive tradition is borne by the church, which is part of the story that it carries on toward its conclusion.[60]

Hence, indubitable certainty (*pace* Descartes) does not enter into the equation, since knowledge does not rest in the mind of the knower, but rather in the Incarnation, which "shows ultimate reality to be personal in nature, which means that it can only be known by self-revelation on the part of the Creator and by an answering response on the part of the human knower. Such knowledge comes by way of an inseparable trust and obedience toward the call of Christ."[61]

As a result, the centrality of one's confidence rests squarely in the One who is known and upon his faithfulness and reliability, rather than in the competence of one's own knowing; in fact, the knower does not *possess* absolute knowledge of final truth, but is merely on the *path* that is leading toward the eschatological clarity of reality that awaits humanity. Again, *trust* is the core feature here, and Polanyi goes to great lengths in demonstrating the virtual universality of the centrality of trust within all scientific (and other) communities—neutrality is thus a fallacious myth.[62]

Newbigin concentrates on the different types of knowledge affirmed *outside* of the narrow ideal of modernity's reduction of all knowledge to "mathematical formulae," along with its withdrawal from the personal realm to impersonal rationalism. The Bible, for instance, holds the primary meaning of "to know" as pertaining to knowing another person, in a

---

Newbigin, 49. Unfortunately, none of the pages Wainwright references contains the exact quotation.

59. Carnell, *Christian Commitment*, ix.

60. From Newbigin, *Proper Confidence*, page not cited, as quoted in Wainwright, *Lesslie Newbigin*, 49.

61. Wainwright, *Lesslie Newbigin*, 50. In effect, *the* gospel must become *my* gospel, personal commitment to the call to *trust and obey* the gospel.

62. For example, see Polanyi, *Personal Knowledge*, 266–67.

trust-centered journey with one who "discloses his own mind and heart to me."[63] Hence, Newbigin looks to epistemology for what he considers the most fundamental task of the church in relation to challenging modernism's presuppositions—"questioning of contemporary assumptions about what is involved in knowing":

> The Enlightenment's exaltation of radical doubt as an epistemological principle needs challenge from *the biblical vision that places at the center a relationship of trust in a personal reality greater than ourselves.* Science needs to be brought into a framework in which "ethical considerations are not merely external regulators of the results of scientific work" but are present from the start, "because all knowing is an activity of persons responsible to God and to one another."[64]

Thus, while the Enlightenment model envisions individuals as autonomous centers of knowing and judging, essentially making interdependence incompatible with human dignity, the biblical model possesses a "relatedness" orientation, humans created to "mirror divine faithfulness by faithful relatedness to one another;" while the Enlightenment focuses on "equal rights" and "atomic equality," the scriptures emphasize God as the center and human "personal mutuality," serving one another.[65] These two paradigms are in obvious conflict. Choosing between them will determine the centrality of one's theological epistemology: knowledge as *personal* or *impersonal.*

Newbigin relentlessly attacks the false dichotomy between "knowing" and "believing," which he saw often characterized in the statements, "We all know" and "Some people believe." This *false distinction between facts and values* claims existence of a world of facts without values and a world of values that have no grounding in facts. However, in ways similar to Christianity, Enlightenment science has been shown to create and depend upon *faith in the authority of its own tradition*—i.e., trust in a community that claims to have knowledge.[66] Hence, all human knowledge is of a fiduciary character.

63. Wainwright, *Lesslie Newbigin,* 66–67. Unfortunately, the Newbigin source is not cited.

64. From Newbigin, *The Other Side of 1984,* page not cited, as quoted in Wainwright, *Lesslie Newbigin,* 256–57. Emphasis mine.

65. Ibid., 257.

66. From Newbigin, *Gospel in a Pluralist Society,* page not cited, as quoted in Wainwright, *Lesslie Newbigin,* 371.

LEARNING IN COMMUNITY

Wainwright notes that Newbigin, drawing from Polanyi's *Personal Knowledge*, "shows that all knowledge is a 'skill' that has to be learned; that all knowledge is 'an activity of persons in community,' involving mutual trust and accountability to certain standards; that all knowledge entails at least a provisional commitment to an existing framework of thought and knowledge, but that advances in knowledge occur only when the risk is taken that one may be proved wrong . . ."[67]

Newbigin never downplays the importance of *personal responsibility* as it relates to knowledge. Yet, being responsible with knowledge also means recognizing one's knowledge as limited: "my judgment is not the last word." Consequently, in respecting the interconnected question of authority,

> my personal judgment must be provisional, tempered by the recognition that I have more to learn. . . . I have to be open to things that I have not yet understood. In this sense, authority has to be external; it refers to a reality beyond myself. But, if it is to be authoritative for me, I must come to the point of recognizing its authority. It has to be internalized.[68]

Hence, an individual's vocation as defined by God's revelation is that of *learner* or *apprentice*—learning how to learn and know.[69] The very nature of apprenticeship requires that one be connected to another (or others) who *knows the way*: in this case, the way to the knowledge of God. Here, Newbigin assigns to the faith community (or tradition) a principal as well as reciprocal role pertaining to shaping the knowledge and worldview of its members:

> All our knowing comes to us through our apprenticeship in a tradition of knowing that has been formed through the effort of previous generations. This tradition is the source of the mental

67. Wainwright, *Lesslie Newbigin*, 348–49. Internal Newbigin quotations are from Newbigin, *Honest Religion for Secular Man*, page not cited.

68. Newbigin, *Truth and Authority in Modernity*, 12.

69. During a brief flirtation with the *secularization of theology* in the early to mid-1960s, Newbigin posited "all knowledge is of a piece," encouraging correlation of the knowledge of God and knowledge of the world. He retains some important elements appreciated within the secular, reorganizing them into the genre of the *public* nature of the gospel and Christian faith; this is the arena in which he engaged as an apologist the remainder of his years (see Wainwright, *Lesslie Newbigin*, 354).

faculties through which we begin to make sense of the world. In this sense the tradition has authority, but it is not a purely external authority. We are responsible for internalizing the tradition by our struggle to understand the world with the help of the tools it furnishes, and in this process the tradition itself develops and is changed. This calls for a combination of reverence for the tradition with courage to bring our own judgment to bear upon its application to new circumstances. The idea that we could construct an entire edifice of knowledge without reliance on the tradition by the exercise of our own powers of observation and reasoning (an idea that was certainly present in the formative process of modernity) is surely illusion.[70]

As we saw earlier, all knowledge is fiduciary in character. Thus, the question for theological knowledge is, Who is to be trusted as to knowledge of God claims? According to Newbigin, the full Christian tradition must be considered:

> Tradition is not a separate source of revelation from Scripture; it is the continuing activity of the Church through the ages in seeking to grasp and express under new conditions that which is given in Scripture. The study of Scripture takes place within the continuing tradition of interpretation.[71]

Moreover, it is critical to remember the *three-way shared relationship* between *individuals, the written word*, and *the lived tradition*: "it is only by 'indwelling' the Scripture that one remains faithful to the tradition. By this indwelling (abiding) we take our place and play our part in the story that is the true story of the whole human race and of the cosmos."[72] Of course, the story is intended to engender devotion by authentic worshipers of the Creator of the story.

Learning in community, therefore, means becoming immersed in the expressions of *worship* within the tradition: an ongoing effort of the worshiping community to "grow in the grace and knowledge of God"—part of the "activity of persons in community" committed to the tradition's worldview. One central aspect of these activities includes theologizing in worshipful contexts. As Newbigin writes, "Worship is the central work of

---

70. Newbigin, *Truth and Authority in Modernity*, 12–13.

71. Newbigin, *The Gospel in a Pluralist Society*, 53.

72. Newbigin, *Truth and Authority in Modernity*, 49.

the church, and everything else in its life has meaning and value as it finds its focus in worship." In fact, Newbigin claims that theology

> is rightly done in the context of worship and discipleship. The central place of theological teaching is the place where, in the midst of the mystery of the Eucharist, the minister seeks to interpret the words of Scripture to those who, having partaken of the Eucharist, will then go out into the world to live out in practice the action of the broken body and shed blood. This kind of theological teaching certainly needs illumination and correction by the work of those whose whole time is given to the scholarly study of the Christian tradition, but it must not be allowed to lose its central place in the life of the Church.[73]

Doing Justice and Mercy

In a mission-focused context involving critique of liberation theology (and later, capitalism), Newbigin declares that "to know the Lord" involves carrying out justice and mercy in tangible situations.[74] Determining what justice and mercy are, however, must be based on the biblical story and the authority of Jesus Christ, rather than on an unquestioned "proletariat praxis," which characterizes the Marxist coercion of much liberation theology. Thus, even while liberation theology may be viewed as being much closer to the biblical models of salvation and liberation than is Enlightenment-driven theology that separates theory from praxis,[75] for those who seem to imply that action itself is the truth, the text of scripture functions "as a source of judgment upon the praxis of those who have the Scriptures in their hands."[76]

Thus, the "supreme moral value" is not a class struggle praxis, based on "the casting of moral passions in the form of scientific affirmations under a facade of objectivity"; instead, it is "obedience to the personal

---

73. Wainwright, *Lesslie Newbigin*, 151, 153. Unfortunately, the source of the quotation for Newbigin is not cited, but is apparently the Constitution of the Church of South India (CSI). See also Newbigin, *Unfinished Agenda*, 85–87.

74. Newbigin, *Open Secret*, 109. Newbigin also states, "Those who claim to know the Lord and do evil are deceived. They are far from God. . . . There is no knowledge of God apart from the love of God, and there is no love of God apart from love of the neighbor." Cf., Jer 22:16.

75. Among liberation theologians, the exodus from Egypt is frequently presented as *the* biblical model of God's supreme saving action.

76. From Newbigin, *Open Secret*, 127–34, as quoted in Wainwright, *Lesslie Newbigin*, 188.

calling of Jesus Christ in and through his community. The ultimate model, in terms of which I am to understand what is the case and what is to be done, is furnished by the biblical story."[77] Newbigin notes that the gospel has always encouraged acts of justice and mercy, e.g., feeding the hungry, helping the poor and helpless, and healing the sick. Therefore, the believing community fulfills God's purposes by means of these deeds, and as a result, reflects the knowledge of God in seeking to make manifest the prayer, "Thy will be done."[78]

MERCY OF GOD   N's individualism

For Newbigin, embracing the gospel presupposes a bold proclamation concerning Jesus as the Way, the Truth, and the Life, while necessarily avoiding both pessimistic exclusivism and fanciful pluralism.[79] Wainwright summarizes the bishop's reasoning:

> "To confess Jesus as 'the true and living way' gives us the freedom and confidence to explore everything that claims to be real, knowing that it all belongs to him." Knowing the wideness in God's mercy, one can "rejoice in all the signs of God's grace at work in the lives of people of other religions or no religion," and yet—in the face also of God's judgment on human sin, there is no substitute for the story of God's redemptive love in Jesus Christ (Acts 10:34–48). The path of life is "marked by the footsteps of Jesus as he went from Bethlehem to Calvary. Because we know that this path is to be trusted, we want to call others to come with us on the way."[80]

77. Ibid., 187–89. This key statement must also be used to analyze much popular and fundamentalist American Christianity, which tends to equate justice and mercy with the praxis of supporting conservative (or liberal) causes wholesale, at the expense of judiciously and sufficiently nuanced deliberation. The problem is evident, for instance, vis-à-vis unapprised yet obdurate "straight-ticket" voting.

78. Ibid., 186.

79. Theologian Veli-Matti Kärkkäinen defines exclusivism as viewing salvation as "available only in Jesus Christ to the extent that those who have never heard the gospel are eternally lost. Exclusivists claim that salvation can be found only in the Christian church." Pluralism, he states, "involves both a positive and a negative element: Negatively, pluralism categorically rejects exclusivism (and often also inclusivism); positively, it affirms that people can find salvation in various religions and in many ways" (*Theology of Religions*, 24).

80. From a series of eleven articles written by Newbigin for *Reform* magazine in 1990, as quoted in Wainwright, *Lesslie Newbigin*, 329. Wainwright provides no addition source information.

This approach known as *biblical realism*[81] is properly viewed as one of several methodologies within the inclusivist category,[82] and is found in various works by Newbigin.[83] As to theological knowledge, this *wideness perspective* necessitates that knowledge of God extends beyond the bounds of Christianity (as a religion), and ought to be anticipated elsewhere since Christ is Lord of all.

In addition, the gospel calls to all people, and rather than asking persons to embrace a religion, offers the grace of God by faith in a person—Jesus Christ. Newbigin utilizes a *drama of salvation* model that includes the following *scenes*: 1) God's creation and mercy over all his works, and the ongoing trace of the presence and goodness of God in all human beings (e.g., consciousness); 2) the apostasy and rebellion against the Lord and his Anointed; 3) the historical reality of the apostasy and God's particular redemptive work with universal intent; 4) the Resurrection of the Crucified and commissioning of his witnesses to proclaim the story to every human soul and all nations; and 5) a judgment remaining to be executed. Wainwright points out that this fifth point, speaking of the knowledge of God in a salvific sense, means for Newbigin that

> the Church's being "the sign and first-fruit of God's purpose to save all" neither entails the exclusion of those who lived without knowledge of the story nor ensures that all in the end are necessarily saved. According to the New Testament, it is possible to miss the way and be lost; and three things are clear about the final judgment that will have to be faced: first, it will be in accordance with what each one has done in regard to the will of God . . . second, the warnings about judgment are directed chiefly against the overconfident; third, there will be surprises. Premature judgment by the Church is precluded (1 Corinthians 4:5).[84]

81. This designation is widely attributed to Hendrik Kraemer.

82. Kärkkäinen maintains that inclusivists "hold that while salvation is ontologically founded on the person of Christ, its benefits have been made universally available by the revelation of God" (*Theology of Religions*, 25).

83. See, for instance, two chapters, "No Other Name" and The Gospel and Other Religions," in *Gospel in a Pluralist Society.*

84. Wainwright, *Lesslie Newbigin*, 226, as a composite of Newbigin's thoughts expressed in Newbigin, "The Christian Faith and the World Religions," and Newbigin, *Open Secret*, 197–205.

WITHIN THE TRINITARIAN RELATIONSHIPS OF THE TRIUNE GOD

Newbigin asserts that while complete mutual understanding between humans is not attainable this side of the eschaton, perfect knowledge of persons does exist *within the Trinity*:

> The Christian testimony is that it is a reality within the being of the Triune God. This testimony rests on the fact that in a life lived as part of our human history, Jesus manifested a relationship of unbroken love and obedience to the one he called Father, a love and obedience sustained by the unfailing love and faithfulness of that same Father, and that those who believe and follow have been enabled through the Spirit actually to participate in this shared life of mutual love, which is the being of the Trinity, by being made one in the sonship of Jesus.[85]

Hence, knowledge of the Triune God involves *participation* in the shared love between the persons of the Trinity, demonstrating that the ultimate purpose for human knowledge of God is *partaking in the life and love of God*—a concept more suggestive of quintessential theological knowledge as characterized in scripture, than originating as a normative philosophical perspective.

Secondary Considerations

EXPERIENCE

Newbigin is rather dubious as to experience serving as a source of authority for theological knowledge. He notes that the way in which the word is used in recent vernacular is not found before the beginning of the nineteenth century, and primarily came to fruition with the work of F. D. E. Schleiermacher, who attempted to provide an apologetic for Christianity to the "cultured despisers" of his age, focusing attention on a supposedly universal "feeling of absolute dependence" upon God.[86]

As with reason and tradition, Newbigin eschews the idea of a stand alone (or separate source of) authoritative experientialism; it, too, belongs within a particular interpretive framework.[87] "It would therefore be mis-

---

85. From Newbigin, *Foolishness to the Greeks*, 89–90, as quoted in Wainwright, *Lesslie Newbigin*, 366.

86. See Schleiermacher, *Christian Faith*.

87. For instance, within a distinctly Christian perspective, an experience of, say, reflecting upon the death of Jesus Christ may generate feelings of gratitude, praise, and humility, whereas from within an alternative framework, the experience will likely include aspects

leading to treat experience as a distinct source of authority for Christian believing because the character of our experience is a function of the faith we hold."[88]

REASON

Ought reason to be considered a separate source of theological knowledge, disengaged from tradition and culture? As we have indicated, Newbigin believes such an idea is entirely mistaken. Instead, reason is a faculty that helps individuals and the communities understand various aspects of their experiences in a way that those experiences make sense. Contrary to Enlightenment trust in rationalism providing an alleged ahistorical, acultural basis of knowledge, he notes that "all rationality is socially and culturally embodied":

> Reason operates within a specific tradition of rational discourse, a tradition that is carried by a specific human community. There is no supracultural "reason" that can stand in judgment over all particular human traditions of rationality. All reason operates within a total worldview that is embodied in the language, the concepts, and the models that are the means by which those who share them can reason together.[89]

If this *particularity* of reason is valid, then how can the Christian worldview possibly escape the apparent relativism? Newbigin answers, "The fact that it is thus rooted in one strand of the whole human story in no way invalidates its claim to universal relevance."[90] The focus must be on the question of *adequacy*—and the testing of Christianity's account of reality against all other accounts. In Newbigin's view, the Christian vision

> will convince people of its superior rationality in proportion to the intellectual vigor and practical courage with which those who inhabit the new plausibility structure demonstrate its adequacy to the realities of human existence. This will call for the most vigorous and exacting use of reason . . . [and] I suspect that one of the

---

of questioning, denial, angst, or other feelings quite different from what is experienced by those immersed within a Christian faith framework.

88. Newbigin, *Truth and Authority in Modernity*, 61. More on the subject of experience later, as the question is raised whether Newbigin's view seriously contrasts with the perspective of evangelical reformists.

89. Ibid., 52.

90. Ibid.

main functions of the church in the twenty-first century will be to defend rationality against the hydra-headed *Volksgeist*.[91]

Commitment to the use of reason does not imply, however, generating a kind of Cartesian indubitable certainty for Christian knowledge and truth since such knowledge is reserved only in the eschaton. Instead, we are presently called to *trust and follow* the One who has reconciled us through the cross, and who says not "follow reason," but rather, "follow Me."

Taking a cue from Martin Buber's *I and Thou*, Newbigin develops the idea of *interpersonal*—rather than impersonal and autonomous—reason: a matter of the role reason is given to play. Autonomous reason remains in my full control as *I* determine and ask the questions, make the claims, force answers, and use reason to service my own sovereign will. Yet, in interpersonal relations with others—for our purposes, *the* Other—control must be surrendered, listening and exposing myself realized, self becoming the one questioned, and reason being the servant of "a listening and trusting openness, instead of being the servant of a masterful autonomy."[92] This does not mean, however, abandonment of reason: only a change in the role given to it.

The wrong-headed masterful autonomy has now caught Westerners in a dilemma between two competing philosophies: the false objectivity of scientific rationalism, and a relativistic, fragmented, rebellious subjectivism. Newbigin finds a direct correlation in the Christian church between the first and fundamentalism, which in some ways mirrors scientism, and between the second and liberalism, which privatizes faith as religious experience and personal opinions. The addition of skepticism aggravates the situation, doubting the possibility of knowing *any* truth, as Nietzschean views have become fashionable among current elites who claim that knowledge is simply concealed assertions of power.[93]

This situation provides the church with an opportunity to use reason in the service of the Master—the gospel may and must now speak into the various collapses of the "plausibility structures" of the world, as it is the nature of the gospel to do so because of the resurrection of Christ, which is "the beginning of a new creation, the work of that same power by which

91. Ibid., 53–54.

92. Ibid., 55–56.

93. Wainwright writes that "deconstruction" is viewed by Newbigin as an "ultimate absurdity" with its premise that "all claims to speak of truth may appear untenable" (Wainwright, *Lesslie Newbigin*, 73).

creation itself exists," and therefore "the starting point for a new way of understanding and dealing with the world."[94]

Our survey of Lesslie Newbigin's approach to theological knowledge has revealed a model that appears strongly committed to both the centrality of the unchanging gospel and a method that authentically (re)presents that gospel in ever-changing contexts. While it would be feasible to stop our examination here and proceed to commend Newbigin's methodology for evangelical theology, it seems preferable to first consider the relationship of his ideas and practices with those of "card-carrying" evangelical intellectuals. This option will probably better facilitate for evaluating which of the theological epistemologies that we have considered in some detail—Newbigin's and postconservatives—may perhaps be the most advantageous for knowledge of God considerations in the present postmodern (as well as whatever "postpostmodern") philosophical and cultural settings we face in the West. Before getting to this, however, we will, in seeking to underscore the common ground as well the distinctions, briefly summarize the relationship between Newbigin's vision for theological knowledge and the classic evangelical traditionalist perspective.

Newbigin's Theological Epistemology Compared / Contrasted with Contemporary Evangelical Thought

Newbigin and Evangelical Traditionalist Theological Epistemology

At many points, Newbigin's theological method substantially diverges from traditionalist models. Nevertheless, general agreement does exist regarding essential Christian doctrine.[95] Among the reasons that could be suggested for the significant differences in methodology are Newbigin's postfoundationalist perspective, disallowing a primarily propositionalist, Enlightenment-led schema for theological knowledge. Of course, many other disparities follow from this macro-distinction, some of which will be seen via a forthcoming Newbigin/postconservatism comparison. For

---

94. Ibid., 72–73.

95. For instance, "belief in God's transcendence and supernatural activity, the Bible as divinely inspired and infallible in matters of faith and practice, Jesus Christ as crucified and risen Savior and Lord of the world, conversion as the only authentic initiation into salvation, and evangelism through communication of the gospel to all people" (see Olson, *Story of Christian Theology*, 595).

instance, Newbigin's unwillingness to embrace the characteristically traditionalist view of the Bible as the *sole* source of theological knowledge—*sola scriptura* in its most restrictive sense—or the emphatic rationalism frequently charged of the traditionalist view, and especially visible within certain contemporary fundamentalist faith communities. Therefore, rather than presenting here a lengthy comparison and contrasting of Newbigin and traditionalists, the next section will concentrate on the connections between Newbigin and postconservatives.

Newbigin and Postconservative Evangelical Theological Epistemology

INTRODUCTION

As we proceed to compare and contrast Newbigin's theological knowledge view with that of evangelical postconservatives, what becomes evident is the existence of a great deal more agreement than disagreement. And while there will be some attempt to consider the broader reformist continuum with reference to theological epistemology, the views expressed will essentially represent the views of the same three postconservative scholars whose efforts were examining in the previous chapter: Stanley Grenz, Kevin Vanhoozer, and Robert Webber.[96] The direction ahead will include 1) delineation of a general hypothesis regarding compatibility of the two perspectives being considered (i.e., Newbigin's and postconservatives'), 2) focus on three major areas of consensus, 3) discussion and proposal regarding one area of apparently significant contrast, and 4) a modest recommendation concerning critically appropriating Newbigin's method as a promising way forward for evangelical theological epistemology.

GENERAL THESIS CONCERNING COMPATIBILITY

As noted above, Newbigin and reformists share significant common ground as to theological knowledge perspectives. For example, one rather obvious area of agreement involves the *particularity of all knowledge*—knowledge as historically, culturally, and contextually grounded. Both Newbigin and reformists unequivocally reject the Enlightenment idea of a pure objectiv-

---

96. Throughout this assessment, rather than constantly restating that each of these three scholars agree concerning a particular feature of theological epistemology, it will be assumed that a general agreement exists among the group; as explicit disagreement arises respecting a specific subject being analyzed, it will be noted.

ity of knowing as potential or real for human beings, although neither diminishes the objectivity of the gospel and its universally-intended meta-narrative. In fact, commitment to the gospel metanarrative as *ultimate* story concerning the knowledge of God and reality is central to both perspectives. This narrative focus stands in contradistinction to a more proposition-oriented approach to the biblical text, without denying or downplaying the explicit didactic assertions respecting truth and knowledge evident within the biblical story and its diverse genres. The chief claim is that not only is *the Bible's own method generally narrative*, but that the story-oriented approach is also highly relevant for the present cultural context.[97] Such fundamental concord between views will prove salient to recommending critical appropriation of Newbigin's thought for a satisfying evangelical theological epistemology.

Both standpoints also embrace the idea of a personal or relational element being intrinsic to all knowledge, plus the associated inherent fiduciary character of all knowledge. While abundant examples could be assembled to support this general and pervasive accordance between Newbigin and reformists, attention will focus on three primary arenas of unity: Christ-centeredness, church community, and personal commitment.[98]

CHRIST-CENTEREDNESS

Both Newbigin and postconservatives insist on a Christ-centered focus. They shift the center of theological knowledge—once determined by traditionalists—from a rational-propositional basis to a Person-oriented one: in other words, replacing what they see as a modernity-driven approach to interpreting the Bible with a relational approach to knowing Jesus Christ. Both agree that traditionalist theology and epistemology have been perverted—sometimes profoundly—by highly questionable Enlightenment principles, such as the scientific method evident in the Old Princetonians' utilization of Scottish Common Sense Philosophy, and the consequent appeal to "neutral" facts.

---

97. It seems evident that most cultures of the world, regardless the historical context, are story-oriented, and that the primarily Western Enlightenment approach to knowledge is more akin to being somewhat of an anomaly in time than a universal given.

98. More precisely, 1) Jesus Christ as central to theological knowledge; 2) the *ecclesia* as the normative orientation by which individuals learn of, and grow with respect to, the knowledge of God; and 3) a holistic framework as intrinsic to theological knowledge.

Instead, both reformists and Newbigin eschew what they view as wrong-headed dualistic distinctions (e.g., fact/value). The Bible, rather than being a so-called storehouse of facts waiting to be unearthed, is instead a particular story of God intended to persuade the reader of the legitimacy and universality of its proclaimed metanarrative—a metanarrative centered in a Person hailed as incarnate Deity. And while Newbigin acknowledges that there "is still a vast ocean of what we do not know and do not understand," he notes that "we know the way, and the way is Jesus. As Bonhoeffer said, 'Jesus Christ alone is the certainty of faith.'" Newbigin concludes that "to look for certainty elsewhere is to head for the wasteland."[99] Overall, postconservatives agree, although some are concerned to explicitly associate this claim more directly with the Christian community.

Newbigin and postconservatives affirm together that Christ-centered theological epistemology is more biblically based and philosophically compelling than Bible-centered traditionalist methodology. A Christ-centered approach also coincides with the *personal* nature of knowledge perspective that is being given increased attention among evangelical scholars and practitioners. Evidently, revisiting scripture's witness to the knowledge of God, together with renewed consideration of ancient Christian exegesis, has effectively produced of recent times more christomorphic than bibliomorphic thinkers.

ECCLESIA COMMUNITY

A second major commonality shared between Newbigin and postconservatives is emphasis on a *church community* orientation regarding theological knowledge. We have noted throughout this study that one of the prized possessions of Enlightenment rationalism was its appeal to the authority of the subject, necessitating individualism. The abandonment of the widely disparaged conception of a "traditionless" self-reliance has meant a search elsewhere for authority, frequently resulting in an emphasis on one's community or communities; in the case of evangelicals, the focus moves to church as Christian community. Reformists and Newbigin essentially concur that since disciples of Jesus throughout the premodern church practiced an *immersed participation* in the faith community, knowledge of God through such communities is primary. Thus, the *sociology of knowl-*

99. Newbigin, *Proper Confidence*, 104–5.

edge model must be brought to the fore. According to Robert Webber, this tradition-oriented move coincides with the present ethos of culture, and is intended to "restore and then adapt classical Christianity to the post-modern cultural situation."[100] Moreover, Webber pictures the premodern church era as "the most productive."[101]

As seen earlier, Newbigin envisions the church as a central source for theological knowledge. Applying Polanyi's appraisal of discoveries/knowledge as found in the sciences, Newbigin asserts that knowledge of God, like all knowing, is always part of a tradition: it comes by means of individuals becoming *learners in an apprenticeship* within the Christian tradition, indwelling its language, concepts, models, images, and assumptions.[102] Theological knowledge is also found within supremely authoritative church practices, i.e., the sacraments of baptism and the Eucharist, where they point *to* Jesus and *through* Jesus to the Trinity. Hence, obedient praxis within the faith community authenticates human knowledge of God. Most reformists are prompt to acknowledge the same basic vision of persons-in-community and the immersed participation necessary to theological knowledge.[103] For instance, we discussed earlier Grenz's proposal in support of the communitarian view of the *individual-within-community*.[104] At the same time, we have shown throughout our study that Newbigin and postconservative evangelicals together affirm the gospel's calling of *individuals* to salvific knowledge of God in Christ, while adding that growing in the knowledge of God occurs primarily as a learner within the context of Christian community.

100. Webber, *Ancient-Future Faith*, 24.

101. Ibid.

102. Newbigin, *Proper Confidence*, 46. Newbigin—like some postconservatives—seems to be overstating their case, at least on its face, by not including instances of individual surrender to and trust in Christ. Certainly one such important exception to the communitarian-apprenticeship model would be the evident faith commitment made by one of the two thieves on the cross; another would be the numerous testimonies of individuals claiming to have come to saving faith in God through Christ outside of any known Christian communities or influences. Presenting a more nuanced account of the church community/Christian tradition view, would likely have alleviated concerns over seemingly unavailable means of grace outside of the ostensibly normative *apprenticeship way* into theological knowledge.

103. However, at least one reformist evidently finds greater substance in a virtue-orientation than in a church community approach (see Wood, *Epistemology*).

104. Grenz, *Primer on Postmodernism*, 168.

Personal Commitment

Thirdly, both Newbigin and reformists emphasize *personal commitment;* they are united in seeking to recapture this premodern vision of *trust* as central to theological knowledge. What both intend to achieve apparently includes a re-fusion of flawed dualisms, e.g., fact/value, believing/knowing; even more importantly, a shift regarding ingrained dependence. Hence, this involves moving away from an *impersonal* Enlightenment and self-centered authoritative standard, toward a biblical *relatedness* direction, wherein God is at the center, and human *personal mutuality* (i.e., serving one another) is the norm.[105] This *commitment orientation* integrates with both Christ- and church community- centeredness, and forms a holistic approach to the knowledge of God; none of the three emphases we have identified exists apart from interrelatedness with the others.

What is the rationale for this holism? It follows necessarily from the triune God being the object of one's commitment, as primarily known in the person of the incarnate Word; the normative context of knowing God being within a Christian tradition, i.e., church community; and the praxis of persons-in-community, e.g., sacraments, worship, preaching. Together, these form a three-strand theological knowledge cord not easily unwound.

Postconservatives point out that commitment-orientation of all knowledge forces a dilemma upon traditionalists; having fused theology with the alleged impartiality of the scientific method, for the sake of consistency, traditionalists must commit to some other basis for their theological epistemology. Reformists, in concert with Newbigin, argue that embracing a commitment-centered theological epistemology is the only method that will ultimately prove judicious.

Both personal and corporate commitment to responsibility and witness are in view, and the local congregation ought to serve as "the local presence of the one holy catholic and apostolic Church that we acknowledge in the creeds."[106] Clearly, theological reflection and praxis must hang together, serving as persuasive evidence for the trustworthiness of an evangelical worldview, including its theological knowledge claims.

105. Wainwright, *Lesslie Newbigin,* 257.

106. From Newbigin, *Truth to Tell,* 28, as quoted in Wainwright, *Lesslie Newbigin,* 74–75.

Past evangelicals paid little attention to interreligious dialogue. In our increasingly pluralistic cultures, however, this phenomenon looms large. Both Newbigin and the postconservatives emphasize the importance of evangelical engagement in these discussions. Yet they both make it clear that such dialogue must begin and end with commitment to the gospel—not dispassionate reason—as the final authority, with the *purpose* of dialoguing for Christians being to witness for Christ in various ways.[107]

POTENTIAL CHALLENGE TO COMPATIBILITY: CONTRASTING VIEWS OF EXPERIENCE?

Most postconservatives appear *prima facia* to embrace *experience* as one among several interrelated sources of theological knowledge.[108] Newbigin, however, finds this unacceptable, assigning experience a significant *supplementary* role: experiences "can continue to provide authority for believers only insofar as they enable the person to 'make sense' of *the rest* of his or her experience" (emphasis mine).[109] Furthermore, one's worldview is central to interpreting experiences, and "the Christian Gospel provides a framework within which all experience is interpreted in terms of the wise and loving purpose of God."[110] Newbigin prefers to see experience as part of the living tradition of the Christian community, reliving the biblical story, and preaching the word that is "reinterpreted and applied to contemporary discipleship." He concludes, "At the heart of all of this is something that may be called experience, but it is specifically the experience of the contemporary power of the Holy Spirit of God, who is the Spirit of Jesus, to bring the atoning work home to the heart and conscience of the worshiping community."[111]

107. This ought to be a normative approach since Jesus is the source by which all other religions, and the totality of experience, is understood (see Wainwright, *Lesslie Newbigin*, 226–27).

108. We have noted that many such thinkers generally accept a Wesleyan Quadrilateralism (or a modification thereof). Significantly, then, the majority of reformists are not "Classical Reformed" or "Modified Reformed" scholars, but rather "Reformed Arminians" or "Wesleyan Arminians." Different theological traditions may help explain potential incompatibilities with Newbigin, who most closely parallels a "Modified Reformed" attitude.

109. See Newbigin, *Truth and Authority in Modernity*, 59–60.

110. Ibid., 60–61. Newbigin notes that this holds true for the crucifixion of Jesus—in one framework, it is "the wisdom of God," in another it is "folly." This point was made quite evident in Mel Gibson's film, *The Passion of the Christ*.

111. Ibid., 62.

What at first appears to be in *contrast* with a postconservative view of experience in actuality *parallels* it. This correspondence stems from a mutual understanding and critical embracing of major epistemological shifts taking place within the culture, conjoined with an ecclesial-focused theological method. Consequently, rather than a developing subjective experientialism, whether of the fundamentalist or liberal variety, reformists view experience within a *communitarian framework*—a move virtually identical to Newbigin's judgment. As Grenz explains, normative evangelical experiences—i.e., encounters—with God in Christ occur within Christian community:

> Most evangelicals would agree that at the heart of their vision of the faith is an emphasis on an experience of being encountered savingly in Jesus Christ by the God of the Bible. This encounter is an identity-producing event. Through Christ, God constitutes us individually as believers and corporately as a community of believers.
>
> This elevation of the role of experience ought not to be confused with the older Protestant liberalism. Two aspects separate the evangelical ethos as delineated here from the liberal project. First, liberalism transformed religious experience into a new foundationalism. . . . Rather than following liberalism in this direction, the evangelical theology proposed here avers that the various religions mediate religious experiences that are categorically different from each other. The encounter with the God of the Bible through Jesus, which is foundational to Christian identity, is shared only by those who participate in the Christian community (even though the experience is *potentially* universal, in that all persons might conceivably embrace the Christian faith).[112]

Grenz explicates his second point of differentiation between liberals and evangelicals on the role of experience. He maintains that

> the evangelical approach takes seriously the experience-forming dimension of interpretive frameworks. . . . Experience does not precede interpretation. Rather experiences are always filtered by an interpretive framework that facilitates their occurance. Hence, religious experience is dependent on a cognitive framework that sets forth a specifically religious interpretation of the world. . . . More

112. Grenz, *Renewing the Center*, 202.

specifically, Christian experience is facilitated by the proclamation of the Christian gospel.[113]

In view of the earlier analysis of Newbigin's ecclesial-centered method, including the idea of *apprenticeship* whereby individuals connect with others within the faith community or tradition who *know the way*, there appears to be substantial agreement with postconservatives on the role of experience vis-à-vis theological knowledge. Webber's emphasis on a holistic immersed participation in the community of faith, where experience is part of the whole rule of faith and praxis, further supports this contention.[114]

Neither Newbigin nor most postconservative scholars seem prepared to adopt experience as a wholly distinct source of theological knowledge. The bishop's Reformed tradition doubtlessly influenced his reserve whereas, to the contrary, the more Arminian-leaning tendencies of most reformists, especially those most closely connected with revivalism and charismatic movements, would likely be expected to possess a strong experience orientation. Somewhat paradoxically, however, the cultural shift away from the Enlightenment model of knowledge and its emphasis on *scientia* and individualism—especially pertaining to authoritative claims—toward a post-Enlightenment return to *opinio* and tradition, has ultimately emerged as even more persuasive. Correspondingly, reformists appreciate this *new light* from God's word and the subsequent returning of experience to what they view as its rightful place—not as a stand-alone source for knowledge of God, but as a constituent part of the holistic church community.

SOME FINAL CONCERNS

Several important potentialities for rejecting Newbigin's approach to theological knowledge for evangelicalism remain to be addressed. First, there are almost certainly some concerns to be vocalized from the theological extremes. At one end, strictly Reformed and traditionalist scholars will surely find fault with several aspects of Newbigin's thought, seeing too many deficiencies: for instance, his openness to certain charismatic movements. At the other end, many Arminian and "tradition-free" postmodern thinkers will likely take issue with Newbigin's liturgical and sacramental emphases. Nevertheless, one possible result may be that more moderate

---

113. Ibid., 202–3.

114. For instance, see Webber, *Ancient-Future Faith*, 24.

thinkers along the theological spectrum may, through exercising patience and tolerance, influence their more unyielding colleagues concerning Newbigin's approach, while also establishing or improving dialogue with their counterparts.

Second, Newbigin's rejection of a strict inerrancy position will loom large for some evangelicals—many within more fundamentalist and decidedly conservative communities.[115] However, a significant number of evangelical scholars would concur with, or at least not stand opposed to, Newbigin's approach to the Bible.[116] Therefore, his high view of scripture's authority and inspiration, coupled with his unbending commitment to orthodox Christian doctrine, leaves little room for advancing arguments against adopting his method on this basis alone.

Third, for those continuing their commitment to foundationalism, it seems likely Newbigin's theological epistemology will receive short shrift, mainly because of unwillingness to acknowledge the virtual collapse of modern rationalistic approaches to knowledge. As the powerful philosophical influences of the modern era fade further into history, it seems probable that traditionalist evangelicals will either move with Newbigin toward embracing a more relational and *credo ut intelligam* approach to theological knowledge, or suffer following theological "or-

---

115. Newbigin's view makes him an extremely unlikely model for fundamentalist evangelicals, and for some others who hold this philosophical position as essential to Christian orthodoxy. For other evangelicals, his commitment to the inspiration and authority of the Bible, as well as his affirmation of *all* conservative Christian doctrines concerning the person and work of Christ, the Trinity, etc., offers evidence of Newbigin's orthodoxy. For him "the Scriptures serve as the supreme & decisive standard of faith" (see Wainwright, *Lesslie Newbigin*, 88–89). Still, Newbigin's opposition to the doctrine of verbal inerrancy because it "is a direct denial of the way in which God has chosen to make himself known to us as the Father of our Lord Jesus Christ" appears to be a *non sequitur*, since it is unclear how a scriptural inerrancy stance actually *denies* God's revealing himself as the Father of Jesus. Perhaps Newbigin is motivated here more by a disparagement of the scientific method and naïve biblicism foisted upon scripture by fundamentalists and certain conservatives than by logical implication of his own position. Nevertheless, for him, the Bible remains the *primary* and *decisive* (though not *exclusive*) theological knowledge source, appealing to the givenness of the revelation of God in Christ content "through the testimony of his first followers."

116. It would appear that for a large and growing number of evangelical thinkers, the commonly held notion that throughout most of the its history, the Christian church has recognized the Bible as the premiere and final authoritative source for faith and practice, provides sufficient validation for the scriptures as fiducial and functional word of God, thus rejecting the idea of subjecting the Bible to modern tests of the scientific method in order to supposedly "verify" its constitution.

phanhood" as the controlling philosophical method eventually slips into irrelevance. Together with Lesslie Newbigin, we would hope for the first of these two alternatives.

Conclusion

Sensitive to the reality that no single scholar can be expected to fully represent the complex evangelical intellectual community, some may wonder about a proposal to consider Lesslie Newbigin's approach to theological knowledge as a model for evangelical thought. But as this analysis has shown, it appears very probable that evangelical academia and ecclesia would stand to benefit substantially from Newbigin's faithful, informed, and constructive reflection: study deeply attentive to the practicable and functional life of the church. While some evangelical theologians evidently appreciate certain insights from Newbigin,[117] to date few postconservatives appear to have embraced his method as paradigmatic for theological reflection and praxis. However, among missiologists, Newbigin's efforts have been received with more interest.[118]

Newbigin's *theological life* calls for an evangelical consideration of his concrete theology and relational epistemology, especially within a culture yearning for authentic and relational praxis.[119] Newbigin has sought

---

117. See, for example, Grenz and Franke, *Beyond Foundationalism*, 151; Vanhoozer, "Voice and the Actor," 105–6.

118. For instance, see Hunsberger, *Bearing the Witness of the Spirit*.

119. Within the business sector, thriving companies are constantly challenged to learn (obviously, through much trial and error) the value of listening to voices *outside* their own area of specialization, recognizing myopia can be debilitating. Evangelical scholars would do well to take a lesson from, say, the Swiss watch making industry of a few generations ago. Presented with an opportunity to capitalize on the then recent invention of LED watches, Swiss watchmakers snubbed the idea as uninteresting and impracticable, assuming the watch-buying world—of which they apparently controlled nearly ninety-five percent at the time—would never consider purchasing such obviously inferior products. To the contrary, within a decade both Japan and the United States had surpassed the Swiss in market share, leaving them about a five percent share of annual sales. A similar example involved the Xerox Corporation's discounting the potential value of a computer pointing device, only later to realize their *rejection of the mouse* demonstrated they has been trapped within their own myopic vision, leading to a near total failure to capitalize on the exploding computer industry. Fortunately for Xerox, enough reformists were able to see the sales potential for computer peripherals and supplies. What is the main point here? The need for being open to seriously consider ideas posed by those not generally considered within one's particular community—they may have valuable, even pivotal, contributions to make for the benefit of the company: possibly for the entire industry. In the same vein, Newbigin's

to comprehend, utilize, and clarify a biblical-based, Christ-centered, Trinitarian-framed perspective, drawing from decades of experience in a multiplicity of cultures and contexts, to the glory of God and the benefit of the church. His wide experience with diverse worldviews, cultures, historical periods, churches, traditions, and denominations, engenders a certain reliability and respect. His outlook is holistic, crossing boundaries of East and West, privileged and oppressed, intellectual and experiential, modern and postmodern, Christendom and post-Christian culture.

Newbigin's lifelong intellectual and theological journey has undergone several major shifts—most central to this work, in the area of epistemology and its relevance to theology. Moving with time and culture through variegated stages of modernity, late modernity, and postmodernity, Newbigin habitually reflected upon and seriously engaged with the research and developments within a wide range of academic disciplines. His assimilation of the thought of Michael Polanyi, for instance, served as a major turning point in his focus on the personal nature of knowledge, including knowledge of God. This direction led him to a deepening appreciation for the primarily narrative and relational character of the Bible, and to theological focus on the metanarrative of the gospel, both in its particularity and its universal intent. Short of the self-revelation of God to humankind, ignorance of the knowledge of God would persist. However, by grace, God chose self-disclosure to human creatures, most manifestly in Jesus Christ. Christians are thus called to fully adopt a trust-based, Christian community-oriented, metanarrative-centered, praxis-habituated, and trinitarian-framed theological epistemology.

A proposal for adopting Newbigin's approach to theological knowledge for evangelical thought will undoubtedly be welcomed more by postconservatives than by traditionalists, by those envisioning *more light breaking forth from God's word* than those believing *all* has been revealed and subsequently *concretized* within certain confessions and catechisms. Still, postconservatives would do well to embrace and focus on the three areas of Christ-centeredness, church community, and personal commitment for theological knowledge—essentials generally shared with Newbigin. In so doing, evangelical theological epistemology seems assured to remain

---

ideas have often met with neglect by the evangelical theological guild. Such bypassing is shortsighted. His "outsideness" actually seems to have more to do with his liturgical and dialogical involvements than with his clearly conservative doctrinal and theological commitments, which ought to be reassuring for most evangelicals on the "inside."

informed via a biblically-faithful and holistic methodology, rather than chiefly through philosophical movements.

Finally, Lesslie Newbigin's *holistic* approach to theology and the knowledge of God might best be viewed metaphorically as representing aspects of *both* types of theologians Stanley Grenz refers to in his vision for evangelicals achieving a desirable contemporary and orthodox apologetic theology:

> What is needed in the post-theological situation . . . is not a re-surgence of the type of traditionalist mentality that would define clearly the boundary of evangelicalism and launch a campaign to oust from the movement any reformists whom they have judged to have moved beyond the pale of evangelical orthodoxy. Nor does the current situation call for the thorough revising of evangelical theology that gives scant attention to the great legacy of which the contemporary generation is the recipient. Instead, what is needed today is a continuation, a transferring into the present situation, of the program that the architects of the neo-evangelical movement inaugurated, namely the creation of an apologetic theology that brings classic orthodoxy into conversation with the contemporary situation. For this to occur, however, requires that the theological task be advanced by *traditional reformists* and *reforming traditional-ists*, by reform-minded theologians who value the tradition and tra-dition-anchored thinkers who are zealous for ongoing reform.[120]

May God grant us more *patient revolutionaries*,[121] as we await the final transition from *theologia viatorum* to *theologia beatorum*.

Although it would perhaps suffice to simply end this study at offering Newbigin's theological epistemology to postconservative-leaning evangeli-cal intellectuals for genial integration, an alternative path has been select-ed—one that draws heavily on Newbigin's work, yet also attends to certain other complementary elements. Hence, we now turn to briefly consider a modest proposal for revitalizing evangelical theological epistemology.

---

120. Grenz, *Renewing the Center*, 183. Emphasis mine.

121. Newbigin, *Gospel in a Pluralist Society*, 209.

5

Constructive Proposal for Revitalizing Evangelical Theological Epistemology

A Holistic Approach

HOW THEN SHALL WE NOW PROCEED? MUCH HAS BEEN MADE OF THE SIGnificant shifts underway within evangelical thought. As we have discussed, repositioning within certain disciplines appears to be shaping the future of evangelical theological method in general and theological epistemology in particular. Real changes are occurring by means of consequential methodological transitions in history, theology, and apologetics: moving from ahistorical to tradition, rationalism to narrative, and evidentialism to embodiment—especially among younger evangelicals. Many postconservatives are embracing these modifications, viewing them as not only connecting with postmodern culture, but as recovering premodern ways of knowing associated with ancient, classical, and medieval expressions of Christian faith. How one views these shifts—as *revitalizing* evangelical theology or *razing* it—likely reveals one's inclination for postconservatism or traditionalism, respectively.

Bearing in mind the warnings and criticisms made herein regarding certain aspects of reformist views, there is still much to commend with reference to the various moves being made. And while a growing number of new proposals seek a new evangelical theological method, it is hoped that the constructive vision presented here will add a new, melodic, and encouraging piece of theological epistemology for the evangelical orchestra to play!

Hence, what remains for this work is to chart a constructive way forward for evangelical scholarship to implement a revitalized, holistic theological epistemology, incorporating many of the characteristics of Newbigin's methodology, while making use of addition suggestions herein. The first step will comprise reflection upon primary presuppositions undergirding the proposal. The content will include mainly reiteration of several important postmodern epistemological insights discussed in previous sections, plus introduction of a few fresh ideas. Next, an outline of the proposal will be offered by means of brief appeal to the distinctive facets integrated into the larger mosaic. Finally, the study will conclude with some recommended practical steps for revitalizing evangelical theological epistemology. We begin with consideration of the philosophical underpinnings at work in this prescription.

Philosophical Factors Supporting the Proposal for a Revitalized Evangelical Theological Epistemology

We recognize that foundationalism—in its stronger versions at least—is a hindrance to our vision for a post-Enlightenment theological epistemology, entailing that evangelical scholarship find appropriate and helpful ways of theologizing in the postfoundational context. Postmodern philosophy, critically appropriated, offers evangelicalism new opportunities relative to constructing models of thought beyond prevalent rationalism-oriented motifs, while retaining a gospel metanarrative focus.

The twin dangers of theological stagnation with built-in irrelevance, and theological fluidity for the sake of relevance, will continue to exist until the eschaton; thus seeking a middle way (however idealistic) is critical, even while knowingly leaning one direction or the other to some degree, yet aiming for balancing and centering. One deep need for the contemporary church is to return to an *essentialist vision of the faith*, thereby working to reinforce unity at the expense of secondary issues to some degree, while acknowledging the value and continuation of diversity. There is growing evidence of a move towards the "center" among evangelical scholars, a positive development within intellectual evangelicalism. Sharing *what is* rather than *what must be* is one such move afoot.[1]

Evangelicalism must be willing to incorporate more of the *Great Tradition of Belief*[2] as a whole into its own theological method, a more ecumenical orientation in an effort to critically appropriate the wisdom, practices, and theological and philosophical insights provided via the

1. Among more recent books taking this tact, perhaps one of the finest is Boyd and Eddy, *Across the Spectrum.*

2. Olson, *Mosaic of Christian Belief,* 32–39, 46–47.

larger tradition of the church, embracing that which has been believed by (nearly) all Christians at (practically) all times and (virtually) everywhere.

Much of intellectual evangelicalism has been hampered by a largely *text-only basis* for theological knowledge—yet symbol, metaphor, mystery, embodiment, and story provide powerful ways into the truth of the knowledge of God, while also moving back towards faith and humility and away from facts alone and overconfidence. Therefore, we must move beyond an exclusively textual referent with respect to the knowledge of God.

Hubris and exclusivist tendencies have been detrimental to the cause of the gospel and its gaining a hearing among competing views of reality. A more gracious and inclusivist approach—yet free of open-endedness and theological pluralism—is the best middle way for remaining true to the gospel story (i.e., Eucatastrophe), while open to the mercy of God by means of grace beyond human comprehension.

Too deep and wide a line has been drawn by certain evangelical scholars (usually with radical immobility strictures) between knowledge of God and *salvific* knowledge of God. While such a line exists—most likely at the point of trust in Christ, or in God where Christ has not been made known—a good deal of room must remain open for God's own work of grace, his character of love, drawing of the Holy Spirit, and ways beyond our own comprehension, yet within the whole of the scriptural vision. Thus, theological knowledge ought to be treated without certain specificity of "savingness" connected to a particular knowledge area (e.g., God as self-revealed in creation or as Creator).

Scripture—the Old Testament particularly—does not regularly focus on differentiating knowledge of God from saving knowledge of God, although certain passages are given to the task.[3] This distinction is ultimately and preeminently important, and while we are prompt to affirm that certain elements of theological knowledge by definition represent a personal trust or knowing of the Lord and are to be viewed as salvific,[4] some aspects do not necessitate this type of knowledge.[5]

Employing an approach that embraces the theological conviction that one's *never-ending trust in Christ* is requisite for salvific knowledge of God would seem to abate the need for consciously or repeatedly address-

---

3. For instance, James 2:18–26.

4. E.g., via the person of Jesus Christ.

5. E.g., being intellectually virtuous.

ing the issue of *whether* theological knowledge has *saving efficacy*. While this author is more inclined towards God-centered perseverance—yet as only known certainly from God's side of the equation and based on union with Christ—the "livedness" of a saved life demands practical persevering from a human perspective, *leaving all ultimacy questions to the sole authority of the Lord.* Such an approach to the knowledge of God will entail the following: 1) a general consideration of theological knowledge without speculation as to the salvific aspect in detail; 2) concentration on employing Quadrilateral sources and beyond; 3) pointing to postconservative evangelical contributions and building upon them; 4) attending to scripture predominantly among other sources of theological knowledge; 5) incorporating broader church perspectives (e.g., Eastern Orthodoxy), critically and appropriately.

The notion that the knower universally and objectively comprehends knowledge ought to be rejected in favor of epistemic particularity and perspectivalism. Far too much evidence has been amassed disconfirming the notion of universality in how and what individuals (and cultures) know. Moreover, notions of an Archimedean point presently available to human beings must be discarded in favor of a non-reductive historicism—one that also presupposes the reality of knowledge and truth constituted in God and the will of God.[6]

As discussed earlier, what was supplanted in the Age of Reason was not irrationality—rather *opinio was replaced by scientia.* Before this development, Aquinas had reiterated that we see through a glass darkly by declaring the balanced view that, although Christians attest to the reality of being able to know God—even in a relational manner—because of the *imago dei* present in our human intellects,[7] the quantitative difference between divine and human limits our speaking of God to an *analogical* sense. This presupposes there is no univocal way of referring to both God and human beings, but rather that we use the language of creatures to speak of God, and thus we cannot *fully* reflect or comprehend God as he is.[8]

---

6. Rejection of *epistemological* objectivity does not require a similar rejection of *ontological* realism, as Grenz, Pannenberg, and others have argued. See, for instance, Grenz, *Renewing the Center*, ch. 6.

7. This conception appears to be a less holistic view of the image of God than understood by postconservative evangelicals today.

8. See Benson, "End of the Fantastic Dream," 158–59.

Enlightenment thinking assumes knowledge to be certain, objective, and good: in principle, accessible to the human mind. This method means that *reason* becomes the authoritative test for reality: an "absolute faith in human rational capabilities." The "autonomous self" is championed—supposing individuals may transcend tradition or community.[9] So in such cases, rather than knowledge being *cognosci*, it is *comprehende*. And as we have discussed, this presumption helped lead to modernity's hubris and inevitable demise. According to Grenz, the critical spirit of postmodernity is actually closer in certain respects to the spirit of biblical faith than the modernist assumptions of objective epistemological certainty. Viewing human reason as suspect and untrustworthy is a *Christian* disposition. Scripture warns of the deceitfulness—even *self-deception*—of reason, and that part of saving truth is *beyond* reason.[10]

Postconservatives have correctly pointed to the *overuse* and *idolizing* of reason in much modernist epistemology, and have also sought to demonstrate the necessity of humility that must accompany claims to knowledge and truth, as opposed to the hubris that has often but not always characterized foundationalism. In postconservative evangelical epistemology, reason has not been *discarded*—only placed as one among relatively equal resources, secondary to scripture, in the quest for knowledge and truth. Other ways of knowing are being given opportunity to rise again. *Opinio* is no longer thought of as only a tertiary support for things known autonomously. Of course, the risk of elevating *opinio* to an idolatrous level needs to be strongly guarded against, and signs are already showing that point to an inordinate amount of epistemic weight being granted to tradition *at the expense of* alternative means of gaining knowledge.[11]

9. Grenz, *Primer on Postmodernism*, 4.

10. Dorrien, *Remaking of Evangelical Theology*, 194.

11. Richard Rorty (see *Objectivism, Relativism, and Truth: Philosophical Papers*) and Stanley Fish (see *Is There a Text in this Class?*) are two thinkers who appear to place the entirety of epistemological considerations within a *shared community*. In doing so, they are apparently working to avoid a full-blown subjective relativism, and in a way, they do. On the other hand, by failing to consult and engage with the larger community (e.g., traditions, churches, charity organizations), it would suggest nothing short of a group of inbred thinkers regurgitating the same views. While Rorty can be heard calling for civil conversation apart from searching for (allegedly non-existent) truth, Fish admits that *he himself* is the primary leader of his community to which others are seeking knowledge and truth. Thus, while some might characterize for instance, Rush Limbaugh's followers as "dittoheads" (a term they themselves now use endearingly—similar to "Christians" in that way), the real dittoheads of a negative sort would be those failing to think beyond their

Even if the result for postconservative evangelical theologians is not a walk on the *Canterbury Trail*, there will doubtlessly continue to be more open dialogue with other Christian—and perhaps non-Christian—traditions that allow greater room for scripture, experience, wisdom, community, and mystery in epistemological matters than conservative evangelical theologians traditionally have permitted. Those who have improperly pedestalled human reason above all else are now being confronted with a new cultural ambiance that does not so easily acquiesce to reason's supposed authority. "Reason is a whore" may go down in history as one of the most decontextualized pieces ever written, alongside "judge not lest ye be judged;" nonetheless, there remains a kernel of truth even in the misquotations: reason can become a whore, as judging can lead to inappropriate judgment. Motivation and means are critical factors. God has provided both, yet the user must beware of the often accompanying "will to power."[12]

Since human knowledge is never complete or absolute, *certainty rests in the future*; theological knowledge, then, has a strong eschatological orientation that ought to be affirmed. Using the concept of *eschatological realism*, Grenz correctly points out that "Christian theology is inherently eschatological, because it is the teaching about the promising God, who is bringing creation to an eternal *telos*."[13]

While human beings presently share in the cultural mandate as God's image-bearers (i.e., *filling the earth* and *constructing the world*), in the future there awaits an as-it-should-be world, based on the new creation that God intends. Then and there, with God as subject and the purposes of God realized, the knowledge of God will be expressed and experienced with the certainty that has been uniquely reserved for the eschaton—faith and hope swallowed up in that which never fails.

Moreover, remembering that the future completion of God's intention is to bring about the eschatological community of God necessitates allowing space for the work of the Spirit within all cultures, contexts, and even religions. Without assuming salvific efficacy, knowledge of God may be exemplified in various ways that connote the truth of the omnipresence of the Spirit, and thus the Triune God's universal accessibility throughout

---

merely human philosophical guru, being confined to the community think tank.

12. See Grenz's relevant and insightful comment in *Primer on Postmodernism*, 166–67.

13. Grenz, *Renewing the Center*, 216–17.

the world. While the problem of Christian particularity and universal human condition is difficult to articulate, it seems clear that God's eschatological goal, though ultimately refused by some, encompasses all people as he elects the people of God for the world's sake.

While perhaps additional philosophical considerations could be adduced, those mentioned above should provide sufficient framework through which a modest proposal for revitalizing evangelical theological epistemology may be articulated.

Outline of Proposed Revitalized Evangelical Theological Epistemology: Elements Composing the Larger Mosaic

Theological Knowledge as Centered in the Person and Work of Jesus Christ

Postconservative resuscitation of the *personal* and *relational* nature of knowledge has served to (re)construct theological epistemology from those dimensions. This move effectively *replaces pride of place for an "I-It" knowledge with an "I-Thou" knowing.* Whether this move in favor of *knowledge as personal* is viewed as reconnecting with premodern ways of knowing, or as a matter of associating with the postmodern relational emphasis, in this author's estimation, it rings true. For too long have too many evangelical theologians and philosophers allowed the standards of "accepted" reason to diminish the ultimate standard-bearer's authority relating to the knowledge of God.

Scholars need not surrender the use of reason, however, in pursuit of theological knowledge and truth, but rather ought to consider reason as one-among-other useful divinely-provided tools—a tool to be employed faithfully and imaginatively within a Christian belief mosaic centered on the Object of faith and knowledge. In terms of evangelical theology, then, this amounts to shifting ultimate attention away from the *words* of the Bible toward (re)centering on the *person and work* of Jesus Christ. The New Testament instrumentally endorses this, pointing out knowledge of God as constituted in Messiah Jesus.[14] Hence, a holistic evangelical theological epistemology will certainly embrace as one of its most crucial facets the knowledge of God incarnated in the self-revelation of God in Christ.

---

14. Likewise, the Old Testament emphasizes the functional-relational realm regarding Yahweh and humankind.

Nevertheless, this Christ-centeredness concerning the knowledge of God will not be an exclusive orientation; on the contrary, it ought to lead naturally to several other important expressions of theological knowledge, consistent with the very teachings and practices of the Son of God. One such way is via the Spirit.

Theological Knowledge as Spirit-Oriented

A progressing shift toward a *pneumatological* approach to theology is detectable among postconservatives.[15] Part of the rationale for this move emerges from reaction against the apparent bifurcation between professional theological work and personal spirituality evident within much modern-period evangelical scholarship, a disjunction essentially diminishing—in extreme cases, denying—a significant role for the work of the Holy Spirit in theology reflection.[16] Particularly pertaining to theological knowledge, we may perhaps view the upshot of recovering a more Spirit-oriented approach to include the following:

1. Emphasis on the subjectivity of knowledge, while retaining objectivity regarding the Source and Object of knowledge, via the Spirit's work in drawing people to God and Christ and revealing the work and love of God for humanity.

2. Characteristic of primarily Arminian- Pentecostal- and Charismatic- leaning traditions focused on robustly integrating theology and praxis, and thus correlating more with postconservative than with traditionalist methodologies.

3. Increasingly practical approach, concretely connecting with the cultural context focused more on experiences and relationships than on intellectual and propositional orientations.

4. Heightened sense of openness to, and trust in, the moving of the Spirit in both the church and world.

5. Part of progressive revelation culminating in the age of the Spirit and the Triadic (i.e., Trinitarian) revelation, entailing knowledge of God via the Holy Spirit, who is continually empowering the church.

15. For instance, see Pinnock, *Flame of Love.*

16. See again the section entitled, "Postconservative Concerns with Traditionalist Theological Epistemology: A Case Study of Old Princeton Theology and its Use of Scottish Common Sense Realism," beginning on page 85.

6. Enhanced sensitivity to the knowledge of God being a gift of the Holy Spirit, and thus increasing dependence upon the Spirit and divine revelation, rather than upon human reason.

7. Intensified commitment in viewing the Holy Spirit as overseer of the authority of church tradition and its scripture.

8. Emphasis on the work of the Spirit within the church, both globally and locally, especially imparting the atoning work of Christ within the worshiping community.

Western thinkers may find it difficult to imagine the reality of literally billions of fellow human beings practicing distinctly non-Christian faiths *consummate with* the Holy Spirit's unending work among all peoples of the world. Perhaps this *prima facie* paradox requires Christians, particularly evangelical believers, to maintain a more open stance toward accepting a certain level of theological knowledge and truth within other world religions and spiritualities, keeping in mind the necessary distinctions and nuances to be made concerning the salvific value of such knowledge and truth.[17] One suggestion involves recognizing the ubiquitous presence and persuasion of the Holy Spirit, acknowledging the complementarity of the Spirit's drawing people to the particular Savior, Jesus; at the same time granting a prethematic awareness (i.e., knowledge) of God (*pace* Pannenberg). This shift among evangelical postconservatives toward greater openness of the Spirit's role in the knowledge of God ought to be enthusiastically—yet critically—welcomed as part of a holistic evangelical theological epistemology.

Theological Knowledge as Biblical Revelation

The difficulty regarding this particular facet for theological epistemology has more to do with the *purpose* of the biblical text than with its ontological status as word of God. The modern approach to scripture among traditionalist evangelicals, especially as promoted within strong foundationalism, seeks certainty via looking *at* the pages of the Bible, rather than looking *through* the writings (i.e., via an *instrumental* use of the biblical text) as part of the larger tradition of the church.

17. For a first-rate relevant discussion on this subject, see Kärkkäinen, *Theology of Religions.*

One of the primary emphases occupying written revelation is the broadcasting of ways in which God is revealed, plus the avenues by which humankind knows—or may come to know—God. Such textual content ought to be anticipated from a religion and spirituality asserting the personal-relational nature of God, together with the crucial importance of human knowledge of God (vis-à-vis the many potential dimensions of this knowledge). The biblical worldview and its intracultural language recognize the distinction between Creator and creature, disclosing the relational means of overcoming the divine-human estrangement. Biblical revelation, in this agential sense, ought to be affirmed as part of a holistic evangelical theological epistemology.

Theological Knowledge as Ecclesia

Theological knowledge is *constituted in the ecclesia*—actualized as a result of immersed participation of its members. Webber, for instance, promotes a theological model encouraging evangelicals to understand the knowledge of God as the church, being or becoming once again the *metaphysical presence* of God on earth: grounded in Jesus Christ and apostolic epistemology. For this author, it seems reasonable to ontologically view the ecclesia as a theological knowledge source in light of the ceaseless divine presence and *deposit of the faith* promised the apostles of the Lord and all subsequent followers of the Way.[18]

Thus, the knowledge of God as embodied in the ecclesia, based on the living Christ and the authority of apostolic interpretation, deserves recognition as part of a holistic evangelical theological epistemology. As will be shown next, it also calls evangelical thinkers to consider their standpoints regarding the epistemological legitimacy of church tradition and community for theological knowledge.

Theological Knowledge as Grounded
in Tradition and Community

A central feature of this study has been the summon to evangelical intellectuals to return more than a modicum of authority to Christian tradition and community. Surmounting long-ruling Cartesian preoccupation with individualism requires commitment to resuscitate and (re)incorporate

18. See John 15:26, Acts 3:19–21, 1 Tim 6:20, 2 Tim 1:14.

opinio into evangelical approaches to theological knowledge. As we have shown, the postmodern critique of allegedly universal-turned-ethnocentric rationality places evangelical traditionalists in a precarious philosophical position respecting authority, knowledge, and truth. Reason utilized *within* tradition certainly deserves a seat alongside other ways of knowing; yet, rationalism's fading pride of place as ahistorical, acultural, acontextual authority ought to concern and call all evangelical theologians and philosophers to re-evaluate their methodology, including the current level of authority offered Christian tradition and contemporary evangelical community in connection with the knowledge of God.

Becoming a testimony of the metaphysical presence of God on earth will require such re-examining, plus distancing from the intellectual hubris indicative of far too much conservative-leaning theology in the modern period. Embracing the authorized epistemology of the apostles is a start; critical integration of early and medieval church theologians moves further in the right direction, giving ancient (i.e., premodern) and postmodern ways of knowing common ground whereby the discussion of the knowledge of God may continue vis-à-vis faithfulness *and* humility. This move will naturally culminate in viewing as parenthetical evangelical utilization of modern epistemological foundationalism, as well as inspiring a more holistic theological knowledge conspicuous in earlier Christian communal tradition and personal praxis.

Practically, to recapture intellectually the value of tradition and community for theological epistemology will mean a reinvigorated attending to, and serious engagement with, the writings and practices of past and present Christian traditions *outside* mainly-Protestant evangelicalism, seeking ways of absorbing methods and rituals essentially compatible with core evangelical convictions, while exercising flexibility toward *adiaphora*, and thereby expressing openness regarding alternative methodologies. The same open attitude must prevail with respect to engagement with contemporary philosophy, psychology, and sociology—especially with reference to historical and cultural factors shaping thought and practice. Evangelical scholars must recognize their calling not only to be heralds of the gospel metanarrative, but also articulators of the entire biblical panorama of the human condition and the divine drama of redemption—tradition and community playing substantial parts in each stage of the biblical play.

Theological Knowledge as Immersed Participation in Ecclesia

Closely connected with the previous aspects of theological knowledge, this facet extends the intellectual and theoretical considerations to the engaged participatory level. Herein, theological knowledge is viewed from *within*, i.e., inside the community of worshipers and learners of the Triune God. From this vantage point, experiencing the knowledge of God implies absorbed partaking in the life of the ecclesia—its rituals, sacraments, symbols, worship, proclamation, etc.

Webber, Newbigin, Grenz, and others rightly envision this *embodied reality* as a central connecting point with a postmodern culture convinced more by authenticity and action than by evidentialist arguments. To its own detriment, modern conservative evangelicalism has for too long allowed *non*participation in the ecclesia a place of legitimacy in both academic[19] and popular arenas.[20] This must end. Nothing less than a radical and irreversible commitment to an *organic* theological epistemology—connection between immersed participation in the ecclesia and the knowledge of God—will effect realization of the church becoming the metaphysical presence of God on earth: doubtlessly a commitment in step with the will and wisdom of God. Moreover, as the knowledge of God is experienced through the embedded sharing of Christian life and intentional discipling together in a worshiping community, the Great Commission is fulfilled in the midst, and outsiders are drawn into a new, interpretive faith community.

Evangelical praxis within the ecclesia extends far beyond the community itself and into local neighborhoods, multiple cultures, and national and international situations. Rather than being limited to events within the "four walls," the walls are replaced with open windows through which embodied participation includes the category of cause—practical application of theological convictions among the poor, the oppressed, and the alienated. Such action gives legitimacy to the theological claim that the body of Christ has been granted the authority to bring universal healing and reconciliation. Healing grace and love expressed through benevolent ecclesial praxis *actualizes* the knowledge of God for partici-

19. Examine the solemn censure leveled against disengaged academic theologians in McGrath, *Future of Christianity*, ch. 6.

20. For instance, consider the large number of "television Christians," convinced that a dose of faith on Sunday morning from their favorite charismatic TV preacher trumps any need for personal interaction and participation within a local church congregation.

pants and recipients alike. Thus, immersed participation in ecclesia, in this active sense, ought to be affirmed as part of a holistic evangelical theological epistemology.

Theological Knowledge as Experiential

The importance of experience connected with knowledge of God seems rather obvious for evangelicals, since part and parcel to evangelicalism itself is the claim of experiential relationship with God. Nevertheless, as we have seen, the question of *authority* granted to experience in determining actual knowledge and truth engenders great diversity of opinions among the committed. Like reason, experience ought not be viewed as a stand-alone entity, but rather, as part of an interpretive tradition or community. Importantly, with reference to premodern and postmodern connectivity, *embodied* experience serves an apologetical role for the Christian faith, thus having an illocutionary part in calling attention to communal and personal experiences of the knowledge of God.

Undoubtedly, critical *safeguards* for testing claims to theological knowledge—often communicated via moral language—have their crucial role to play, yet not at the expense of humans being granted various ways of accessing the knowledge of God. For instance, the book of Genesis deliberately reminds its readers of the significance of the ultimate divine-human encounter, including God's intention that creatures made in the *imago dei* experience relationship (i.e., fellowship) with their Creator. Such is an instance of moving beyond Enlightenment boundaries of purely objective and neutral knowledge, to *personal* and *subjective* knowledge of God.

The generally *loving and relational theological models* characteristic of postconservative scholars fit well with the aspect of experiential knowledge of God, focusing attention on God's willingness and desire to be known by all of creation—especially creatures made in the *imago dei*. Pietistic emphases envision the primary divine goal as having relationship with humanity: bringing the same into union with the Trinity. But theological knowledge experiences are not disconnected from (i.e., independent of) interpretive traditions or faith communities; instead, such experiences are elucidated through these matrices.[21] Thus, a holistic evangelical theologi-

---

21. Recall the ways John Wesley pictured experience as part of the Christian life and knowledge of God in our discussion under the section, "The Wesleyan Quadrilateral, or Wesley and the Quadrilateral," beginning on page 144.

cal epistemology rightly pictures experience as part of a fully-integrated Christian faith and life worldview.

Negatively, it would appear transparent that evil practices are devoid of the love of God and others; nonetheless, countless numbers who have committed dastardly acts have made the claim of possessing knowledge of God. They are deceived, and are far from God, since "there is no knowledge of God apart from the love of God, and there is no love of God apart from love of the neighbor."[22] Positively, it seems equally valid to affirm that practicing love of God and neighbor reflects some level of theological knowledge. Such spiritual praxis has seldom received its due attention related to theological method in modern evangelical academia—often segregated to "practical theology" and "spirituality" disciplines. Recouping a *spiritual theology* will be vital to evangelicalism in contextualizing the *evangel* in a postmodern context.[23] Certainly, reasserting the cruciality of *loving praxis* within theological studies ought to expedite vital habits of the faithful. Evangelical scholars seeking a revitalized theological epistemology would do well to consider the important factor of practicing love toward God and neighbor as an integral part of a holistic approach to the knowledge of God.

Theological Knowledge as Creation and Culture

Evangelicals are predictably at some variance as to the profundity of theological knowledge manifest in creation and culture. With relevance to the knowledge of God in creation, most reject a thoroughgoing Barthian perspective. Few appear prepared to accept a Pannenbergian *prethematic awareness* model. Presumably, most are inclined toward visions that are more classical, such as found in Augustine, Aquinas, Anselm, Calvin, Wesley, and George Fox—each involving some level of theological knowledge being revealed within creation. More controversy surrounds claims of the knowledge of God in culture, yet some reformists are warming to the idea in light of the potential contextualization advantage for the Christian metanarrative.

A revitalized evangelical theological epistemology will foster critically appropriation of both creation and culture—to some degree. Denying this important step would encourage an anemic rather than robust holistic view

22. Newbigin, *The Open Secret*, 109.
23. See Newbigin, *Open Secret*, 102–27.

of theological knowledge, tending to underestimate the witness of divine revelation in the work of divine and human activity. A challenge for evangelical scholars will be in developing and refining theologies of culture, religions, and emergent movements as the twenty-first century continues to unfold, both in ways anticipated and ways presently unimaginable, but always in the presence of the Holy Spirit in creation, and thus in culture and religions necessarily. And as such, creation and culture provide a window on the knowledge of God, however dark the glass may actually be.

Theological Knowledge as Virtue and Telos

Comprehension of the human *telos* and cultivation of communal and personal virtues are preeminent purposes with respect to human knowledge of God. The call to cultural and personal transformation through being and becoming *the right sort of persons* echoes the biblical mandate to moral or right living—a theme clearly identifiable throughout both Testaments.[24] Moreover, this specific element of theological knowledge bears unmistakable reconnection with ancient and medieval emphases on *telos* and virtue, providing postmodern evangelicals desired theological moorings stretching to and before the Reformation period. God takes interest in "properly ordered" human emotions and behavior. Associating these with the potential for knowledge of God both aligns with the biblical data and serves an important apologetical role in the present era. Therefore, any attempt to construct a holistic evangelical theological epistemology suited for the postmodern condition must integrate virtue and *telos* within its comprehensive paradigm.

Consideration of the aforementioned elements comprising a holistic approach to evangelical theological knowledge has raised several important questions: What practical steps may be taken toward actualizing implementation of a revitalized theological epistemology? Are certain activities or attitudes prerequisite? What about connectivity between the two evangelical "worlds"—academia and the church? And how will such an approach influence apologetical methods? These and other concerns will be the focus of our final chapter, drawing heavily again from the monumental work of Lesslie Newbigin.

---

24. See the important work on this topic in Wood, *Epistemology*, passim.

6

Conclusion

Selected Practical Steps for Revitalizing Evangelical Theological Epistemology

ALISTER MCGRATH HAS STATED THE SITUATION FACING EVANGELICAL theologians in the new millennium:

> What about the status of the theologian . . . ? What role might the Christian intellectual play in the twenty-first century? Is all well in the playground of the theologians? . . . it is most certainly not. The time is ripe for some serious new thinking about the place and role of theology in the life of Christianity. Perhaps this is one aspect of Christianity which will change most radically.[1]

Moving the unchanging gospel forward via the changing garb of new historical and cultural contexts is more than an option—it is *a biblical and theological mandate*. Approaches to the knowledge of God must successfully bridge the two worlds: the biblical and the contemporary; the communicated word and the receiving world. May the contribution herein modestly contribute to the realization of this vision for revitalizing evangelical theological epistemology, as part of the broader need for re-envisioning evangelical thought for the new millennium.

A holistic theological method ought to be embraced as it pertains to evangelical academic *intercommunity* dialogue. This move envisions evangelical scholars committing to civil and constructive discussions on questions of the shaping role and effects of modernity and postmodernity upon evangelical thought, e.g., in regard to the knowledge of God. Furthermore, it imagines a willingness to submit theological systems to the scrutiny and authority of the biblical record, intertwined with fidelity to the gospel metanarrative in present historical and cultural contexts, as well

1. McGrath, *Future of Christianity*, 119.

as embracing a scholarly *believing criticism* or *critical anti-criticism* stance.[2] As with Newbigin, such dedication necessitates painstaking effort, time, sacrifice, patience, and an attitude of genuine openness.[3] Conducting such dialogue seems most feasible via major entities like the World Evangelical Alliance, the National Association of Evangelicals, evangelical seminaries, and other professional evangelical societies. At the very least, commitment to ongoing dialogue respecting theological knowledge and other key topics ought to stimulate and further critical reflection and praxis advantageous to the evangelical cause. More hopefully, it may generate a broad consensus among evangelical thinkers as to authoritative sources of theological knowledge, especially by scholars open to considering a wide variety of views both within and beyond evangelicalism.[4]

Next, evangelical intellectuals need to hear the clarion call to return theological reflection—theological knowledge included—to the proper place of immersed participation in the church community. Partaking in the sacraments and worshiping together ought to be the focal point of growing in the grace *and knowledge* of the Lord (*pace* Newbigin). Perhaps, *combined with strategic development of a Christian worldview among the congregation*, a unifying vision among God's people may be ignited.

Therefore, a reconnection between evangelical scholars and the ecclesia, both locally and globally, will be necessary. One reasonable

2. Details of these two broad evangelical scholarship orientations, focused mainly on biblical criticism, are found in Noll, *Between Faith and Criticism*, 156–73. In short, both critical anti-criticism and believing criticism scholars affirm the inspiration and revelatory truthfulness of the scriptures, yet approach the question of criticism from different angles, based on, for instance, differing degrees of commitment to the infallibility or inerrancy of the Bible (strongest among critical anti-criticism scholars) and dependence upon the practices and results of critical research (highest among believing criticism academics). Naturally, strict fundamentalists and others absolutely opposed to biblical, theological, or epistemological critique would be quite likely to refrain from engagement with either of these two orientations.

3. Ideally, this type of dialogue would involve a balanced representation of evangelical communities. Conferences may best suffice as the communication environment. More realistically, however, likelihood of engaging in such discussions would be among those open to new light breaking forth from God's word, as well as new methods of expressing the faith. Consequently, it seems probable that reformists would comprise the vast majority of participants, while attending traditionalists and fundamentalists would be highly underrepresented though deeply respected for their commitment to interact with divergent perspectives.

4. This could include attention to typically non-evangelical Christian traditions (e.g., Roman Catholic, Eastern Orthodox), as well as to, say, newer charismatic or Pentecostal faith communities.

way to accomplish this bridge building involves moving advanced theological education "classrooms" into local churches, rather than keeping such opportunities for learning at arms-length from the many parishioners unable to attend an evangelical seminary, university, or college.

A new emphasis, though, would center on theologically-based training and dialoguing among congregations: seekers and followers of Christ otherwise unlikely to experience systematic theological learning beyond the church walls. Christian higher education satellite campuses ought to be welcomed by evangelical pastors, elders, and other leaders, as one way of training people to *love God with all their minds*, in a Christ-honoring local community milieu, and among fellow laypersons. Yet, the situation requires great attentiveness on the part of evangelical professors addressing ordinary church member audiences, as R.T. France has perceptively underscored:

> The professional scholars tend to press doggedly on with their researches without considering how their results are likely to affect the evangelical public. . . . There is need for care in presenting our material so that the non-specialist reader will not be misled. It is an exercise in communication, which is sadly not always the scholar's greatest aptitude. So unnecessary hostility is sometimes created towards new interpretations because they have not been presented with sufficient care and consideration for the natural reactions of the ordinary Christian.[5]

Evangelical academics ought also to consider adopting a Newbigin-like *centrality of Jesus Christ* and *Trinitarian framework* approach. This would mean embracing a relationally or personally oriented standard for theological knowledge. It is past time to reject, as controlling for theology, the modern scientific method and its hard evidentialism saturated with fact/value and other faulty dualisms.[6]

5. From R. T. France, "Evangelical Disagreements About the Bible," as quoted in Noll, *Between Faith and Criticism*, 170. "Baby boomer" audiences, for instance, may need considerable explanation from an academic who is excited about the latest evangelical scholar's commitment to a virtue-oriented epistemology based primarily on Aristotelian or Thomistic thought—likely a more difficult philosophical pill to swallow for evangelical "moderns" steeped in Enlightenment dualisms than for their evangelical counterparts raised in post-Enlightenment culture. Nevertheless, a patience, nuanced, and modest presentation should provide the venue through which evangelical epistemological perspectives viewed as less sacrosanct will receive fair hearing among local congregations.

6. As mentioned before, this does not imply a rejection of utilizing evidences regarding

Properly attending to the *personal* expression of theological knowledge will not only guard against future developments of aberrant Christian groups[7] seeking to connect with the biblical God—the One who is at once transcendent and immanent—but will likely ensure that the theological center of attention does not move "off camera" to focus on peripheral matters, instead remaining centered on the person of Jesus Christ, God-with-us. Two additional benefits attending this are alignment with the personal nature of the biblical drama and connectivity with postmodern sensibilities to relationality over rationalism.

Possibly one of the most important contributions Newbigin makes to evangelical scholarship is his commitment to learn from—and critically analyze—so many different fields of knowledge and interest. His example bodes well for evangelicals who will heed the call to go beyond specialization and preference, and to enter into consequential conversation with various related or interrelated disciplines. Although Newbigin is by no means the first to move in arenas wider than his trained expertise, in modern times his résumé demonstrates the kind of breadth of subject and cultural mastery that rarely arises in this era of ever-narrowing concentration.

Following Newbigin's epistemological lead, including his approach to theological knowledge, will likely entail a much wider consideration of the subject than often emerges within evangelical thinking. Willingness to listen to *other voices* beyond the evangelical community who may have something valuable to contribute to the current discussion will represent a crucial step forward. This could conceivably take the form of revisiting the long history of virtue epistemology, as at least one evangelical academic has done recently.[8] It will also likely suggest careful reading and critiquing of French and other postmodern philosophers, whose epistemological views have radically altered both intellectual and popular scenes on the Continent.[9] Research and developments in sociology, linguistics, phi-

---

the Christian faith, both to compel the yet unconverted, and as edification for followers of Christ. It would imply, however, returning evidence to its rightful place, alongside experience and reason, as *part of* a holistic interpretive framework.

7. Both Mormonism and Christian Science arose in the nineteenth century partly in reaction to a lopsided, mainly strict Puritan presentation of God as extraordinarily transcendent, at the expense of God also being truly immanent.

8. See Wood, *Epistemology.*

9. Happily, some evangelicals have engaged (or are beginning to analyze) these intellectuals. See, for example, Carson, *The Gagging of God;* Dockery, *The Challenge of Postmodernity;* Erickson, *Truth or Consequences;* Grenz, *A Primer on Postmodernism;* Lundin, Walhout, and Thiselton, *The Promise of Hermeneutics;* Thiselton, *Interpreting God and the Postmodern Self;* Vanhoozer, *Is There a Meaning in This Text?*

losophy, hermeneutics, and other disciplines related to theology must be understood and evaluated. And this task, rather than being accomplished in isolation by individual scholars, ought to be a concerted effort among groups of evangelical intellectuals, most feasibly by way of both mutual study and conference opportunities, as well as through shared tasks as part of sponsored endowments and grants. For this to be successful, it appears that the urgency would need to be communicated on both global and national scales as well as local and communal levels.

Modern proclivity toward hubris noticeably affected much nineteenth- and twentieth-century evangelical thought. Combined with an often distrustful and intolerant view of others, especially among fundamentalists, a sort of evangelical overconfidence characterized Enlightenment-related assertions of theological knowledge. The unmasking of certain related false ideologies of the modern period has actually been healthy for evangelical scholars in the area of character and attitude; a growing teachableness and humility is evident in the work of many younger theologians and philosophers who have been chastened by some of the justified criticisms of reason-centered methodologies.

While never being rightly accused of anything short of total commitment to the gospel and its claims to truth and knowledge of God in Christ, Newbigin was one to lead the way in willingness to learn and to change, and in his attitude of true appreciation and patient understanding of others and their perspectives, no matter how wrong he felt they were. Deep recognition of God's grace provided the impetus for his own beneficence toward others. Evangelical scholars will not only increase their sensitivity to multifarious theological and epistemological views by following the *irenic yet full confession of faith* approach Newbigin epitomized, but will undoubtedly augment their own God-honoring constructive and creative thinking as they take seriously the dictum, "All truth is God's truth," and agree with Abraham Kuyper's statement, "There is not one square inch of the entire creation about which Jesus Christ does not cry out, 'This is Mine! This belongs to me!'"[10]

Reactionary apologetics is virtually unnecessary—moreover obstructive—for evangelical theology and theological knowledge claims in the postmodern era.[11] Contemporary evangelical thought presently enjoys, or

---

10. From a university lecture presented in Amsterdam, as quoted in Mouw, *Uncommon Decency*, 147.

11. In fact, pertaining to Newbigin's own methodology, he sought to avoid using the term "apologetics" in favor of "witness." He viewed apologetics as a peculiarly modern

at least has access to, critically-engaged scholarship revealing the fiduciary character of *all* knowledge. Such valid insights should encourage apologists to take initiative to defend the *functional/relational emphasis* of God's revelation to humanity[12] and, moreover, to graciously commend a more biblically-derived theological epistemology.

This effort ought to be carried out within a broad evangelical context in order to judiciously test claims to the knowledge of God claims made by members of the body of Christ, and as a means for understanding and evaluating these claims in light of scripture, tradition, virtue, and Christian maturity. Intercommunity dialogue among academics of various evangelical traditions on particular theological knowledge topics (e.g., "knowing/doing God's will" or "hearing God's voice") is bound to meet with difficulty and disagreement. Nevertheless, evangelical interlocutors will need to press toward constructive engagement on these issues and their biblical criterion, in a spirit of peace and tolerance, as exemplified by Newbigin. Concentrated discussion on the composition of an evangelical worldview—and what it calls for—will be required to move the conversation in productive directions. Once again, incorporating an ecumenical and dialogical spirit will be a determinative ingredient in the potential for respectful interaction among evangelical intellectuals, as well as toward fruitful advancement of Christian apologetics in the twenty-first century.

The practical steps suggested above represent merely a handful of ideas that perhaps may help to guide evangelical theology toward a revitalized theological epistemology in the context of postmodernity. Taking a holistic approach to the knowledge of God will force evangelical intellectuals beyond the comforts of the familiar territory marked out by modernity: traditionalism, modernist-fundamentalist categories, foundationalism, ahistoricism, aculturalism, acontextualism, propositionalism, triumphalism, objectivism, ethnocentrism, certainty, hubris, et al. In its place will be a model of theological knowledge incorporating biblical perspectives and insights of various Christian traditions, along with critically-evaluated postmodern epistemology ideas: a holistic approach to the knowledge of God offered principally by evangelical scholars emulating and building on the lead of Lesslie Newbigin—scholars of the *tradition-conserving reformist* and *conservative tradition-reforming* varieties.

---

approach, primarily adopted by fundamentalists, diminishing the usefulness of the term, and thus calculated to fail with postmodern people.

12. A central thesis of Murray, *Problem of God.*

Bibliography

Ahlstrom, Sydney E. "The Scottish Philosophy and American Theology." *Church History* 24 (1955) 257–72.

Audi, Robert. *Epistemology: A Contemporary Introduction to the Theory of Knowledge*. New York: Routledge, 1998.

———, editor. *The Cambridge Dictionary of Philosophy*. Cambridge: Cambridge University Press, 1999.

Barth, Karl. *Church Dogmatics, I/1*. Translated by G. Bromiley. 2nd ed. Edinburgh: T. & T. Clark, 1986.

———. *Church Dogmatics, II/1*. Translated by T. Parker, *et al*. Edinburgh: T. & T. Clark, 1957.

Bebbington, D. W. *Evangelicalism in Modern Britain: A History from the 1730s to the 1980s*. London: Unwin Hyman, 1989.

Beegle, Dewey M. *Scripture, Tradition, and Infallibility*. Grand Rapids, MI: Eerdmans, 1973.

Benson, Bruce Ellis. "The End of the Fantastic Dream: Testifying to the Truth in the 'Post' Condition." *Christian Scholar's Review* 30.2 (2000) 145–61.

Botterweck, G. Johannes. In *Theological Dictionary of the Old Testament*, ed. G. Johannes Botterweck and Helmer Ringgren, 5:448–81. Grand Rapids, MI: Eerdmans, 1986.

Boyd, Gregory A., and Paul R. Eddy. *Across the Spectrum: Understanding Issues in Evangelical Theology*. Grand Rapids, MI: Baker Academic, 2002.

Brook, Peter. *The Empty Space*. New York: Atheneum, 1968.

Bultmann, Rudolph. In *Theological Dictionary of the New Testament*, ed. Gerhard Kittel, I, 689–719. Grand Rapids, MI: Eerdmans, 1964.

Burnham, Frederic B., editor. *Postmodern Theology: Christian Faith in a Pluralist World*. San Francisco: Harper & Row, 1989.

Callen, Barry L. *Clark H. Pinnock: Journey toward Renewal: An Intellectual Biography*. Nappanee, IN: Evangel, 2000.

Calvin, John. *Institutes of the Christian Religion*. Translated by Ford Lewis Battles. Vol. 1. 2 vols., edited by John T. McNeill. Philadelphia: Westminster, 1960.

Campbell, Ted A. "The Interpretive Role of Tradition." In *Wesley and the Quadrilateral: Renewing the Conversation*, ed. W. Stephen Gunter, Scott J. Jones, Ted A. Campbell, Rebekah L. Miles and Randy L. Maddox, 63–75. Nashville: Abingdon, 1997.

Carnell, Edward John. *Christian Commitment: An Apologetic*. New York: The MacMillan Company, 1957.

Carson, D. A. *The Gagging of God*. Grand Rapids, MI: Zondervan, 1996.

Clapp, Rodney. "How Firm a Foundation: Can Evangelicals Be Nonfoundationalists?" In *The Nature of Confession: Evangelicals and Postliberals in Conversation*, ed. Tim. R. Phillips and Dennis L. Okholm. Downers Grove, IL: InterVarsity, 1996.

Colson, Charles, and Richard John Neuhaus, editors. *Your Word Is Truth: A Project of Evangelicals and Catholics Together*. Grand Rapids, MI: Eerdmans, 2002.

Conn, H. M. "Liberation Theology." In *New Dictionary of Theology*, ed. Sinclair B. Ferguson, David F. Wright and J. I. Packer, 387–91. Downers Grove, IL: InterVarsity, 1988.

Dalzell, Thomas G. "Lack of Social Drama in Balthasar's Theological Domatics." *Theological Studies* 60 (1999) 457–75.

Davis, Stephen. *Debate About the Bible: Inerrancy Versus Infallibility*. Philadelphia: Westminster Press, 1977.

Denney, J. "Knowledge." In *A Dictionary of the Bible*, ed. James Hastings, 3:8–10. Edinburgh: T. & T. Clark, 1898.

Descartes, René. *Discourse on the Method of Rightly Conducting the Reason and Seeking for Truth in the Sciences*. Translated by Elizabeth S. Haldane and G. R. T. Ross, 1:79–130. 2 vols. The Philosophical Works of Descartes. New York: Dover, 1955.

———. *Meditations on First Philosophy*. Translated by Elizabeth S. Haldane and G. R. T. Ross, 1:133–99. 2 vols. The Philosophical Works of Descartes. New York: Dover Publications, 1955.

Dewey, John. *John Dewey: The Later Works 1925–1953*. Edited by J. Boydston. Vol. 8. Carbondale, IL: Southern Illinois University Press, 1982.

Dockery, David S., ed. *The Challenge of Postmodernity: An Evangelical Engagement*. Grand Rapids, MI: Baker, 1997.

Dorrien, Gary. *The Remaking of Evangelical Theology*. Louisville: Westminster John Knox, 1998.

Erickson, Millard J. *Christian Theology*. 2nd ed. Grand Rapids, MI: Baker, 1998.

———. *The Evangelical Left: Encountering Postconservative Evangelical Theology*. Grand Rapids, MI: Baker, 1997.

———. *Postmodernizing the Faith: Evangelical Responses to the Challenge of Postmodernism*. Grand Rapids, MI: Baker, 1998.

———. *Truth or Consequences: The Promise and Perils of Postmodernism*. Downers Grove, IL: InterVarsity, 2001.

Escobar, Samuel. "Liberation Theology." In *The Blackwell Encyclopedia of Modern Christian Thought*, paperback ed., ed. Alister E. McGrath, 330–35. Malden, MA: Blackwell, 1995.

Fackre, Gabriel. *Ecumenical Faith in Evangelical Perspective*. Grand Rapids, MI: Eerdmans, 1993.

Ferguson, Sinclair B., David F. Wright, and J. I. Packer, editors. *New Dictionary of Theology*. Downers Grove, IL: InterVarsity, 1988.

Frame, John M. *The Doctrine of the Knowledge of God*. Grand Rapids, MI: Baker, 1987.

Fretheim, Terence E. In *New International Dictionary of Old Testament Theology & Exegesis*, ed. William A. VanGemeren, 2:409–14. Grand Rapids, MI: Zondervan, 1997.

Grenz, Stanley J. "Conversing in Christian Style: Toward a Baptist Theological Method for the Postmodern Context." *Baptist History and Heritage* 35 (2000) 82–103.

———. *A Primer on Postmodernism*. Grand Rapids, MI: Eerdmans, 1996.

———. *Renewing the Center: Evangelical Theology in a Post-Theological Era.* Grand Rapids, MI: BridgePoint, 2000.

———. *Revisioning Evangelical Theology: A Fresh Agenda for the 21st Century.* Downers Grove, IL: InterVarsity, 1993.

———. *Theology for the Community of God.* Nashville: Broadman & Holman Publishers, 1994.

Grenz, Stanley J., and John R. Franke. *Beyond Foundationalism: Shaping Theology in a Postmodern Context.* Louisville: Westminster John Knox, 2001.

Gunter, W. Stephen. "The Quadrilateral and the "Middle Way"." In *Wesley and the Quadrilateral: Renewing the Conversation*, ed. W. Stephen Gunter, Scott J. Jones, Ted A. Campbell, Rebekah L. Miles and Randy L. Maddox, 17–38. Nashville: Abingdon, 1997.

Gunter, W. Stephen, Scott J. Jones, Ted A. Campbell, Rebekah L. Miles, and Randy L. Maddox. *Wesley and the Quadrilateral: Renewing the Conversation.* Nashville: Abingdon, 1997.

Hall, Christopher A. *Learning Theology with the Church Fathers.* Downers Grove, IL: InterVarsity, 2002.

Hart, Trevor. *Faith Thinking: The Dynamics of Christian Theology.* Downers Grove, IL: InterVarsity, 1995.

Hauerwas, Stanley, Nancey Murphy, and Mark Nation, eds. *Theology without Foundations: Religious Practice and the Future of Theological Truth.* Nashville: Abingdon, 1994.

Henry, Carl F. H. "Know, Knowledge." In *The International Standard Bible Encyclopedia*, ed. Geoffrey W. Bromiley, 3:48–50. Grand Rapids, MI: Eerdmans, 1986.

Hicks, Peter. *The Philosophy of Charles Hodge: A 19th Century Evangelical Approach to Reason, Knowledge and Truth.* Lewiston, NY: Edwin Mellen, 1997.

Hodge, Charles. *Systematic Theology.* Vol. 1. 3 vols. Grand Rapids, MI: Eerdmans, 1952.

Hoffecker, Andrew W. *Piety and the Princeton Theologians: Archibald Alexander, Charles Hodge, and Benjamin Warfield.* Grand Rapids, MI: Baker, 1981.

Holmes, Arthur F. *All Truth Is God's Truth.* Grand Rapids, MI: Eerdmans, 1977.

———. *Contours of a World View.* Grand Rapids, MI: Eerdmans, 1983.

———. *Faith Seeks Understanding: A Christian Approach to Knowledge.* Grand Rapids, MI: Eerdmans, 1971.

Hubbard, David Allan. "The Knowledge of God in Hosea: The Meaning of the Concept and Its Relevance to Biblical Theology." Master of Theology, Fuller Theological Seminary, 1954.

Hunsberger, George R. *Bearing the Witness of the Spirit: Lesslie Newbigin's Theology of Cultural Plurality.* Grand Rapids, MI: Eerdmans, 1998.

Jones, Scott J. "The Rule of Scripture." In *Wesley and the Quadrilateral: Renewing the Conversation*, ed. W. Stephen Gunter, Scott J. Jones, Ted A. Campbell, Rebekah L. Miles and Randy L. Maddox, 39–61. Nashville: Abingdon, 1997.

Kärkkäinen, Veli-Matti. *An Introduction to the Theology of Religions: Biblical, Historical, and Contemporary Perspectives.* Downers Grove, IL: InterVarsity, 2003.

Kerr, Fergus. *Theology after Wittgenstein.* Oxford: Basil Blackwell, Ltd., 1986; London: SPCK, 1997.

Kuhn, Thomas. *The Structure of Scientific Revolutions.* 2nd ed. Chicago: University of Chicago Press, 1970.

Lindbeck, George W. *The Nature of Doctrine: Religion and Theology in a Post Liberal Age.* Philadelphia: Westminster, 1984.

Lindsell, Harold. *The Battle for the Bible.* Grand Rapids, MI: Zondervan, 1976.

Lonergan, Bernard J. F. *Method in Theology.* Toronto: University Press, 1971. Reprint, 1999.

Lundin, Roger, Clarence Walhout, and Anthony C. Thiselton. *The Promise of Hermeneutics.* Grand Rapids, MI: Eerdmans, 1999.

Luther, Martin. *Three Treatises.* 2nd ed. Philadelphia: Fortress, 1970. Reprint, 1986.

MacIntyre, Alasdair. *Three Rival Versions of Moral Enquiry: Encyclopedia, Geneology, and Tradition.* Notre Dame: University of Notre Dame, 1990.

Maddox, Randy L. "The Enriching Role of Experience." In *Wesley and the Quadrilateral: Renewing the Conversation*, ed. W. Stephen Gunter, Scott J. Jones, Ted A. Campbell, Rebekah L. Miles and Randy L. Maddox, 107–27. Nashville: Abingdon, 1997.

Marsden, George. "The Collapse of American Evangelical Academia." In *Faith and Rationality: Reason and Belief in God*, ed. Alvin Plantinga and Nicholas Wolterstorff, 219–57. Notre Dame, IN: University of Notre Dame Press, 1983.

McGrath, Alister E. "An Evangelical Evaluation of Postliberalism." In *The Nature of Confession: Evangelicals and Postliberals in Conversation*, ed. Tim. R. Phillips and Dennis L. Okholm, 23–44. Downers Grove, IL: InterVarsity, 1996.

———. *The Future of Christianity.* Malden, MA: Blackwell, 2002.

———, editor. *The Blackwell Encyclopedia of Modern Christian Thought.* Malden, MA: Blackwell, 1995.

Miles, Rebekah L. "The Instrumental Role of Reason." In *Wesley and the Quadrilateral: Renewing the Conversation*, ed. W. Stephen Gunter, Scott J. Jones, Ted A. Campbell, Rebekah L. Miles and Randy L. Maddox, 77–106. Nashville: Abingdon, 1997.

Moltmann, Jurgen. *Experiences in Theology: Ways and Forms of Christian Theology.* Translated by Margaret Kohl. Minneapolis, MN: Fortress, 2000.

Montgomery, John Warwick, editor. *God's Inerrant Word: An International Symposium on the Trustworthiness of Scripture.* Minneapolis, MN: Bethany Fellowship, 1974.

Mouw, Richard J. *The Smell of Sawdust: What Evangelicals Can Learn from Their Fundamentalist Heritage.* Grand Rapids, MI: Zondervan, 2000.

———. *Uncommon Decency: Christian Civility in an Uncivil World.* Downers Grove, IL: InterVarsity, 1992.

Mundle, W., O. Flender, J. Gess, R. P. Martin, and F. F. Bruce. "Image." In *The New International Dictionary of New Testament Theology*, ed. Colin Brown, 2, 284–93. Grand Rapids, MI: Zondervan, 1986.

Murphy, Nancey. *Beyond Liberalism and Fundamentalism: How Modern and Postmodern Philosophy Set the Theological Agenda.* Valley Forge, PA: Trinity Press International, 1996.

———. *Theology in the Age of Scientific Reasoning.* Ithaca, NY: Cornell Paperbacks, 1993.

Murray, John Courtney. *The Problem of God: Yesterday and Today.* New Haven: Yale University Press, 1964.

Newbigin, Lesslie. "The Christian Faith and the World Religions." In *Keeping the Faith: Essay to Mark the Centenary of Lux Mundi*, ed. Geoffrey Wainwright, 310–40. Philadelphia: Fortress, 1988.

———. *Foolishness to the Greeks: The Gospel and Western Culture.* Grand Rapids, MI: Eerdmans, 1986.

———. *The Gospel in a Pluralist Society.* Grand Rapids, MI: Eerdmans, 1989.

———. *Honest Religion for Secular Man.* London: SCM Press, 1966.

———. *The Light Has Come: An Exposition of the Fourth Gospel.* Grand Rapids, MI: Eerdmans, 1982.

———. *The Open Secret: Sketches for a Missionary Theology.* Grand Rapids, MI: Eerdmans, 1978.

———. *The Other Side of 1984.* Geneva: WCC, 1984.

———. *Proper Confidence: Faith, Doubt, and Certainty in Christian Discipleship.* Grand Rapids, MI: Eerdmans, 1995.

———. *The Reunion of the Church,* 2nd ed. London: SCM Press, 1960.

———. *Truth and Authority in Modernity.* Valley Forge, PA: Trinity Press International, 1996.

———. *Truth to Tell: The Gospel as Public Truth.* Grand Rapids, MI: Eerdmans, 1991.

———. *Unfinished Agenda.* 2nd ed. Edinburgh: University of Saint Andrews Press, 1993.

Noll, Mark A. *Between Faith and Criticism: Evangelicals, Scholarship, and the Bible in America.* San Francisco: Harper & Row, 1986.

———. *The Scandal of the Evangelical Mind.* Grand Rapids, MI: Eerdmans, 1994.

_____, editor. *The Princeton Theology 1812–1921: Scripture, Science, and Theological Method from Archibald Alexander to Benjamin Breckinridge Warfield.* Grand Rapids, MI: Baker Academic, 2001.

Oden, Thomas C. *After Modernity . . . What?: Agenda for Theology.* Grand Rapids, MI: Academic, 1990.

———. *The Rebirth of Orthodoxy: Signs of New Life in Christianity.* San Francisco: HarperSanFrancisco, 2003.

Olson, Roger E. "The Future of Evangelical Christianity." *Christianity Today,* February 9, 1998, 40–48.

———. *The Mosaic of Christian Belief.* Downers Grove, IL: InterVarsity, 2002.

———. "Postconservative Evangelicals Greet the Postmodern Age." *The Christian Century* (May 1995) 480–83.

———. "Reforming Evangelical Theology." In *Evangelical Futures: A Conversation on Theological Method,* ed. John G. Stackhouse, Jr., 201–7. Grand Rapids, MI: Baker, 2000.

———. *The Story of Christian Theology: Twenty Centuries of Tradition & Reform.* Downers Grove, IL: InterVarsity, 1999.

Pannenberg, Wolfhart. *Systematic Theology.* Translated by Geoffrey W. Bromiley. Vol. I. 3 vols. Grand Rapids, MI: Eerdmans, 1991.

Phillips, D. Z. *Faith after Foundationalism: Plantinga-Rorty-Lindbeck-Berger—Critique and Alternatives.* Boulder: Westview, 1995.

Phillips, Tim. R. "Knowledge of God." In *Baker Theological Dictionary of the Bible,* ed. Walter A. Elwell, 458–59. Grand Rapids, MI: Baker, 1996.

Phillips, Tim. R., and Dennis L. Okholm. *A Family of Faith: An Introduction to Evangelical Christianity.* Grand Rapids, MI: Baker Academic, 2001.

_____, editors. *Christian Apologetics in the Postmodern World.* Downers Grove, IL: InterVarsity, 1995.

Pinnock, Clark H. "Appendixes: Selections from the Writings of Clark Pinnock and Pinnock's 1999 Comments on 'How My Mind Has Changed'." In *Clark H. Pinnock: Journey toward Renewal*, edited by Barry L. Callen, 219–67. Nappanee, IN: Evangel, 1999.

———. *Biblical Revelation: The Foundation of Christian Theology*. Chicago: Moody Press, 1971.

———. *A Defense of Biblical Infallibility*, 1967.

———. "Evangelical Theologians Facing the Future: An Ancient and a Future Paradigm." *Wesleyan Theological Journal* 33.2 (1998) 13–16.

———. *Flame of Love: A Theology of the Holy Spirit*. Downers Grove, IL: InterVarsity, 1996.

———. "Limited Inerrancy: A Critical Appraisal and Constructive Alternative." In *God's Inerrant Word: An International Symposium on the Trustworthiness of Scripture*, ed. John Warwick Montgomery, 143–58. Minneapolis, MN: Bethany Fellowship, 1974.

———. *Most Moved Mover: A Theology of God's Openness*. Grand Rapids, MI: Baker Academic, 2001.

———. *A New Reformation: A Challenge to Southern Baptists*. Tigerville, S.C.: Jewel Books, 1968.

———. *Reason Enough: A Case for Christian Faith*. Downers Grove, IL: InterVarsity, 1980.

———. *The Scripture Principle*. New York: Harper & Row, 1984. Reprint, 1998, Wipf and Stock Publishers.

———. *Set Forth Your Case: Studies in Christian Apologetics*. Nutley, NJ: The Craig Press, 1968.

———. *Tracking the Maze: Finding Our Way through Modern Theology from an Evangelical Perspective*. New York: Harper & Row, 1990.

———. *A Wideness in God's Mercy: The Finality of Jesus Christ in a World of Religions*. Grand Rapids, MI: Zondervan, 1992.

———, editor. *The Grace of God and the Will of Man*. Minneapolis, MN: Bethany, 1989.

Pinnock, Clark H., and Robert C. Brow. *Unbounded Love: A Good News Theology for the Twenty-First Century*. Downers Grove, IL: InterVarsity, 1994.

Pinnock, Clark H., and Delwin Brown. *Theological Crossfire: An Evangelical/Liberal Dialogue*. Grand Rapids, MI: Zondervan, 1990.

Pinnock, Clark, Richard Rice, John Sanders, William Hasker, and David Basinger. *The Openness of God: A Biblical Challenge to the Traditional Understanding of God*. Downers Grove, IL: InterVarsity, 1994.

Piper, John, Justin Taylor, and Paul Kjoss Helseth, editors, *Beyond the Bounds: Open Theism and the Undermining of Biblical Christianity*. Wheaton, IL: Crossway, 2000.

Piper, O. A. "Knowledge." In *The Interpreter's Dictionary of the Bible: An Illustrated Encyclopedia*, ed. George Arthur Buttrick, I:42–48. New York: Abingdon, 1962.

Placher, William C. *Unapologetic Theology: A Christian Voice in a Pluralistic Conversation*. Louisville: Westminster John Knox, 1989.

Plantinga, Alvin. *Warranted Christian Belief*. New York: Oxford University Press, 2000.

Pojman, Louis P. *What Can We Know?: An Introduction to the Theory of Knowledge*. 2nd ed. Belmont, CA: Wadsworth, 2001.

Polanyi, Michael. *Personal Knowledge*. Chicago: University of Chicago Press, 1958.

Ramm, Bernard L. *After Fundamentalism*. San Francisco: Harper & Row, 1983.

————. *The Devil, Seven Wormwoods, and God*. Waco, TX: Word, 1977.

Rausch, Thomas P., editor. *Catholics and Evangelicals: Do They Share a Common Future?* Downers Grove, IL: InterVarsity, 2000.

Rorty, Richard. *The Linguistic Turn*. Chicago: University of Chicago Press, 1967.

Schleiermacher, Friedrich. *The Christian Faith*. Translated by H. R. Mackintosh and J. S. Stewart. 2nd ed. Philadelphia: Fortress, 1928.

Schmitz, E. D. "Knowledge, Experience, Ignorance." In *The New International Dictionary of New Testament Theology*, ed. and trans. Colin Brown, 2, 390–409. Grand Rapids, MI: Zondervan, 1976.

Stackhouse, John G., Jr. "Evangelical Theology Should Be Evangelical." In *Evangelical Futures: A Conversation on Theological Method*, ed. John G. Stackhouse, Jr., 39–58. Grand Rapids, MI: Baker, 2000.

Stout, Jeffrey. *The Flight from Authority: Religion, Morality, and the Quest for Autonomy*. Notre Dame: University Press, 1981.

Thiel, John. *Nonfoundationalism*. Minneapolis, MN: Fortress, 1994.

Thiselton, Anthony C. *Interpreting God and the Postmodern Self: On Meaning, Manipulation and Promise*. Grand Rapids, MI: Eerdmans, 1995.

————. *The Two Horizons: New Testament Hermeneutics and Philosophical Description with Special Reference to Heidegger, Bultmann, Gadamer, and Wittgenstein*. Grand Rapids, MI: Eerdmans, 1980. Reprint, 1993.

Thompson, Marianne Meye. *The God of the Gospel of John*. Grand Rapids, MI: Eerdmans, 2001.

Toulmin, Stephen. *Cosmopolis: The Hidden Agenda of Modernity*. Chicago: University of Chicago Press, 1990.

van Imschoot, P. "Knowledge of God." In *Encyclopedic Dictionary of the Bible: A Translation and Adaptation of A. Van Den Born's Bijbels Woordenboek Second Revised Edition, 1954–1957*, ed. and trans. by Louis Hartman, 1290–93. New York: McGraw-Hill, 1963.

Van Inwagen, Peter. *God, Knowledge, and Mystery: Essays on Philosophical Theology*. Ithaca, NY: Cornell University Press, 1995.

Vanhoozer, Kevin J. *First Theology: God, Scripture & Hermeneutics*. Downers Grove, IL: InterVarsity, 2002.

————. *Is There a Meaning in This Text?: The Bible, the Reader, and the Morality of Literary Knowledge*. Grand Rapids, MI: Zondervan, 1998.

————. "The Voice and the Actor: A Dramatic Proposal About the Ministry and Minstrelsy of Theology." In *Evangelical Futures: A Conversation on Theological Method*, ed. John G. Stackhouse, Jr., 61–106. Grand Rapids, MI: Baker, 2000.

von Rad, Gerhard. "The Divine Likeness in the OT." In *Theological Dictionary of the New Testament, Translation Of: Theologisches Worterbuch Zum Neuen Testament*, ed. Gerhard Kittel and Gerhard Friedrich, II, 390–92. Grand Rapids, MI: Eerdmans, 1964.

Wainwright, Geoffrey. *Lesslie Newbigin: A Theological Life*. Oxford: Oxford University Press, 2000.

Ware, Bruce A. "Defining Evangelicalism's Boundaries Theologically: Is Open Theism Evangelical?" *JETS* 45.2 (2002) 193–212.

————. *God's Lesser Glory: The Diminished God of Open Theism*. Wheaton, IL: Crossway, 2000.

Webber, Robert E. *Ancient-Future Faith: Rethinking Evangelicalism for a Postmodern World*. Grand Rapids, MI: Baker, 1999.

———. *The Younger Evangelicals: Facing the Challenges of the New World*. Grand Rapids, MI: Baker, 2002.

Wells, David F. *God in the Wasteland: The Reality of Truth in a World of Fading Dreams*. Grand Rapids, MI: Eerdmans, 1994.

———. *No Place for Truth, or Whatever Happened to Evangelical Theology?* Grand Rapids, MI: Eerdmans, 1993.

Westphal, Merold. "A Reader's Guide to 'Reformed Epistemology'." *Perspectives* 7.9 (1992).

Wittgenstein, Ludwig. *Philosophical Investigations*. Translated by G. E. M. Anscombe. Malden, MA: Blackwell, 1997.

———. *Tractatus Logico-philosophicus*. Translated by D. F. Pears and B. F. McGuinniss. New York: Reutledge, 1994.

Wolterstorff, Nicholas. *Reason within the Bounds of Religion*. 2nd ed. Grand Rapids, MI: Eerdmans, 1999.

Wood, W. Jay. *Epistemology: Becoming Intellectually Virtuous*. Downers Grove, IL: InterVarsity, 1998.

Yong, Amos. "The Demise of Foundationalism and the Retention of Truth: What Evangelicals Can Learn from C.S. Peirce." *Christian Scholar's Review* 29.3 (2000) 563–88.

Zimmermann, Heinrich. "Knowledge of God." In *Bauer Encyclopedia of Biblical Theology*, edited by Johannes B. Bauer, 472–78. London: Sheed and Ward, 1970.

Pinnock 45